# POETS
## of
# OUR TIME

*by* RICA BRENNER

*author of* "TEN MODERN POETS"

HARCOURT, BRACE & WORLD, INC.

NEW YORK

# THE FRENCH CABINETMAKER
*(France)*

## Author's Notes on THE FRENCH CABINETMAKER

This farce is set in France. The general plot for the play is taken from an old seventeenth-century French farce, *Crispin Medecin*, by Noel de Breton. Although the farce is, in part, a development from the Italian *commedia del' arte*, as a modern dramatic form it is uniquely French. The word *farce*, in fact, is from a French word meaning "stuffing." And that is exactly how the French thought of the farce: a play "stuffed" with tricks and pranks, disguises, physical violence without physical pain, exaggerated characters.

So much of French literature is in the "grand manner," formal dramatic poetry in which exalted characters speak only the refined language of sentiment, that France's role in the development and origin of farce may seem surprising. But during the 17th century, the theater of France was the theater of the court, and the theater of England was closed by the order of the government. Thus in both of these countries there was no professional stage for the common people. Wandering actors and clowns filled this gap, and thus the farce was born. It was the ideal play to take from place to place, and it was then—and is now—the kind of a play that people love to see. Farce doesn't teach a lesson, nor explain life logically. It has only one intention: to make people laugh.

# POETS OF OUR TIME

# TABLE OF CONTENTS

# PREFACE

"But the noblest poetry is not merely a nice arrangement of consonants and vowels, of stresses and pauses; it is also stained and roughened by a concern for human experience, by the maculations of philosophy. It remembers, with anger and pain, the loneliness and impotence of the old, the impotence and loneliness of the young, the breath on our necks of that guttler, death, and the humbling net of circumstance about our feet."
— Babette Deutsch, *Potable Gold*

"This result, to the propagandist undesirable, would seem to be due to the fact that Sophocles (even in a translation) uses freely all the faculties that can be possessed by a writer; and suggests, therefore, that if we use art to propagate political opinions, we must force the artist to clip and cabin his gift to do us a cheap and passing service."
— Virginia Woolf, *Three Guineas*

An earlier book, *Ten Modern Poets*, was written with the hope that simple articles on the poets of our times, sketching biographical backgrounds and suggesting points of view, might bring to readers of their poetry clearer understanding and so deepened enjoyment. At the time the book was published, some apology seemed necessary because its physical restrictions limited the number of poets who could be thus presented and compelled the omission of some who should, otherwise, have been included. This book is, to some degree, an effort to make amends for that compulsory exclusion. Its purpose is no less strong to increase the pleasure of reading poetry.

But since the publication of that earlier book, a number of years have passed and new names have been added to the list of those who make our poems. So, poets like W. H. Auden and Stephen Spender appear together with those who have been writing longer.

Those intervening years have been years of world-wide upheavals, of changing social attitudes, of conflicting economic and national philosophies. Some of the poets included in this book, like Sara Teasdale and Elinor Wylie, died before these forces were let loose in their fullest fury. The very youngest, like Auden and Spender, have been influenced by them since they first took up pens to write. What have these poets in common? Are all of them poets of our times? In short, can the term *modern* be applied to the nine poets who are the subjects of this book?

If we refuse to accept chronology, alone, as a proof of modernity, if we hesitate to call a poet modern simply because he has written within our life's span, have we some other guide by which to judge? There is, first, the test of function. All nine poets have performed the task which one of the youngest of them, Stephen Spender, has declared to be the task of the modern poet: "to interpret permanent human values in forms which have a significant bearing on our environment and the circumstances of our life."

But more than this, all nine have in common one quality, an attitude of freedom—freedom to look for truth and beauty where one wills and not where one is ordered to find them, freedom to express them as one thinks most suitable and best, and freedom to maintain while doing so one's independence and integrity. In this respect, these poets are modern poets, however widely they may differ in their responses to life and in the methods by which they expressed for readers of their poetry these responses.

This very variety, in fact, has been—at least until the present—the outstanding characteristic of our century. The century's first four decades cannot be neatly tied up and put away labeled with one or two qualifying phrases. Nor can its poets be grouped and have said of them, "This and this alone is what a twentieth century poet sings and this is how he sings it." In these years, as always, the unchanging elements of life—birth, love, and death—have been the material of poetry; and a modern poet, like Sara Teasdale, made them the subjects of her poems. But wars, too, marked these times, and depressions, and persecutions; and a poet, like W. H. Auden, chose them as his themes. Some, like Yeats, responded to the pressure of life by evolving a mystic philosophy; others, like Archibald MacLeish, by a conviction of the need of a new social order.

In that freedom and variety lies a clue to the answer to a question which may very naturally have arisen: Why, in times like the present, read poetry at all, why seek thus to escape from bitter reality into a world of words and fancies? Poetry is no escape from life;—it is, or should be, a deepening of life's experiences, a clarification and enlargement for us by one more sensitive than we are of our thoughts and feelings. But more than this, if the present war is being fought for anything more than economic and imperialistic motives, it is being fought that our culture may survive, that

there may continue for poet and reader alike the spirit ani-
mating modern poetry—the spirit of freedom. That spirit
can endure only if it is nurtured. Poetry can live only if it is
read and loved.

So these chapters are written for young people to help
them understand and enjoy the poetry of the present. May
they, in turn, help keep it alive for the future!

What has been written here with the hope of turning the
reader to the poets themselves has gained significance by
quoting what the poets have written. For the privilege thus
to use selections from their works, I owe a pleasant debt of
gratitude. This indebtedness is acknowledged to the following holders of the copyrights:

D. Appleton-Century Company—for selections from *Going-to-
the-Sun* and *The Candle in the Cabin* by Vachel Lindsay.
Stephen Vincent Benét and his agents, Brandt & Brandt—for
permission to reprint selected lines from volumes of his
poems which are copyright as follows: *John Brown's Body*,
published by Farrar & Rinehart, Inc. Copyright, 1927, 1928,
by Stephen Vincent Benét. *Ballads and Poems*, published by
Farrar & Rinehart, Inc. Copyright, 1918, 1920, 1923, 1925,
1929, 1930, 1931, by Stephen Vincent Benét. *Burning City*,
published by Farrar & Rinehart, Inc. Copyright, 1933, 1935,
1936, by Stephen Vincent Benét. *A Book of Americans*, published by Farrar & Rinehart, Inc. Copyright, 1933, by Rosemary and Stephen Vincent Benét. *Heavens and Earth*, published by Henry Holt & Company. Copyright, 1920, by
Stephen Vincent Benét. *Young Adventure*, published by the
Yale University Press. Copyright, 1918, by Stephen Vincent
Benét. *The Beginning of Wisdom*, published by Henry Holt
& Company. Copyright, 1921, by Henry Holt & Company.

Duell, Sloan & Pearce, Inc.—for selections from *America Was Promises* by Archibald MacLeish.

Farrar & Rinehart, Inc.—for selections from *The Fall of the City: A Verse Play for Radio,* copyright, 1937, and *Public Speech,* copyright, 1936, by Archibald MacLeish.

Harcourt, Brace & Company—for selections from *Collected Poems, Murder in the Cathedral,* and *The Family Reunion* by T. S. Eliot; *Land of the Free* and *Air Raid* by Archibald MacLeish.

*Harvard Advocate*—for selections from "Song" and "Song— The Flowers I Sent Thee" by T. S. Eliot.

Houghton Mifflin Company—for selections from *The Destructive Element* by Stephen Spender; *The Happy Marriage, The Pot of Earth, Streets in the Moon, New Found Land, Conquistador, Poems,* and *Panic* by Archibald MacLeish.

Alfred A. Knopf, Inc.—for selections from *Collected Poems* by Elinor Wylie.

The Macmillan Company—for selections from *Dark of the Moon, Flame and Shadow, Helen of Troy and Other Poems, Love Songs, Rivers to the Sea, Strange Victory* by Sara Teasdale; *Collected Poems, The Golden Whales of California, Every Soul is a Circus* by Vachel Lindsay; *New Voices* by Marguerite Wilkinson; *Autobiography, Collected Poems, Last Poems and Plays, The King of the Great Clock Tower* by William Butler Yeats.

Edgar Lee Masters—for permission to reprint "Come" by Vachel Lindsay from *Vachel Lindsay* by Edgar Lee Masters.

Random House—for selections from *On This Island, Letters from Iceland, Journey to a War, Another Time* by W. H. Auden; *Poems, Vienna, Forward from Liberalism, Still Centre* by Stephen Spender.

Charles Scribner's Sons—for selections from *Vachel Lindsay* by Edgar Lee Masters.

Wheaton College Press—for selections from *Prose and Poetry of Elinor Wylie* by William Rose Benét.

Yale University Press—for selections from *The Tower of Ivory* by Archibald MacLeish.

I am also indebted to W. W. Norton & Company for permission to quote from *Potable Gold* by Babette Deutsch and to Harcourt, Brace & Company for permission to quote from *Three Guineas* by Virginia Woolf. Both of these quotations appear in this preface.

I am grateful to Miss Mabel A. Bessey, Miss Mary McLees, Miss Ella Suydam, and Miss Mabel Williams for helpful suggestions in the preparation of this book. There are others, whose names do not appear, who have been generous and patient in their help; they, too, know that I am grateful.

R. B.

August 1940

*STEPHEN  VINCENT  BENÉT*

## STEPHEN VINCENT BENÉT

POSSIBLY the most amazing thing about Stephen Vincent Benét is that the early poetic promise that he gave has been fulfilled and maintained. Frequently enough, some prodigy in his teens publishes a book which critics hail as a work of genius; thereafter, over a span of a few years, he produces further work, adequate but far from great; and then he lapses into a silence from which he emerges but fitfully and, on the the whole, feebly. This has not been true of Benét. The book of poems which he published at 17, *Five Men and Pompey*, a book which Louis Untermeyer called "little short of astounding," marked only the beginning, not the high point, of his career as a poet.

Stephen Vincent Benét, the son of James Walker and Frances Neill Rose Benét, was born July 22, 1898, in Bethlehem, Pennsylvania. The Benét family, of Spanish descent, originally from the island of Minorca off Spain, had in the early days of this country settled in St. Augustine, Florida. The family cherished a strong tradition of army service. The poet's grandfather, for whom he was named, had been the first appointee from Florida to West Point; had become Chief of Ordnance of the United States Army with the rank of Brigadier General; and, during the Civil War, had remained loyal to the

3

Northern cause. The poet's father was also an army officer, a Colonel.

Demands of army life transferred the Benét family from one part of the country to another and made impossible a geographically fixed home for the boy. When he was seven, he moved to California where his father was then stationed. Later, the family returned East, to Georgia:

"Here in the heart of this remembered land
  That holds so much of boyhood for me still,
  The smoky pines in winter on the hill,
  The May who walks with peach-bloom in her hand."

The boy's schooling, begun in California, was continued at the Summerville Academy in Augusta, Georgia. So, early in his life, he touched the vastness of America and came to know its varying aspects; his college years in Connecticut added to this knowledge and intensified the essential Americanism of his spirit:

"This flesh was seeded from no foreign grain
  But Pennsylvania and Kentucky wheat,
  And it has soaked in California rain
  And five years tempered in New England sleet."

There was still another strong element in the family influence. Something in inheritance and background must have pointed the boy's interest so directly toward writing; for both his older brother, William Rose, and his sister, Laura, devoted themselves to literature.

4

"Poetry was yet from the first a bright valour in his blood," wrote * the older brother about the younger. "It was a direct inheritance from a father whose love of the ringing line was well known to the evening circle in a certain home."

The tie between father and son was strong; their community of interest, great. This the elder brother points out in the same article:

"Indeed I recall many a conversation between a spectacled small boy and an older man who always reminded one rather of a rapier, the latter biting his mustache and drawling his argument with twinkling eyes. Both draped themselves quaintly over their respective chairs; the tendency on the part of the males of that family being never to sit straight in a chair if one could possibly avoid it. They may have been discussing the Wilderness or Antietam. It was in the midst of my brother's most pronounced pro-Southern period, which had followed on a period of polemic Socialism during which time he would receive letters in red ink from his parent addressing him as 'Dear Comrade—!' "

Colonel Benét had a large library, from which the young Stephen widened his knowledge of people and of places. Freely accessible to him were books of adventure, of history, of pure literature—among the latter of which the poet fondly recalled a gray-bound copy of *The Rose and the Ring,* which he "helped to read to pieces." According to his older brother, army records

* William Rose Benét: "Round About Parnassus," *Saturday Review of Literature,* December 27, 1930.

5

and accounts of the Civil War all "helped to ruin his eyesight."

The boy lost himself completely in the books he read. Legends of the past for him took on an aspect of current reality. He lived the characters of fiction and of history; they became part of his life. Always there stirred in him a desire to transmute his experiences, both actual and fancied, into words. He contributed verses to the League department of *St. Nicholas,* where so many of America's writers received their first literary encouragement; he won the League's Silver and Gold Medals and for a poem, "The Regret of Dives," received a special money prize. He soon put such apprenticeship behind him. When he was seventeen, his first book of verse was published, *Five Men and Pompey.*

This book consists of six longish poems, written predominantly in iambic pentameter—some in blank verse, some in rhymed couplets, some with a still more flexible rhyming scheme; each poem contains as interludes in its statelier measure lyric passages. The poems, in method and spirit very much like Browning's dramatic monologues, are based on the lives of ancient Romans. Sertorius, Lucullus, Crassus, Cicero, Caesar, and Pompey are rescued from musty Latin texts and are revealed in moments of common human emotions rather than in those of epic grandeur. Cicero, for example, ponders over a letter he is about to write to his friend Atticus; he grieves over the tragedies of the civil war waged by Caesar and Pompey; but in the midst of his

6

grief, he rejoices that his wife Tullia is safe. Pompey, after his final defeat by Caesar, reflects that enduring beyond Caesar's victories are the ideals of a Republic for which he, himself, fought, "a dream no conquests can dispel." Lucullus, recalled to Rome without a triumph, while longing for his former military life, still contents himself with thoughts of his farms:

> "I, I have my trees,
> My cherries, rooted firm in Roman soil,
> Shedding a delicate whiteness on the hills
> When spring comes. A far greater triumph that
> Than all my conquests."

All this—knowledge of his country and of books and his own auspicious entrance into the literary world— were already part of his experience when, in the fall of 1915, Benét entered Yale University. The thoughts, the feelings, the development of a boy such as he had been are described in *The Beginning of Wisdom,* his novel which was published in 1921, shortly after he had finished his college studies. There is always danger of reading too much autobiography into a young writer's first novel. But in that book Benét says of his hero Philip Sellaby, "himself is the only person the jejune artist knows with any degree of certainty"; so it may be safe to assume that much of Philip is a reflection of Stephen Vincent. Philip is represented as a boy, keenly sensitive to his surroundings; disliking the military atmosphere and discipline of his prepara-

7

tory school, yet able by sheer intelligence and adapt-
ability to fulfill its requirements of conduct and of
work; enjoying to the utmost long summer vacations
with his family; and entering Yale to live a college
life as rich in human contacts as in classroom studies.

Of the courses that Philip Sellaby took, Benét
writes:*

"His first courses were mainly voluntary—four of
them under first-class teachers—Billy Phelps, the most
gracious and attractive of all the literary traditions of
Yale—Stanley Cathcart, that acrid, eccentric genius
with a mind that had the illuminated solidity and continuous fluctuating brilliance of a fire-opal—a professor
of paleontology who made the dinosaur as familiar a
beast as the camel and showed the solid crust of the
earth with its eternal hills flowing and melting like a
wave in the vast empty spaces of geologic time—an
assistant professor of history with an eye for the purple
and scarlet of kings and queens."

A companion piece to this picture, a portrait of his
poet-student, is drawn by William Lyon Phelps, the
beloved Billy Phelps of Philip's memories:†

"He was universally popular, having a peculiarly lov-
able disposition. His gift for satire and irony was exercised in such a manner that it charmed its victims.
He is one of the most sparkling conversationalists I

* Stephen Vincent Benét: *The Beginning of Wisdom,* Henry Holt
and Co.

† William Lyon Phelps: "Men Now Famous," *The Delineator,*
September 1930.

have met anywhere. . . . He has a combination of northern energy with southern relaxation that makes him irresistible."

The Yale days were filled with literary activity. Benét contributed light verse to the *Yale Record* and, in his Junior year, became its literary editor. From the beginning of his Sophomore year he contributed regularly to the more literary and more serious *Yale Literary Magazine*. His Junior year saw him a member of the editorial board of that magazine, also; and, for his Senior year, he was made its chairman. Meanwhile, the United States entered the World War of 1914-1918; college men became soldiers overnight; college work and college activities had to be reorganized. Benét enlisted in the army, served three days until his defective eyesight was discovered, and was discharged. He later acted as a cipher clerk in the State Department and for this period had his name listed in the *Literary Magazine* among the "Editors in Service." With the January 1919 number, under the reorganization of the college after the end of the war, Benét resumed his office as Chairman of the Board.

As an editor, he wrote book reviews, comments on a variety of subjects, and editorials. In these last, one can see his attitude toward the war—a clear-eyed recognition of its horrors and a fear of its futility, combined with a strong determination to do one's part and a hope that some good might be gained for some distant future:

"But modern war, except for the incurable romantics of the Aviation, and in some degree other independent corps, is not—to state a truism—an adventure; it is a disgusting, muddy, thorough, card-index sort of business. . . .

"We shall fight for an end unknown to us, under a cause which we do not entirely understand. Unless we are utterly broken, there will always be the rack of thought—and we shall drive ignorantly toward a hidden and bloody consummation. Whether the thing we get will seem worth the price we pay must rest indifferent to us. For it is by such means that men buy their freedom."

In another editorial, called "The Island of Refuge," he speaks of the Utopias rising in men's war thoughts, the Utopias of which they dream and which they never can attain for themselves. "For us it is enough that through the smoke, the confusion, the useless and wanton sacrifice, we have seen gleam bright and vanish for an instant those white walls we know of—and the way to them lies forward, and in the last agony of assault."

In his poetry, too, the war was a theme. *The Literary Magazine* of April 1917, the month in which the United States entered the war, contained his group of "Campus Sonnets." Among these is "Return—1917" with its ironic introductory note from the college Catalogue: "The college will reopen in Sept.—" and its still more ironic ending:

"Lord, what a dream that was! And what a doze
Waiting for Bill to come along to class!
I've cut it now—and he—Oh, hello, Fred!
Why, what's the matter?—here—don't be an ass,
Sit down and tell me!—What do you suppose?
I dreamed I . . . *am* I . . . wounded? *'You are
    dead.'* "

The war, however, did not absorb all his interest or
provide the only inspiration for his verse. He was writing poems steadily and receiving recognition for them.
For "The Drug-Shop, or, Endymion in Edmonstoun,"
a poem about Keats, he received the Professor Albert
Stanburrough Cook award given for the best unpublished verse written at Yale; and the very first award
of the John Masefield Poetry Prize was given to him
in 1917 for his poem "Music."

During the years that Benét was in college, there
was a widespread and pronounced new interest in
poetry. Poetry was being written and—surprisingly—
being read to an extent that suggested a poetic renas-
cence. The technique of the "new poetry" was being
developed; free verse became accepted; the field of
poetic subject matter lost its limiting bounds. This
poetic quickening gave impetus to the publication of
*The Yale Book of Student Verse, 1910-1919.* The war
had delayed the original plans for the project. Of the
book in its final form, Benét was one of the editors
and was well represented among the list of contributors

that contained such now familiar names as John Farrar, Thornton Wilder, and Archibald MacLeish.

There were some ten or twelve of Benét's poems in this collection. These, however, were but a few of those he had written, which now formed a sufficient number for a volume of his own. While still an undergraduate, in 1918, he had the honor of having his own university press publish his book, his second volume of verse, *Young Adventure.*

This volume of "weedy rhymes," dedicated in an affectionate sonnet to his older brother, could not be considered merely as further evidence of precocity. It was the expression of poetic maturity. One sign of that maturity lay in Benét's evident determination to write his poetry in the mode he thought best for his purpose. True, he had been influenced by earlier writers. The influence of Browning, for example, still persisted, as it did markedly in "Alexander VI Dines with the Cardinal of Capua." Some of the romanticism of William Morris appeared in "Three Days' Ride." As for contemporary poets, it is unquestionably Alfred Noyes who was reflected in both the subject and the method of "Come Back":

"Run, and be as darting as the sunlight through a tree!
Sit, and sing a silly song of apricots with me!
Innocence, O Innocence, with whiteness on your names,
Come into the crooked wood and help a child play
    games!"

But no one poet, no one method dominated him. Nor did he yield himself an unquestioning follower of the "new poetry." He was not unaware of its tenets; its principles of meter he accepted and followed in "Road and Hills," written in free verse. In that period of poetic experimentation, however, old forms were ruthlessly abandoned and for them was substituted, too often, formlessness. To that extreme, Benét could not go. In all but a very few of his poems, he followed traditional forms, molded to his own use.

Such preference for the traditional must not be considered symptomatic of a withdrawal from life, of a retirement into a cloistered academic atmosphere. Benét touched life, modern, bustling, complicated life. He reflected it in such poems as "Dinner in a Quick Lunch Room," "Rain After a Vaudeville Show." He had keen insight into people, a psychological understanding of their needs and motivations, as he showed in "Young Blood," "The Breaking Point," "Poor Devil." Far from the timidity of a literary recluse, he manifested the courage of youthful spirit:

"Icarus, Icarus, though the end is piteous,
  Yet forever, yea, forever we shall see thee rising thus,
  See the first supernal glory, not the ruin hideous."

Humor, too, colored his poems, as in "Portrait of a Boy."

From this humor developed one of Benét's most characteristic qualities, his ironic spirit, "delicate, bitter food of the clear-eyed, careless and melancholy solution for all base frets." If one of the elements in humor is a recognition and appreciation of the incongruous, one of the elements of irony is the emphasizing of that incongruity. One can note the early poetic expression of his ironic spirit in the poem "Music." A friend, playing the piano, had expressed the deepest emotions that stir men.

". . . And my friend swung round on his stool, and
    from gods we were men,
 'How pretty!' we said; and went on with our talk
    again.''

It was still more poignantly expressed in "The General Public," an indictment of the public's reception of genius. An old man recounts his boyhood memory of seeing his schoolmate Shelley stoned by his fellow students:
       " 'And you?' I said.

'I? I threw straighter than the most of them,
And had firm clods. I hit him—well, at least
Thrice in the face. He made good sport that night.' "

Benét's irony might focus upon callousness and cruelty; but of itself, it was not cruel. Without bitterness, it became for him a way of looking at life, of seeing things in their proper relationships and proportions.

The student with two volumes of poetry already to his credit was chosen Class Poet. He was graduated in

1919 with the degree of B.A. After one more year at Yale, doing graduate work in the English department, he received his M.A. in June 1920.

Some little while later, he went to France where, on a fellowship, he studied at the Sorbonne. While he was abroad, he met Rosemary Carr of Chicago, a writer on the staff of *The Chicago Tribune*. On their return to this country, they were married in Chicago, on November 26, 1921.

The young husband was now confronted with the pressing problem of earning a living. He had had some brief business experience in advertising and for a short time had done editorial work on a magazine. But all his hopes and desires were bound up in his writing. The publication in 1921 of his first novel, *The Beginning of Wisdom*, its instant and popular success, placed him surely among the clever younger generation of writers.

Clever, however, was not a satisfying adjective to be applied to him. There was a deeper note than cleverness in the poetry that he continued to write and publish. There was the steady perfection of his art and there was the expression of a constantly maturing attitude toward life. In 1920, *Heavens and Earth* had been published; 1925 saw the publication of *Tiger Joy*. The former divided with Sandburg's *Smoke and Steel* the Poetry Society Prize; the latter contained the long satiric poem, "King David," which had been published February 14, 1923, in *The Nation* as *The Nation* prize poem.

In addition to his poetry, and as a more certain source of income, Benét was writing fiction. But the short stories which were helping to provide him a livelihood failed to satisfy the rigorous standards he set for himself and for his work. He had plans for a noble poetic theme, large and soul-satisfying, for which he needed unharried time and respite from the insistence of daily finance. The solution to his combined literary and economic problem he found in a Guggenheim Memorial Foundation Fellowship, granted to him in 1926. The Fellowship, established to encourage "creative work in writing following certain historical researches," carried a money award which enabled him to sail with his family for France. The original term and grant were extended. As a result, he spent a year and a half outlining, writing, and polishing the theme that had possessed him.

What was this all-absorbing subject? The epic of America's Civil War. Into its execution went the interests and studies of his boyhood. It was colored by his intense love of his own country, deepened and vivified by his absence from it in a foreign land.

For this telling of a purely American tale, Benét was not without preparation. His understanding of people, his ability to depict their feelings and thoughts, could be traced back to his very first volume. His interest in the American scene, his grasp of native spirit and idiom, he revealed in *Tiger Joy*. In that volume he told several essentially American tales: "The Hemp," a Virginia legend of the revenge of Sir Henry Gaunt

16

upon the pirate Captain Hawk; "The Ballad of William Sycamore," the story of a character as indigenous as John Bunyan; "The Mountain Whippoorwill," a Georgia Romance subtitled "How Hill-Billy Jim Won the Great Fiddlers' Prize."

The result of this training and of the eighteen months of steady activity was *John Brown's Body.* In cinematic fashion, projecting widely separated episodes, depicting numerous characters, varying its tones, interjecting comments like the captions of the old silent moving-pictures, it presents a sweeping drama of the Civil War, quite unlike

> "the careful, ponderous histories
> That turn live men into dummies with smiles of wax
> Thoughtfully posed against a photographer's background
> In the act of signing a treaty or drawing a sword."

It is the story of the war in terms of human beings, primarily as it affected the two chief protagonists, Jack Ellyat, representative of the North, and Clay Wingate of the South. The book has no single, well-organized plot. It occasionally lapses into a confusion of time sequence. Yet in spite of this, it succeeds in producing out of innumerable varied details a unified picture, the re-creation of an entire era.

Opening with a slave-ship episode as prologue, Benét roots his story in John Brown's raid and carries it on to the end of the war, to the social and economic consequences which became the determining factors of the industrial United States of today. He shows the intensity and fervor of John Brown; he draws unforgettable pictures of cabinet members and army officers; he depicts battles and outlines campaigns; he narrates the personal adventures of a number of characters, particularly those of Ellyat. Always, it is the story of people that he tells; a purpose consistent with the viewpoint he was later to express when, receiving the Roosevelt Medal, he said that while history is made by economic forces, "it is the men of the time who dramatize these forces and stir us to hope or despair." And always, his story glows with his love for his country. He sings it in the Invocation, a tribute to the elements that have entered into the making of America: cowboys and Indians, velvet Massachusetts lawns and gray Maine rocks, prairie-schooners and cheap automobiles, Southern gardens, bare New England farms, and grainlands of the Middle West. His song of devotion is no less strong at the poem's end with its uncompromising picture of the America of today:

"Out of John Brown's strong sinews the tall skyscrapers
    grow,
  Out of his heart the chanting buildings rise,
  Rivet and girder, motor and dynamo,
  Pillar of smoke by day and fire by night,
  The steel-faced cities reaching at the skies,
  The whole enormous and rotating cage
  Hung with hard jewels of electric light,

Smoky with sorrow, black with splendor, dyed
Whiter than damask for a crystal bride
With metal suns, the engine-handed Age,
The genie we have raised to rule the earth,
Obsequious to our will
But servant-master still,
The tireless serf already half a god—"

The book's success was instantaneous and widespread. Selected as a book club's choice, it had a first
edition of 70,000 copies. The speed with which it seized
popular imagination was remarkable. On August 5,
1928, it was reviewed in the book section of *The New
York Times*. Little more than a week later, on August
14, its author, not yet having seen a printed copy of
his book, arrived from France to be greeted by the
ship-news reporters with word that he had created a
hitherto unknown phenomenon, a poetic best seller.
*John Brown's Body* won for Benét the Pulitzer Prize in
1929. Its popularity and influence persisted. For it, in
1933, the Roosevelt Medal was awarded to him, next
to Lindbergh the youngest person to receive it.

*John Brown's Body* was a remarkable achievement
and one which gave further impetus to Benét's literary
career. After a brief return to France, he came back
with his family to this country, at first making his
home in Rhode Island and then, since 1930, in New
York. Here he has continued his writing. Besides novels
and books of short stories, there have appeared *Ballads
and Poems, 1915-1930*, a collection of his earlier verse,

with a few changes and a few additions; and in 1936, *Burning City*.

Still another volume bears his name as author, a book of poems, published in 1933, *A Book of Americans,* written with his wife Rosemary and dedicated to their three children, "our other works in collaboration." This is a collection of brief, humanized pictures of personalities in American history, ranging from Columbus who discovered our country "by thinking it couldn't be there" to President Woodrow Wilson. Typical of the manner of the whole book is the poem about Abigail Adams, which traces to Abigail the power of the Adams family and then goes on:

> "This accounts for the Adams,
> How then could they fail?
> But *what* were the forces
> That made Abigail?"

The final poem sounds an essentially Benét note. It is difficult to prophesy who of the present will become the heroes of the future, for time is a "curious capsizer" of reputations,

"And we shan't know all the answers till we're history, ourselves."

There is little likelihood that time will capsize Benét's reputation. His books, appearing over a period of more than twenty years, have shown unquestioned poetic mastery.

It has been pointed out that his early reading left an impress upon Benét and his poetry, that in his early poems he was affected to some extent by Browning, Morris, and Noyes. The influence of Noyes persisted into a later time, into the period of *Tiger Joy*. Of that volume, "The Hemp" is slightly reminiscent of the English poet. Even more forcefully in "Moon-Island" is he suggested, both in the concept of the whole fantastic tale and in its method.

In Benét's treatment of other stories and legends there is a note less sophisticated, less highly-wrought than this; it was a note similar to that which Vachel Lindsay was hearing and reproducing in his basic, elemental poems. "The Mountain Whippoorwill," for example, in its depicting of the simple, fundamental character of Hill-Billy Jim uses such exaggerated figures as would have appealed to Lindsay:

"He could fiddle down a possum from a mile-high tree.
 He could fiddle up a whale from the bottom of the
     sea."

and it catches the rhythm of song and dance as Lindsay, himself, might have caught and recorded it.

"Swing yore partners—up an' down the middle!
   Sashay now—oh, listen to that fiddle!
   Flapjacks flippin' on a red-hot griddle,
   An' hell broke loose,
   Hell broke loose,

Fire on the mountains—snakes in the grass.
Satan's here a-bilin'—oh, Lordy, let him pass!
Go down Moses, set my people free,
Pop goes the weasel thu' the old Red Sea!"

It is an acknowledgment of Lindsay's significance to him that Benét makes in his poem of tribute, "Do You Remember, Springfield?" In form and language that might be Lindsay's own, the poem suggests the lack of appreciation that Lindsay felt in life:

"A man is another affair.
We understand that, in Springfield
If he sings, why, let him sing
As long as we need not hear."

Some of the poems evoke the spirit of still another poet, that of Walt Whitman,

"the giant lode we quarry
For gold, fools' gold and all the earthly metals,
The matchless mine."

Not only in the "Ode to Walt Whitman," from which these lines are quoted, is one aware of his influence. One feels it in those poems that cry out for liberty, for human dignity, for a democracy of individuals; in such a poem, for example, as "Litany for Dictatorships," in which a plea is made for those who suffer tortures "to make perfect states, in the names of perfect states," in which the very listing of horrors is done in the manner of Whitman:

22

"For the wrecked laboratory,
The gutted house, the dunged picture, the pissed-in
 well,
The naked corpse of Knowledge flung in the square
And no man lifting a hand and no man speaking."

Though one finds in some of his poems such qualities
reminiscent of other writers, it would be completely
erroneous to assume that Benét's work is derivative.
Others did exert some influence, suggesting directions
and methods. But Benét succumbed no more to any one
of them than he did to the "new poetry." He learned
from all of them, modifying their characteristics to his
own purposes. His aim dictated method; as the content of his poetry developed, so evolved his own technique.

The basic tool of a poet is words, instruments for the
creation of beauty as well as for the expression of
thought. Quite aside from their meaning and associative powers, Benét has a feeling for them as sounds:

"Who can be hopeless saying, 'Bethmacoon'?
'Aleery' is an opiate for all pain."

Sometimes he overindulges this fondness, unfortu-
nately disregarding the appropriateness of the word in
its context. This one feels when in a poem on so modern
a subject as automobile tires, he speaks of "latest laud";
or again, when he calls Love a pugilist with "glance
enskied." Occasionally, too, for the sake of a rhyme,

some word is ruthlessly forced into use. To rhyme with *size*, a person has a "vague beard and guise"; to rhyme with *walk*, "Deep in a Morris chair, Bill scowls at 'Falk' "—(and the poet calls attention to his creation by using quotation marks!)

It would be pointless to hunt through the poems for further similar weaknesses. In any case, they would be few; and they would be without significance compared with such dexterous use of words and sounds as in lines like these from "The Lost Wife":

"And worse than the clods on the coffin falling
Are the clothes in the closet that no one wears now."

Or consider the amazing use of sounds to produce the soothing, soporific effect of "In a Glass of Water Before Retiring":

> "Snails that creep,
> Silver-slow;
> Streams that flow,
> Murmuring,
> Murmuring;
> Bells that chime,
> Sweet—clear—co-o-l;
> Of a pool
> Hushed so still
> Stars drowse there,
> Sleepy-fair."

In the arrangement of words for the creation of flowing meter there is, again, an occasional lapse from the most severe demands of perfection. In so rigid a form as the sonnet, it is unfortunate to come upon such lines as:

> "More than all these, it was a spirit apart,
> Purely of fire and air and the mind."

It is equally unfortunate in so undemanding a form as free verse to find a violation of one of its few principles —that of relation between line and thought, a violation most noticeable in:

"He came out in a cleared place, then. He saw the red
  Sun spell over the trees."

Such lapses—if one insists upon discovering them— must be painstakingly sought for in the vast body of his writing. That any are to be found is quite surprising, for Benét's metrical dexterity is amazing and happy. He seems to have no favorite meter or stanza form; he uses so wide a variety that none may be called typical. His lines vary in length from the short ones of the already quoted "In a Glass of Water Before Retiring" to the long ones of "Nomenclature":

"When God looked at the diffident cherubs and dropped
      them out of the sky,
  He named them like Adam's animals, while Mary and
      Eve stood by,
  The poor things huddled before him in scared little
      naked flocks

—And he gave you a name like sunlight, and clover,
    and hollyhocks."

There is equal variety of stanza form. Stanzas may
range from the traditional ballad form of "The Retort
Discourteous" to the more limpid form used by Hood
in his "Bridge of Sighs" and found in "Elegy for an
Enemy":

> "Say, does that stupid earth
>     Where they have laid her,
> Bind still her sullen mirth,
>     Mirth which betrayed her?
> Do the lush grasses hold,
>     Greenly and glad,
> That brittle-perfect gold
>     She alone had?"

There are six-line stanzas and seven-line ones; and
these in a single poem may display almost as many
changes in rhyming scheme as mathematics permits. Or
there may be stanzas as unpredictable in length as are
prose paragraphs and with a rhyming scheme most ir-
regular and casual, yet completely satisfying.

Such flexibility suggests that free verse might provide a congenial medium for him. He uses it with telling effect in such poems as "Notes to be Left in a
Cornerstone," "Metropolitan Nightmare," and "Road
and Hills":

"My horse snuffs delicately
    At the strange wind;

26

He settles to a swinging trot; his hoofs tramp the dust.
The road winds, straightens,
Slashes a marsh,
Shoulders out a bridge,
Then—
Again the hills."

He shows command not only of free verse, but of those other verse forms, more unyielding, more demanding in meter or in rhyme. Blank verse which, in strict adherence to rules of prosody, frequently results in only a metronomic regularity, with Benét has a fluidity, a singing quality, as in these lines from "The Drug-Shop":

"Do the bees
Still moan among the low sweet purple clover,
Endlessly many? Still in deep-hushed woods,
When the incredible silver of the moon
Comes like a living wind through sleep-bowed branches,
Still steal dark shapes from the enchanted glens,
Which yet are purple with high dreams, and still
Fronting that quiet and eternal shield
Which is much more than Peace, does there still stand
One sharp black shadow—and the short, smooth horns
Are clear against that disk?"

Heroic couplets, used in a traditional manner in *Five Men and Pompey,* become something fresh when used in so modern a setting as "Rain After a Vaudeville Show":

"The last pose flickered, failed. The screen's dead white
Glared in a sudden flooding of harsh light
Stabbing the eyes; and as I stumbled out
The curtain rose. A fat girl with a pout
And legs like hams, began to sing 'His Mother.' "

The sonnet, that challenging and restricting form, has finished expression in the sequences "Campus Sonnets" and "The Golden Corpse" and in "X-Ray," "A Minor Poet," "Lone Burial." In "The Trapeze Performer," it becomes a joyous, self-conscious accomplishment: in the octet, the artist gets ready for his act; while in the sestet

"Over the sheer abyss so deadly-near,
He falls, like wine to its appointed cup,
Turns like a wheel of fireworks, and is mine.
Battering hands acclaim our triumph clear.
—And steadfast muscles draw my sonnet up
To the firm iron of the fourteenth line."

It is this metrical dexterity that is most characteristic of Benét—dexterity and variety. There is no ceaseless repetition of a single pattern. Among the longer poems, one poem will have within itself a variety of forms to express changes in thought and in mood. This is true of poems like "The Drug-Shop" and "The Mountain Whippoorwill." It is most especially true of *John Brown's Body.*

In that book the varying verse forms are used almost as musical themes are used in operas. The sections concerned with Jack Ellyat are, for the most part, in blank verse broken by interpolated passages of shorter measure. Those centering about Clay Wingate and Southern life are in a four-stress line, rhyming in couplets, frequently with feminine rhymes:

> "She was at work by candlelight,
> She was at work in the dead of night,
> Smoothing out troubles and healing schisms
> And doctoring phthisics and rheumatisms,
> Guiding the cooking and watching the baking,
> The sewing, the soap- and candle-making,
> The brewing, the darning, the lady-daughters,
> The births and deaths in the negro-quarters."

Minor themes are introduced, variations and contrasts. There are the seven-stress and the six-stress lines of the Judith Henry episodes; there are passages in free verse; there are songs—John Brown's Prayer in hymn meter, Negroes' songs like spirituals, the lovely Hiders' Song, "This is the hidden place that hiders know"; there are passages of rhythmic prose. Interweaving one with the other, they form a musical background varied and quickening.

Rhyme and rhythm are but two of the elements of poetic technique. One may have a piece of verse, perfectly rhymed, metrically flawless, and yet hopelessly dead. The life-giving spirit comes from the beauty of the chosen words, from the associations stirred up, the pictures evoked. Benét proves himself an artist with

words. He may use a single word with startling aptness. Jack Ellyat, thirsting and suffering, turns his head
"through stiff ages"; flowers blow an "iron-noise." Or,
he may draw a quick, high-lighted sketch. Autumn is
rubicund, "red as a cardinal"; a person is caught in
the "terrier mouth of rain." Again, he presents fuller
pictures. He speaks of Lincoln,

"Whose wit was a coonskin sack of dry, tall tales,
 Whose weathered face was homely as a ploughed
     field."

His ability to sustain a figure throughout a poem is
exemplified in "P.P.C.—Madam Life." In that sonnet,
a man's years upon earth are compared to a formal
afternoon call paid to Dowager Life, the whole comparison given point by the last lines:

  "Such a nice chat! Oh, taking leave is hard!
   But—here's my body for a calling-card!"

To what use has Benét put the technical ability
which he so surely possesses? It has already been noted
that from the time he first wrote there has been an
interest in the re-creation of the past. Ancient times—
Biblical in "King David," Greek in "Two Visions of
Helen," Roman in *Five Men and Pompey*—and the
Middle Ages in such poems as "The Retort Discourteous" and "Alexander VI Dines with the Cardinal of
Capua" suggest poetic material to him. Eventually
there came a shift to subjects closer to him in time

and in space, to American scenes and legends. He became essentially an American writer; his idiom, native American idiom,

"American wheat, firm-rooted, good in the ear."

This tendency reached its culmination, of course, in *John Brown's Body*.

Benét, however, is nowhere concerned with the minutiae of historical pedantry, but with the men and women who peopled an era. He sees them as human beings motivated by causes which he understands and recognizes as universal; he sympathizes with them because of their common humanity. He does not, even in the full-length *John Brown's Body*, create complete characters; his Ellyat and his Wingate, for example, remain types rather than individuals. But his characters, though they may not be fully drawn and three-dimensional, have human qualities and they are revealed vividly and with penetrating insight. Emphasis on a single quality may throw so bright a light upon a character that it becomes rounded and full. Thus do a few lines give a clue to John Vilas, the "Hider" in *John Brown's Body:*

"I have an elder daughter that I love
And, having loved from childhood, would not tame
Because I once was tamed."

*John Brown's Body* is particularly rich in word portraits, thumbnail sketches that flash the essential

31

quality of a person. How more succinctly, for instance, could Emily Dickinson be described?

> "A moth of a woman
> Shut in a garden, lives on scraps of Eternity
> With a dog, a procession of sunsets and certain poems
> She scribbles on bits of paper."

There are brilliant, if brief, portraits of Judah P. Benjamin; of Jefferson Davis, "you are the South in word"; of Stonewall Jackson, concerned in the midst of battle with a Sunday-School for Negro children and with profanity among his soldiers. There are heart-warming glimpses of Lee:

> "Perhaps you see a man like that go on
> And then you have to follow."

The essential inscrutability of the man is emphasized:

> "And kept his heart a secret to the end
> From all the picklocks of biographers."

Less elusive, but fully as appealing, is Grant:

> "It is five years
> Since he sat, with a glass, by the stove in a country
> store,
> A stumpy, mute man in a faded Army overcoat,
> The eldest-born of the Grants but the family-failure,
> Now, for a week, he shines in the full array

STEPHEN VINCENT BENÉT

Of gold cord and black-feathered hat and superb blue
    coat,
As he talks with the trim, well-tailored Eastern men.
It is his only moment of such parade.
When the fighting starts, he is chewing a dead cigar
With only the battered stars to show the rank
On the shoulderstraps of the private's uniform."

Lincoln, too, is of course pictured, "the lank man,
knotty and tough as a hickory rail," who seemed to his
secretary John Hay

". . . dignified past any neat, balanced, fine
    Plutarchan sentences carved in a Latin bronze."

However real and striking he looms in direct description, he is possibly most vividly presented when is
shown his effect upon others. The Northern soldiers on
review finally see him:

" 'So that was him,' they say. 'So that's the old man.
  I'm glad we saw him. He isn't so much on looks
  But he looks like people you know. He looks sad all
      right,
  I never saw nobody look quite as sad as that
  Without it made you feel foolish. He don't do that.
  He makes you feel—I dunno—I'm glad we could see
      him.' "

These are only a few of the men and women who
make rich Benét's story of the American Civil War and

help to bring it to glowing life. But however compellingly Benét re-creates and vivifies the past, it must be instantly noted that the past has not been for him an escape from the reality of the present. He is essentially a modern writer, absorbed in the incidents and life of today, looking upon them with a point of view that is today's. "Dinner in a Quick Lunch Room," "Rain After a Vaudeville Show," "Lunch Time Along Broadway," "Boarding-House Hall," these all find their material in present-day city life, in the small activities of present-day men and women. These may be touched by a bit of sentimentality and of romanticism; they may tell "about Love and Death and Beauty, fly-spotted and tarnished."

But Benét does acknowledge the fly-spots and the tarnish and so his romanticism is a diluted one, mixed with an unshrinking realization of things as they are. Consider, for example, the unyielding rightness of "Mortuary Parlors," its pitiless detailing of the trappings of genteel—and commercialized—sorrow, its cry against the incongruity of such places with "racked and horrible grief," its consummate last line:

"And Death, the obsequious gentleman, comes rubbing
    black gloves and talking!"

No, Benét neither flees into the past nor shuts his eyes to those aspects of the present he would prefer did not exist. He looks upon them with the cold light of truth. As under the X-ray

34

> "the weak flesh contests but cannot stay
> The passionless search for the eternal bone."

His own "passionless search" leads him to a knowledge of life today that is not pretty, but does ring true. "Face the facts," he cries. In "For City Lovers," an old house is being demolished; do not seek to know the lives of those who once lived there, he admonishes:

> "There are no ghosts to raise. There is the blank
> Face of the stone, the hard line of the street,
> The boys crying through twilight. That is all."

It is the same objectivity with which he presents the picture of industrial America in the concluding passages of *John Brown's Body*. It is the same objectivity with which he exposes modern city life in "Notes to be Left in a Cornerstone." But if the search is dispassionate, the results of the search do not leave the poet untouched and cold. He is moved by the plight of mankind, he understands men and feels with them. All his pity, his embracing sympathy wells up in that last line of the last-named poem:

> "He will forget his joy before his loneliness."

That is the poet's message to the man of the future who, eager for clues to truth, searches in the dust of his past which is our present.

It is interesting that in this objective facing of reality, Benét has little concern with a number of subjects

that engross other poets. There is scarcely any looking
back, any yearning for youth that is past. What little
there is, is to be found, as in "Come Back," in his early
poems, when the poet, himself, had barely outgrown
youth. Nor is there any great obsession with the idea
of the passing of time and the coming of death. Years
with their changes pass; death comes. Benét realizes
this in his poetry, but the thought of death as the end
of the inevitable process of change concerns him but
little and upsets him not at all. It is but part of man's
total experience. Spring, summer, and fall have gone,
he says in "Ancient's Song"; winter has come; but

> "I cannot hate this winter on the stream,
> If 'twas a dream, it was a lordly dream
> And men are right to die when they are old."

Life, not death, is the burden of his songs. Life is not
easy; it brings sorrow and pain.

> "But vinegar Time must scour the cup
> Till it's clean for a draught worth drinking."

And it is bravery in the face of pain and courage in
the face of sorrow that distinguish man, distinguish
him from the gods, themselves. So, in "Complaint of
Body, the Ass, against His Rider, the Soul" these gods
are to be told, these gods

> "who sit above the show,
> How, in this world they never stoop to know,

Under what skies, against what mortal odds,
The dust grows noble with desire and pain,
And that not once but every day anew."

Out of his awareness of the effects of life upon the individual, the individual's thoughts, and feelings, joys, and sorrows, grows Benét's social consciousness, his awareness of the effects of life upon the social group. There is a steady development from the early poem, "The Walkers," a poem about strike pickets, whose "march is over my heart," to his latest volume, *Burning City*.

One obvious subject toward which he directs his thoughts is that of war. He is of the generation that saw the World War of 1914-1918 at its closest and knew it for what it was. "Return—1917" reveals his reaction to this country's entrance into the war; there is in it no glamorous appeal to emotions. War plays a necessarily large part in *John Brown's Body;* but again, though there is shown a steady determination on the part of the soldiers to do their duty as they see it, there is no glorification of that duty. Rather, there is a challenge to learn the causes of war—and its results:

"we'll do all we can.
But I wish we could show everybody who stays at home
What this is like."

In *Burning City,* there is that moving appeal, that cry against future wars, that prophecy of the present one, "1936":

37

"All night they marched, the infantryman under pack,
But the hands gripping the rifles were naked bone
And the hollow pits of the eyes stared, vacant and
    black,
When the moonlight shone.

The gas mask lay like a blot on the empty chest,
The slanting helmets were spattered with rust and
    mold,
But they burrowed the hill for the machine-gun nest
As they had of old.

And the guns rolled, and the tanks, but there was no
    sound,
Never the gasp or rustle of living men
Where the skeletons strung their wire on disputed
    ground. . . .
I knew them then. . . .

'It is eighteen years,' I cried. 'You must come no
    more.'
'We know your names. We know that you are the
    dead.
Must you march forever from France and the last,
    blind war?'
*'Fool! From the next!'* they said."

Horrible is the war between nations. But there are
other struggles, equally terrible, in which men engage.
There is the struggle for freedom within one's own

nation, the fight for independence of thought. This is the theme of "Ode to the Austrian Socialists—(February 12–February 15, 1934)":

"They believed in peace.
But they'd seen what happened next door, in another
      country,
To people who believed in peace and elections.
And the same tide was rising here."

The complexities of our civilization, furthermore, cause other problems which man, not as an individual but as a social being, must solve and suffer in solving. "Notes to be Left in a Cornerstone" suggests the effects of city life upon man. The results of economic maladjustments are depicted in "Ode to Walt Whitman":

"They burn the grain in the furnace while men go
      hungry.
They pile the cloth of the looms while men go ragged.
We walk naked in our plenty."

In the three grotesque nightmare poems other dangers and fears that beset man are brought to light. Fantastic and weird they seem. But they have the validity that nightmares have while they are being dreamed. And they have that residuum of truth that a nightmare frequently leaves after the dreamer wakens. There is so much assurance of verity that one is quite willing to accept the statement in one of the poems that mankind cannot be saved by the scientific and philosophic panaceas on which hopes are pinned:

"You will not be saved by General Motors or the prefabricated house.
You will not be saved by dialectic materialism or the Lambeth Conference.
You will not be saved by Vitamin D or the expanding universe.
In fact, you will not be saved."

One is almost ready to envision a stage in mechanical invention when machines will master men.

"Slaves? Well, in a way, you know, we were slaves before."

One accepts these ideas as the imaginings of a poet. And then one pauses. Stripped of the fantasy, stripped of the nightmare element, does not much truth remain?

No answer to these problems is explicitly stated. One may infer that there is need for clear-sightedness and the same need for courage and bravery in the face of danger that there is for the individual in the face of hardship. The cause—the cause of truth and freedom—may, indeed, require the sacrifice of the individual.

"We die here singing, but Rome, Rome goes on!"

There is earnestness and there is sincerity throughout the poems. There is high-hearted courage. But there, too, is humor. Benét retains his sense of humor and that for him is a strong defense and a powerful weapon. He regards, for example, the Prohibition Era in America. He looks at the ban which prohibition places upon drinking. He regrets not the liquor which presumably can no longer be obtained, but the precedent that Prohibition establishes. Not only is this world affected; but now "they've stopped the Lethe, down in Hell." This is the same joyousness, the same robustness of mood that one finds in "For All Blasphemers":

> "He ripped the Sinful Pippin
> From its sanctimonious limb.
> Adam was my grandfather—
> And I take after him."

His humor, at other times, can be light, touched with gentle irony. The young lover broods on the exquisite joys and pains that would be his were his beloved with him and then realizes that he finds

> "just as perfect satisfaction
> In analyzing these, and other moods!"

In "Sparrow," there is a plea that he may be numbered among these humble birds; he builds a structure of sobriety and humility and overturns it in his last lines:

> "And, one thing, Lord—the times are iron, now.
> Perhaps you have forgot.
> They shoot the wise and brave on every bough.
> But sparrows are the last things that get shot."

This irony is the development of the discovery he made as a young man, the discovery of "a working doctrine of irony that healed as it seared the mind with its freezing wit." His ironic spirit manifests itself in his poems in various forms. It may show itself in an abrupt change from one mood to another, in the juxtaposition of apparently contradictory thoughts. Keats in the poem "The Drug-Shop" is interrupted in his delicate, beautiful reveries by the clanging of the shop bell and the order for a drug. Alexander, in "Alexander VI Dines with the Cardinal of Capua," turns casually from the poisoning of an enemy to a welcoming greeting to his daughter Lucrezia on her way to a ball. Or there may be the irony of a situation as there is in "Music." Still another form it may assume is the irony of an idea. This, in its supreme form, is the irony of "Nightmare Number Three," wherein man's creations become man's destroyers, man-made machines devour man.

One may object to irony as a working philosophic doctrine that of itself it is not constructive. But, indirectly, it may prepare the way for constructiveness and it is not necessarily destructive of good. It is merely a manner of looking at things in order to find the truth. It is thus that Benét employs it. It is in this fashion that it is explained by his early hero, Philip Sellaby, in *The Beginning of Wisdom:*

"To see all things without shame or fear in the mind or sentimentality. To test by irony as one tests with burning acid for counterfeit coin, yet not to be swallowed up completely with irony and so merely stay preserved like a specimen abnormality in a jar full of alcohol."

Benét does not allow himself to be swallowed up with it. The ironic is but one aspect of his poetry. Quite different from it are the kindliness, the warmth, the affection that mark others of his poems. His lyrics have an unashamed tenderness. Simply and straightforwardly he sings his emotions in such poems as "Chemical Analysis," "8:30 A.M. on 32nd Street," and "To Rosemary," the lovely dedication to his wife.

Through his poems, one recognizes the poet as a man of strength and of tenderness. What he feels, he feels deeply; what he thinks, he thinks sincerely. He can look at the world objectively; the truth that he thereby finds stirs his sympathy and his affection. It is rare, indeed, for brothers to commend one another publicly in print. Yet that is what William Rose Benét did in his review of Stephen Vincent Benét's *Poems and Ballads*. "A good poet," he said of him, "a man of strong affections; a good man at a venture!" That is an elder brother's judgment based on a personal knowledge of his life. That, too, is a reader's judgment based on his poetry.

### POETICAL WORKS

| | |
|---|---|
| FIVE MEN AND POMPEY | *The Four Seas Co.* |
| YOUNG ADVENTURE | *Yale University Press* |
| HEAVENS AND EARTH | *Henry Holt and Co.* |
| KING DAVID | *Henry Holt and Co.* |

## POETS OF OUR TIME

TIGER JOY                *George H. Doran Co.*

JOHN BROWN'S BODY    *Doubleday, Doran and Co.*

BALLADS AND POEMS, 1915-1930

                      *Doubleday, Doran and Co.*

A BOOK OF AMERICANS (with

     Rosemary Benét)    *Farrar and Rinehart, Inc.*

BURNING CITY          *Farrar and Rinehart, Inc.*

*ARCHIBALD MACLEISH*

## *ARCHIBALD MACLEISH*

M Y development as a poet is of no interest to me and of even less interest, I should suppose, to any one else." So Archibald MacLeish wrote in the foreword to a collection of his poetry, *Poems, 1924-1933*, a collection which he insisted was not to be formally entombed between quotation marks as a "collected edition," nor to serve as a guide in tracing the poetic development in which he disavowed all interest. One has no right, of course, to question the sincerity of the poet's statement so far as it involves himself.

He insists, somewhat further on in the same foreword, that the creative artist dislikes and resents his "old work with its stale problems and its abandoned technique." Were poetic development synonymous with technical development, one might understand MacLeish's indifference to the outgrown past of his method and material. But poetic development is concerned with much more than just technical problems. Moreover, the reader of MacLeish's poetry, he who reads more than a single isolated poem and so is aware that he has

"come upon this place
By lost ways, by a nod, by words,"

must be interested in the various emotional and intellectual stages through which the poet passed to reach his present status.

Archibald MacLeish was born on May 7, 1892, in Glencoe, Illinois, a suburb of Chicago. His father was Andrew MacLeish, fifty-four years old when the child was born; his mother, Martha Hillard, was his father's third wife. The father, "a cold, tall rigorous man of very beautiful speech," was a merchant, who had left his native city of Glasgow to become one of Chicago's early settlers. The mother was the daughter of a Connecticut Congregational minister, one of a New England seafaring family of "very passionate people with many mad among them." She was a graduate of Vassar College and, for a time, had been an instructor there. Her son described * her as "intelligent and energetic and entirely self-less and beloved." From that joint Scotch and New England heritage, the poet must have derived his introspective nature, his philosophic questioning of man's place in the universe, his deep feelings, his artistry with words.

Added to these general inheritances was one specific influence, an attachment to the sea which provided a symbol and an echoing background for many of MacLeish's poems. One who has once known and loved the sea cannot soon forget it. So his mother must have carried with her from the East memories of the ocean and family stories about it:

* Schreiber: *Portraits and Self-Portraits,* Houghton Mifflin Co.

"Tales we know of the lost sea
Tales of the great waves and the wind there."

But even though the Atlantic Ocean did not sound in
the boy's ears, he did know the real joys of beach and
water. The great wooden MacLeish home overlooked,
through oak trees and sandy bluffs, the shores of Lake
Michigan. Lake and beach provided a happy play-
ground for him and the other three children of the
family. Sea gulls, waves, and mighty waters form recurring images in his poems; these made up the indeli-
ble memories of his childhood, these with other tender
associations of country life:

"I can remember times more near
And longer past than that strange year:
Hip-booted springs, half faun, half boy,
Over the lakes in Illinois,
Following the swollen runnels down
To beaches where the waves broke brown
Shaking the air, and the landward breeze
Smelled of fresh water and far pine trees
And overnight in the steep ravine
The first hepatica grew green."

MacLeish's boyhood was uneventful, made up of at-
tendance at local public school, of play, of the ordinary
joys and sorrows of childhood. In his early teens he
left the familiarity of the Middle West to attend, before entering college, a preparatory school in Connecti-

cut, a school which he came cordially to detest. Thence he matriculated at Yale, a member of the class of 1915.

In the atmosphere of college his life expanded. His scholastic record was more than good, bringing him election to Phi Beta Kappa in the spring of his Junior year. He was a member of a fraternity and of the Senior Society, Skull and Bones. He combined scholarly and athletic interests in his extra-curricular activities. Not only was he on the football team and on the swimming team, but he was a member of The Elizabethan Club and The Pundits, and, in his Senior year, he was Class Poet and editor of the *Yale Literary Magazine*.

These two positions were the fitting recognition of the literary activity that had marked his college life. As early as October 1912, he had contributed a story, "The Shears of Atropos," to the *Literary Magazine*. Thereafter, almost every issue contained some contribution, verse, essay, or story; frequently an issue contained more than one. The first of his poems to appear, in December 1912, was called "The Marshes." Its general tone and method are well represented by this stanza:

> "There it is the white tides sleep—
>     Tides that serve the waning moon,
>     Weary over waste and dune,
> Moaning when the grey gods reap."

This poem, conventional in manner, was typical of most of his college writing. It was all quite according

to college standards of the time, conventional in its
tender, wistful air and in its introspective sentimental
concern. Suffused by a tenuous, romantic light, it expressed an unreal, idealistic attitude toward the life
about him:

"For a dreamer am I, and I follow my dreams over the
world and away
To a land as far as the last faint star, the Land of the
Dawning Day."

The poet, in his search for reality, the core of existence that all seek, placed his reliance not on his senses
or on factual knowledge but on his dreams, his intuition. Nor was this a manifestation of his poetic self
only; it was characteristic of the complete MacLeish.
His first editorial in the college magazine expressed it
definitely, if in interrogative form: "But what then if
the Real lives only in the Vague?"

Four years of college courses might give facts and
knowledge but would not necessarily reveal or even
help reveal the ultimate truths of existence. Memories
that evoke emotions may prove a surer guide. So he
summed up his college life in the poem "Baccalau-
reate":

"A year or two, and grey Euripides,
And Horace and a Lydia or so,
And Euclid and the brush of Angelo,
Darwin on man, Vergilius on bees,
The nose and dialogues of Socrates,

Don Quixote, Hudibras and Trinculo,
How worlds are spawned and where the dead gods
   go,—
All shall be shard of broken memories.

And there shall linger other, magic things,—
The fog that creeps in wanly from the sea,
The rotten harbor smell, the mystery
Of moonlit elms, the flash of pigeon wings,
The sunny Green, the old-world peace that clings
About the college yard, where endlessly
The dead go up and down. These things shall be
Enchantment of our hearts' rememberings.

And these are more than memories of youth
Which earth's four winds of pain shall blow away;
These are youth's symbols of eternal truth
Symbols of dream and imagery and flame,
Symbols of those same verities that play
Bright through the crumbling gold of a great name."

After his graduation from Yale in 1915, the question
of his career had to be decided. The law, with its rigid
principles and its insistence upon fact, would seem
a peculiar choice of profession for such a dreamer of
dreams as was MacLeish. Yet that was his choice, a
choice, however, that was only a half-hearted one; for,
in later years, he admitted that he had never believed in
the law. Nevertheless, he entered Harvard Law School,
led his class, and in 1919 received his LL.B.

The delay in receiving his degree was due to the interruption of his studies by his service in the World War of 1914-1918. A genuine desire to be of service must have prompted his enlistment. For, in 1916, while still a student, he had married Ada Hitchcock, a singer; and so, because of his marriage, could have claimed exemption from compulsory military duty. This he did not do. When the United States entered the war, he enlisted in a hospital unit. Soon, however, he transferred to the Field Artillery. In June and July 1918, he saw active service at the front, north of Meaux. Shortly after, he was ordered home to train recruits and was stationed at Camp Meade. It was as Captain of Field Artillery there that he was demobilized.

The war held for MacLeish none of the glamor or romantic aura that it held for many. He had entered it as a conscientious fulfillment of duty; he left it disillusioned, if not embittered. Much later he wrote of it: "My own experience of it was neither heroic nor particularly hard, but it destroyed my brother, many of my friends, two years of my life."

The poignant memory of his brother Kenneth's death in Belgium lived with him and colored many of his poems.

"My brother's grave is over the north water
In the land where they fought."

It is thus expressly recalled in "Anonymous Signature"; but it is no less implied in such a poem as "Memorial Rain."

53

Though war memories did not cease suddenly with demobilization, they must have been thrust somewhat into the background of consciousness by new problems that presented themselves. MacLeish now had a wife and a son, born in 1917, to take care of. So, after finishing his law training and after a year of teaching at Harvard, he entered the Boston law office of Charles F. Choate, Jr. For three years he was engaged in the technicalities of the legal profession, trying cases, seeking precedent and example in leather law books,

"Adjudicated quarrels of mankind,
  Brown row on row!—how well the lawyers bind
  Their records of dead sin."

But law did not content him; it could not engross his spirit. His main interest lay in the writing which he was doing when legal demands permitted. His one wish, his only desire, was to write—"to write the poems I wanted to write and not the poems I was writing."

How could this be accomplished? MacLeish decided that it would be possible only if first there was a complete break from the past.

To understand the decision, it is first necessary to realize the kind of poetry MacLeish had been writing and the underlying point of view that colored his outlook on life and was reflected in his work. In 1917, while he was in France, there appeared a volume of his verse, *The Tower of Ivory,* collected by a friend of his, Lawrence Mason, an assistant professor of English at Yale. These are well characterized by Harriet Monroe as "creditable, youthful poems." They are romantic, introspective, based on fancy and revery, rather than on life experience. They contain much strained diction, expressions like "shooken leaves," "fairy quinqueremes," "music of the spheres." They are marked by such metrical lapses as:

> "Oh, the nerves grown dull with flinging
> Up the mind's o'er written sands,"

and by such ineptitudes as this:

> "Lily, red wood lily,
> Flaunting, fairy lily,
> Lily springing where the heel
> Was down-impressed of Pan;
> Lily at whose throat the moon
> Flutters like a moth a-swoon—
> Round and round thy shining reel
> Deft-foot things of Pan."

A brooding melancholy pervades them. They mourn the swift passage of beauty, love, and happiness; "only old and endless are our tears." The awareness of the transitoriness of life and an adolescent preoccupation with death motivate many poems: "My Body and I," for example, "The Silence," and "Immortality," with its suggestion of Wordsworthian thought:

> "From slumber into slumber all things go;
> Our yesterday is dawned from infinite

Oblivion; tomorrow's fading light
Shall darken to that misted morn, and lo!
No terror clothes the oblivion we know.
Breathe deep the glooming of death's second night."

But basic to the whole volume is that point of view which Professor Mason in his introduction insists the reader must recognize: "Under various symbols he is passionately appealing for the intuitive apprehension of reality as against the baffling limitations of the reason and the senses."

The opening poem, "Our Lady of Troy," a poem cast in dramatic form, makes clear this view. Faust, the Faust of old legend, declares to a group of students:

"There's nought to fear from Heaven through to Hell;
  Nothing that mind can't solve. Mind is the king—"

and insists that all his magic is but trickery. That master of realism is himself confounded by the apparition of Helen, "a rose the world has dreamed," evoked at the request of the students and animated by their very faith. Defeated and crushed, Faust is forced to admit that which is MacLeish's own conviction:

"I sold all things
To know that all I knew was all the world
Of knowledge; and I bought—why, nothing then,—
Or only this at last—a space to know
That out beyond my farthest reach of thought
All knowledge shines—a radiance of stars."

In poem after poem this belief recurs. In "Realities," it is explicitly stated:

> "Yet when the splendor of the earth
>     Is fallen into dust,
> When plow and sword and fame and worth
>     Are rotted with black rust,
> The Dream, still deathless, still unborn,
>     Blows in the hearts of men,
> The star, the mystery, the morn,
>     Bloom agelessly again."

This reliance upon the dream, upon the intuitive, as the only permanent, the one true reality, was not for MacLeish a philosophy of escape. In "Jason," he answers whoever might so accuse him of cowardice:

> "Ah, voice that singeth bravely there,
>     Dost think that dreams are peace?
> Dost think it cowardice to dare
> Eternity of blind despair
>     For gold of fairy fleece?"

The pursuit of the ideal is always difficult and painful; and no less so when it is the spirit rather than the mind that gives it direction, when it is intuitive rather than rational apprehension that gives it authority.

While he was at college and at law school, this was MacLeish's sincerely felt philosophy. Imagine, then, a young man with such conviction, exposed to the horrible reality of war, to the impingement on his senses of

57

all that he would deny as unreal. Consider him, on his return to his own country, going through the adjustments of the armistice and the first post-war years. Life here was seething with unrest; values were shifting so that what had once seemed valuable and permanent appeared to be worthless and ephemeral; the new freedom came to be interpreted as excuse, indeed as reason, for excesses of thought and of conduct. Consider, finally, the poet engaged in a profession which was distasteful to him. The one solution to his unease was a complete change, a shaking off of the habits of his past. To him, as to many of his compatriots, his refuge, his spiritual haven had to be in some country other than his own. So MacLeish decided to leave America.

In the winter of 1923, with his wife and two children, he sailed for France. From that time he dates "the beginning of my more or less adult life." For five years, except for occasional summers in the New England Berkshires, he lived in Europe, in Paris and St. Cloud, on the Mediterranean, in Normandy, and, for one spring, in Persia.

The European scene gave fresh impetus to his writing. It was certainly not because post-war conditions in Europe were any less strained or chaotic than those in the United States. But Europe provided a gathering place for all those restless souls who rebelled against what they considered the crudities of their own land, who had reached a stage of disillusionment and frustration that could be assuaged, they felt, only in the refined atmosphere of older civilizations. France, moreover, had the tradition of being as hospitable to artists of every kind as other lands might be to financiers and industrialists. In her sympathetic atmosphere, the arts flourished. Experimentation in art forms, at first hesitantly begun, was accelerated by the desire to express new moods by new methods. There was an interplay between the various arts, a tendency to adopt for one some of the techniques of another. In literature, as in the graphic arts, movements developed—symbolism and impressionism among others—that had for their purpose not the exact true-to-life re-creation of an object or event but the evoking of a mood or impression caused by the object.

This fresh esthetic activity appealed to MacLeish. He read French poets who, some few decades earlier, had planted the seeds of the new literary movements. He read T. S. Eliot and Ezra Pound who, in English, were exponents of the current philosophy of despair and who were expressing that philosophy in newly tried forms. In a congenial environment, MacLeish found himself able to do the writing he had wished to do.

*The Happy Marriage* appeared in 1924. Its poems manifest some of the earlier poetic mannerisms that might better have been abandoned. There persists a mannered diction: "whist and whispering," "a garden unrumorous of surf." Words are tortured into rhyme: the usual word *assortment,* for example, is rejected for *assortal,* because some rhyme must be found for *im-*

*mortal.* There is an occasional flat poetic failure, fortunately not always so egregious as:

> "Delicious damps and odors filled
> The musings of his thoughtful nose."

But in spite of such imperfections, there is evidence that the poet has a greater command of his medium, has more surely developed his technique. It is at its best in the unerring choice of words for their tonal qualities and their associated values in this gentle picture:

> "It was all quiet on that little hill,
> And through the dusk a hazy quiet fell,
> Quiet as lulled as after a slow bell
> The silver quaver falters and is still.
> There was no stir among the trees at all
> Nor any lift of air along the ground;
> Only soft rain that settled with no sound,
> And raindrops on still leaves too stilled to fall."

The book displays, too, a great variety of verse forms: sonnets, blank verse, couplets, quatrains, free verse. The opening poem, which gives its title to the book, shows within itself a great range. Essentially a sonnet sequence, it varies its form so that monotony may be avoided and changing mood be more appropriately suggested by changing meter. So the sonnets are interspersed with stanzas—some of long lines, some of short—of varying rhyming schemes, with sequences of free verse and with passages of unpredictable line length and rhyme, such as:

"Withdraws
  The mist momentarily, flows
  The dark down and away; and they muse
  On a pattern of sky and a leaf there that blows.
  And a happiness, sudden, unmeaning, unmeant, with-
      out cause,
  Arises, renews,
  In that leaf, in that pattern of sky and there gathers
      and grows."

Of still greater significance, however, is the frequent appearance of a line form which MacLeish was later to use more and more frequently and to make characteristically his. It is a stately, measured line, marked by strong alliteration, a line like:

"Have you heard music at morning of far sea singing?"

But what of the content of *The Happy Marriage?* The title poem is a long one, describing fondly the growth of love between two people, the fears it engenders, the doubts, the hesitancies, and the certainties. One feels that in it MacLeish has depicted his own emotional experience. The entire volume, in fact, is intensely subjective, introspective, concerned above all with the poet's absorption in his individual perplexities and emotions. Throughout is the sense of his tragic

**realization** of the transitory quality of love, of beauty, of life itself.

> "Always the shadow ranges,
>   Always the hour estranges,
>   Always tomorrow's morrow's at the brow."

But "tomorrow's morrow" suggests no faith in the future: it rather echoes the despair that is distilled in the line:

> "Things he had loved because he knew them lost."

This recognition of the fleeting quality of life does not preclude a continuance of MacLeish's search for the "enduring grace," "the perfected thing, the hope made real." It but adds greater poignancy to the quest; for the poet, unable longer to believe in the inevitable rightness of intuition, has not yet found any other source of help. He is confronted with blankness, with nothingness. The cry of futility is the carousel chant of "Chevaux de Bois."

> "Who'll ride on the Merry-go-round!
>     *Toot! Toot!*
>   Who'll ride on the Merry-go-round!
>     Who'll undergo birth
>     For a whirl on the earth,
>   Who'll ride on the Merry-go-round!
>     Ump! Ump!
>   Who'll ride on the Merry-go-round!"

The wooden horses move unceasingly; but arrive nowhere. The dizzy, aimless ride exacts its toll. "You pay as you enter," the final stanza begins; and ends in that epitome of disillusionment:

"And you pay when you leave us, my dear."

However unlike in mood, in manner the poem suggests the poetry of Vachel Lindsay. Other poems in the volume reflect the influence upon MacLeish of other writers. "The Lord Chancellor Prepares His Opinion," for example, in its fine, though indirect, psychological revelation of character, is reminiscent of Robert Browning.

Yet it would be inaccurate to assume that all, or even most, of the poetry of *The Happy Marriage* is derivative. It is far too personal for that, too much the cry of a bewildered soul, lost in the universe. It is true that other souls have felt themselves lost and have said so in poetry. But, in this volume, MacLeish, though reflecting a general mood, is already modifying it by his own individual perspective, tempering it with his own kind of humor:

"No more nor ever like the bright brave gull
 Will I go hawking in the windy world.
 I am turned robin and I wisely pull
 A worm occasional from garden sod,
 Thankful to dodge the dreadful acorns hurled
 In jest or malice by the garden god."

63

This process of individualization was not a process of isolating himself from the rest of mankind. On the contrary, quite the opposite was taking place. For Mac-Leish came to see his search for the eternal verities of life as a repetition of a pattern already set by humanity, came to identify his experience with the experience of the race.

The common fund of human experience is often best discovered in folk-lore. From a collection of such lore, *The Golden Bough* by Frazer, MacLeish uses a quotation as the theme for his next volume, *The Pot of Earth,* published in 1925. This quotation tells the story of an ancient rite of Adonis: the planting of seeds in baskets of earth so shallow that though the seeds sprouted, they could not take proper root. At the end of eight days, the baskets of growing plants, together with images of the god, were taken to the seas and rivers and there thrown into the waters. Thus, in symbols, was repeated the cycle of birth and death and birth again, the endless round of existence. Against the elaborated background of this ancient custom, MacLeish tells the story of a young girl from her adolescence through her marriage and the birth of her child. Her cry for the answer to the problems of life is MacLeish's cry:

> "There are things I have to do
> More than just to live and die,
> More than just to die of living."

Her effort to find an answer in the continuity of the race is MacLeish's effort:

"the salt stone
That the sea divulges does not fructify.
It sits by itself. It is sufficient. But you—
Who was your great-grandfather or your mother's
    mother?"

Her effort is unrewarded. Even the birth of her child
brings no answer; it is merely the beginning of the
repetitive process of life, another turn through space
of the endless cycle. At one point in the poem, the girl
compares herself to a room entered at the end of a long
journey, a room of which the windows open "Upon the
night or perhaps nothing." "Nothing" and "nothingness" seem to bear the burden of the refrain of Mac-
Leish's thought.

But if *The Pot of Earth* shows no change in the conclusion of his philosophical pondering, it does show,
on the side of manner, a still further development of
technique. There is continued use of the alliterative
line. Repetition, too, is used as an effective device—
both the repetition of idea, such as:

"Tell me, do the dead come out of the sea?
  Does the spring come from the sea?
  Does the dead god
  Come again from the water?"

and the insistent, haunting repetition of words:

"She could not sleep,
Feeling the dead thing by her bed, feeling

The slow fingers feeling, feeling the earth
Divided by the fingers of the grass,
Of trees, of flowers, by the pressing fingers,
Of grass pierced, feeling the earth pierced
And the limp stalk flowering."

There is still another marked characteristic, that of transposition or change in the normal and expected order of words.

"The grass
Burdened and nothing blossoms, grows
In the fields nothing, and the garden fallow."

At times, the startling effect of an unexpectedly placed word is most emphatic; at times, it must be confessed, it is merely confusing. It is a device that MacLeish uses with increasing frequency in his later work.

*The Pot of Earth* is a single poem. It was followed, in 1926, by a volume of poems, called *Streets in the Moon*. In this volume, MacLeish is further concerned with technical problems; but the result is that many of the poems appear too studied, too mannered. Words are used to astonish, not to clarify. What, for example, is a "gerundive voice"? Exactly what is gained by the deliberate choice of such words as these of "Hearts' and Flowers' "?

"The delicate lepidopteran tongue
Uncurls
Invades, insinuous penetrant,

Through vulnerable whorls
The cloven stigma of that fluctuant
    That palpable among
      Impalpable soft flowers, sea
Anemone
Whose labial perianth
Closes."

However grotesque, this is still understandable. As much can scarcely be said of "Ombres Chinoises."

    "The sun fell
     In a pattern of Whose,
     I thought, face
     Would be all just
     Turning and not
     Yet and a white
     Hard replacing
     Brightness precisely
     Afterwards."

As if this were not sufficiently bewildering, there is in a number of poems an absence of punctuation that makes for confusion. A valid answer to such criticism might be made; punctuation is, after all, a visual aid and poems are meant for the ear and not for the eye. But in several poems, the poet seems to have forgotten that poems are primarily auditory; words are so placed on the page as to intensify meaning, spacing thus becoming an actual poetic device. "Primitive" uses it. So, too, does "Post-Card," where space suggests separation:

> "I     here: you     then
> And the days and the nights that divide us—
> How shall we cross them again?
> By what wind? On what tide?"

Quite evidently the poet is using new devices and trying new effects to create a style suitable to his own needs and purposes. He experiments further with the sound of words and develops a tendency to replace rhyme with assonance:

> "I do not wonder stones
> You have withstood so long
> The strong winds and the snows."

He modifies even so fixed a form as the sonnet. "Against Illumination," for example, though a sonnet metrically, has no rhyme. "The End of the World," on the other hand, uses one of the conventional rhyme schemes; but the feminine ending of several lines—the presence of an additional final unaccented syllable—produces a slightly new sonnet rhythm.

Such technical experimentation was, of course, not limited to MacLeish. The literary world, American and European, generally, was trying new devices and trying them, moreover, not in an esthetic vacuum of isolation from the rest of mankind. Writers, like others, were influenced by the currents of thought, psychological and social, that were changing man's outlook on the world. Scientific theories, on the one hand, were displacing man from his assumed position as the center of the universe; psychology, on the other, was revealing the vast and hitherto unknown realm of man's unconscious and stressing its importance as the motivating force of conduct. While science was belittling man as a negligible factor in the scheme of things, psychology was making significant man's every feeling and gesture.

How did this affect writing generally and, specifically, MacLeish's poetry? It provided both new subject matter for literature and a new method of presenting material. Musings, seemingly unrelated associations, scarcely expressed thoughts that revealed character more clearly than articulate thought or outward action became the legitimate material for writers. Material from these different layers of consciousness was presented in close juxtaposition; a character's expressed words contrasted with his unexpressed, and frequently unadmitted, thoughts; or a series of external, objective events projected against a background of aroused, associated ideas. This is MacLeish's method in "Ancestral" and is very definitely employed in "Memorial Rain," wherein the facts of a dedication of a war memorial in Belgium are thrown into cruel contrast with the poet's own thoughts of his own war dead.

So introspective a literary method is obviously congenial to MacLeish, still absorbed in the problem of his relation to the universe.

> "Is it I then, only I,
> I who have such need to know,
> I alone that cannot read?"

He still is without an answer to his consuming question, seeking for it within himself.

> "No lamp has ever shown us where to look"

is his avowal of helplessness. Nature refuses an answer; nature refuses and so does the mind of man.

> "We have eyelids to be blind."

Even the trained mind, even science, gives no help. MacLeish is forced to reach the same conclusion that he earlier did, the utter inexplicability of life. The theme of the earlier "Chevaux de Bois," that of the aimless passage of existence, is repeated in "Mother Goose's Garland":

> "Around, around the sun we go:
> The moon goes round the earth.
> We do not die of death:
> We die of vertigo."

The poem in this volume that outstandingly epitomizes this quest and its failure, this fruitless search for reality, security, an answer—call it what you will—is the poem "Einstein." Symbolically, the figure of the modern scientist represents the failure of man's intellect. But, significantly enough, humor enlivens this poem, so that the reader no longer senses a devastating despair; and, still more important, a new note is struck, a note of dignity, of human inviolability in the face of overwhelming odds.

> "But still the dark denies him. Still withstands
> The dust his penetration and flings back
> Himself to answer him. Which seems to keep
> Something inviolate. A living something."

This acceptance of man's fate is the conclusion of *The Hamlet of A. MacLeish,* published in 1928, that strange poem which expresses the extreme of self-probing. Into a running prose comment derived vaguely from Shakespeare's *Hamlet* are fitted poetic pictures of the unconnected meditations of a soul sensitive to the world's upheavals. The poem contains no built up drama of action or even of ideas; coherence of thought yields to the layers-of-consciousness method. The poem is difficult to understand. "It is perhaps the chief merit of this poem," writes one critic,* "that often its lines do not need to be understood in order that their emotional content be apprehended, so admirably does the sound suggest the sense." Incomprehensibility is scarcely a virtue. Yet it is true that the reader not only recognizes MacLeish's self-identification with Hamlet struggling with his inability to "set things right," but the reader comes in turn to identify himself with

* Lewis Galantière: "Hamlet for Our Times," *The Nation,* April 17, 1929.

the double Hamlet–MacLeish protagonist. The poem, though highly intellectualized, still fails to give an intellectual answer to the poet's besetting problem. Its conclusion is a felt, not a reasoned, acceptance of inevitability:

> "We must consent now as all men
> Whose rage is out of them must do,
>
> .   .   .   .   .
>
> It is time we should accept. . . .
>
> *Thou wouldst not think*
> *How ill all's here about my heart!"*

With *The Hamlet*, MacLeish evidently reached the depths of his self-examination. It was necessary to turn elsewhere for help. Once before, in *The Pot of Earth*, he had turned to the past, but that was the vague, indefinite past of the human race. Now he turned to a more direct, a closer past. He recognized that one of the elements of security is a sense of continuity, a realization of inherited custom and tradition. France had seemed a possible haven because of this very sense.

> "They live together in small things. They eat
>  The same dish, their drink is the same and their
>     proverbs.
>  Their youth is like."

But it became increasingly apparent that the French past was not his, that the ties that bound the French, one to another, did not bind him. In spite of his deep and abiding love for France, he knew that his roots were, after all, in America. So, in 1928, he returned with his family to the United States, to a farm in Farmington, Connecticut, a pleasant little town in the foothills of the Berkshires.

"It is a strange thing—to be an American," he writes in "American Letter." He appreciates that America is "neither a land nor a people"; that it is made up of many peoples, with no homogeneity, talking only "taught speech and the aped tongue." Yet it still speaks with authority; and it succeeded in calling MacLeish back from Europe:

"This, this is our land, this is our people,
  This that is neither a land nor a race. We must reap
  The wind here in the grass for our soul's harvest:
  Here we must eat our salt or our bones starve.
  Here we must live or live only as shadows."

"American Letter" appears in *New Found Land,* published in 1930, a volume composed of poems some of which were written in America, some in Europe. As though unwilling to throw off completely the influences of his earlier European years, MacLeish retains some of his old mannerisms. He still indulges in some peculiar tricks of typography and there is still evidence of a disdain for punctuation.

But the idiosyncrasies are again offset by the sureness of his craftsmanship. His early experiments with line form apparently satisfied him, for in *New Found Land* he uses with consummate skill this line in the old Anglo-Saxon tradition, a line of measured rhythm, of balanced vowel and consonant sounds, strong in alliteration, and using alliteration and assonance as a frequent substitute for the more ordinary rhyme. A splendid example of this verse with its balanced halves, its double alliteration of *w* and *s* is the line

"Their word for the sea is a word meaning sorrow."

Two other MacLeish characteristics are marked: the feeling for letter sounds, as in the *b, r, l* sounds of

"Branches bearing a round leaf and bridles;"

and the old habit of word transposition, as in

"Weakener let the wings
Descend of dawn on our roof-trees!"

Just as his technique, though still retaining peculiarities, became surer, so did the subject of his poetry assume a greater certainty. MacLeish continues to pursue his quest, as he does in "Reproach to Dead Poets"; and, at times, as in "Men," it is attended with despair. But for the greater part, there is now a sense of direction to the search, a feeling that there is some hope of an answer. The loneliness, the isolation is gone. The poet is beginning to break through the walls that shut him within himself and to grope toward other people.

This is the tenor of "American Letter." A warm humanity has entered his poetry, as in the lovely "Immortal Autumn," that poem in praise of "the human season." Man and nature approach a reconciliation, an embracing instead of the earlier rejection. And in "You, Andrew Marvell," the life of one man, the life of all men, and the very sun in its heavenly course seem unified.

This change in philosophical outlook can be explained only by those impulses within MacLeish that carried him from Europe back to his native land. His homecoming, both physical and spiritual, became an extended one—in time and in space. He decided that he must learn to know his new home, not only in its present but in its past as well. However old may be the tradition of the United States, south of the United States is a continuous culture still older, derived through the Spanish from the aboriginal Indians. So in 1929 MacLeish went to Mexico, traveling alone up from the coast over the route taken by the conqueror Cortez in the sixteenth century. An idea grew, an idea already in his mind in France, where he had written a poem later to be used as a prologue; enriched by the material of his trip, it was expanded into plans for a long narrative on the Spanish Conquest.

The result was *Conquistador*, published in 1932. It is one of the few examples of long English poems written in *terza rima*. The basis of this verse form is a three-line stanza, the first and third lines rhyming, the second providing the rhyming scheme for the first and third line of the succeeding stanza:

"Standing with morning to an island shore:
  And the wind was toward us and we knew that place:
  We few—Grijalva's soldiers that before

Sailed in those waters where the low sun paces—
  We did remember: and with sideways eyes
  Sought and yet looked not in each other's faces."

It is evident, even from these two stanzas, that the form, as used by MacLeish, undergoes modifications: *place,* for example, is, of course, not an exact rhyme for *paces.* There is still greater freedom in rhyme in such schemes as: *feel of, charge, wheel at; strangeness, Medina, rain; seen, Montezuma, leaving; plumes, city, rooms.* Such a scheme, wherein the rhyming syllables are not the final ones, gives the effect of assonance rather than of rhyme, and it is by his use of assonance that MacLeish makes the *terza rima* peculiarly his own:

" 'This is an undiscovered and dark land:
  'All this that you say is true; but the words of your
  'Fear are not true: there is one ship: man her!

  'Take what you will of the stone: a keel's burden.' "

In these lines, there is no rhyme at all; there is, however, enough similarity of sound in *land* and *man* and in *words of your* and *burden* to carry along the flow of the poetry.

Occasionally a line stumbles. Weakly ending lines like

"Sadness to seek for our thirst—as a maker of words
        to an"

are disquietingly present. So, too, are those that show the retained habit of transposition. But these are relatively few and become unimportant in the face of the vast total of the book which proceeds with a fluent dignity, derived from the balanced, alliterative line that is typically MacLeish's.

The poetry is further heightened by an increased vividness of expression. "Sea-remembering land" creates an instantaneous and definite picture. So, too, do lines like

"Pursing the nib of a No on his lips"

and these describing a boat cutting its way through the water:

"Water under the bow-wash green: the wading
 Keel clean in the eddyless swirl of it: rinse of the
 Salt wake slaking the sea: and we came to the

 Outmost ocean."

This sensitivity to detail builds in the tenth book of the poem a picture, startling in its vividness, of an old Mexican market town. Combined with great force of feeling, it produces that moving speech of Cortez to his

77

men, a speech that contrasts the life the soldiers know with the dangers that may confront them.

With a mastery of material and poetic technique, MacLeish gives an account of the conquest as revealed through the personality of one Bernal Diaz del Castillo, a soldier under Cortez. An old man, now,

> "unused to the combing of
> Words clean of the wool while the tale waits,"

the Spaniard indulges in his reminiscences, which differ widely, he realizes, from the historical accounts of the scholars.

But even as a personalized account, *Conquistador* does not present a consecutive history of the occupation. The events of the narrative are hazy, difficult to follow. There is no suggestion of continuity of action, of sequence, of cause and effect; there is no building up of climax; there is not even an effort at the dramatic. *Conquistador* is not history. Indeed, it is not sustained narrative; nor does it appear to be, as some would have it, an exposition of contrasting civilizations, symbolizing through the figures of Montezuma and Cortez the past and the industrialized, mechanized present. It seems much more to be a further exploration by Mac-Leish into personality, this time not his own but that of another. It is Bernal's poem, the poem of a man who, in the face of old age, regrets his vanished youth, the power to act and to feel acutely. His regret is not simply for a past that will not return, for a past, once fervent but now desiccated in history:

"Now are our deeds words: our lives chronicles."

It is rather a mourning for the steady and inevitable disintegration of personality, for the loss to the individual and to the world of feelings and emotions.

"The sad thing is not death: the sad thing
Is the life's loss out of earth when the living vanish."

*Conquistador* was enthusiastically received. MacLeish had already become known to poetry lovers. Quiet-mannered and shy, he had appeared before groups of them and had been accepted by them as the spokesman of a changing world. In 1929, *Poetry* had awarded him the John Reed Memorial Prize. With *Conquistador,* however, his circle of readers increased. For in recognition of its merits, he was awarded in 1933 the Pulitzer Prize and so gained the publicity and prestige that accompany that award.

When the announcement of the award was made, MacLeish was in England gathering material about the English department store, Selfridge's, for an article that was to appear in the magazine *Fortune*. He had become a contributing editor of that magazine in order to earn the living that poetry by itself could not provide. His association with this magazine has great significance, for *Fortune* is devoted to the description and analysis of large businesses and of influential business men. That MacLeish should have allied himself with a magazine of that nature was an indication that he had climbed down from the remote ivory tower of his youth and was becoming an observer of and a participant in the activity of the busy, confusing world of the day. He could not restrict himself to hoped-for, indefinite ideals; he had to concern himself with objective, realistic facts.

At this period, there was still another activity that contributed to MacLeish's increasingly rounded point of view. Beginning in February 1937, he was a guest professor at Princeton University, giving lectures there on poetry and conducting a course in creative writing.

For a present-day poet to speak with any authority, it is most important that he have an embracing point of view. He must know the craft of his profession and he must have the spirit and insight that always from remote times have been necessary to artistic creation. But today, if he wishes to be heard and listened to by more than a small group of esthetes, it is necessary that he be aware of what is happening in the world about him, that he may throw upon these events the light of his own sensitivity, and distill from them the universal, the poetic qualities.

The effect upon MacLeish of this widening of interest was amazing. His attitude became almost diametrically opposed to his earlier one. *Frescoes for Mr. Rockefeller's City,* a slender volume of poems published in 1933, reveals this change. In it appears "Oil Painting of the Artist as the Artist," a satiric study of "plump Mr. Pl'f," an artist who "is washing his hand of America" because he feels that only in Europe can pure art flourish. How well could this have been called "Portrait of A. MacLeish as a Young Man!" Surely this is a transformed poet who is now writing, one who feels himself part of the American scene and believes in that America as a source of beauty and poetry.

Yet even greater than this change in temperamental outlook is the change in the subjects that engross the poet. He turns away from the introspective probing into his own thoughts and feelings and from the wishful reliance on abstract intuition as the source of truth, turns from these to the social and political ideas agitating the minds of his contemporaries. He appreciates the labor that has entered into the making of America; he is aware of the part that finance plays; he knows the bitter conflict between labor and capital:

"There's nothing good in the world but the rich will
     buy it."

But scathing as are his denunciations of those who have grown wealthy through the exploitation of labor, just as biting are his comments on the pretended friends of labor, on "parlor Socialists and Communists"; on "Comrade Devine," for example, who would write of America, though all he knows of it is what he has learned by going between New York and Hoboken by ferry; on "Comrade Grenadine" who seeks for "something to feel strongly about in verses, his personal passion having tired." Underlying these pictures of the elements in America's economic life are a firmly established faith in America as a molding and modifying force and a conviction of America's strength, a ringing insistence (that echoes slightly of Sandburg) that

"She's a tough land under the corn mister."

These social-minded poems are included in *Poems, 1924-1933,* that volume which MacLeish said was not to trace his development as a poet, but which, in spite of the poet's insistence, does present a developing picture of his writing. His very earliest poems, one finds, are not included. Some of his later poems appear in a somewhat altered form. But the great body of his poetry is there, as it was originally written. One sees reflected in it the lyric poet who, first as an expatriate, then later returned to his native land, is concerned primarily with his own individual emotions, with his personal search for the eternal verities, for something to which he can pin his hope and his conviction. One notes the change that the search undergoes; how first it is intensely subjective and looks to the intuitive; then it includes personality other than the writer's alone; and finally breaks through to the objective, concrete world. The method of the poetry, so far as generalization is possible, is, for the most part, simple: a presentation, often without any recognized reason for their order, of a number of instances which evoke memories and stimulate emotions. The style undergoes modification until a distinctive one is evolved: a sturdy, masculine sentence form, often with involved word order and complicated syntax; poetic lines, long and rhythmically balanced; words chosen with a keen regard for their true values; alliteration and assonance as the most prominent poetic devices.

*Poems* must not be considered to mark the end of a period, to draw a line of demarcation between earlier and later work. True, some of the earlier subjects and earlier methods were later completely abandoned; but others were continued into MacLeish's later writing. Already in *Poems* there is indication of an awakened social consciousness, an inclusion into the sphere of the poet's interests of other people with their activities and their problems. The "Frescoes" do more than suggest that. "1933," the Harvard Phi Beta Kappa poem, expresses it definitely. A poet unaware of or indifferent to the life outside himself could not write, as MacLeish writes in that poem, of "millions starving for corn with mountains of waste corn"; could not urge an avoidance of "childhood utopia" and of copy-book maxims; could not exhort

"You have only to push on
To whatever it is that's beyond us

Showing the flat of your sword and they'll
Lick sand from before you!

Bring yourselves to a home:
To a new land: to an ocean

Never sailed."

So, in *Public Speech,* published in 1936, there is a continuation of the technical devices which MacLeish has developed and employed. At the same time, there is increased distinction in the poetry: a deepening of feeling, a more vivid and effective expression. "The Late Meeting," a poem in "The Woman on the Stairs" series, is as lovely a poem as any MacLeish has written, one instinct with feelings which, though personal, can be universalized: the realization that emotions change with time and that in those who once loved each other may now be found only the "fault of strangeness." Equally effective is " 'Dover Beach'—a note to that poem." This, too, having for its theme the passage of time, is a poem of the philosophy of middle age. Life has reached the ebbing tide; but it is "the outward wave that spills the inward forward." So the poet waiting, as wave waits for wave, for the younger generation that will replace his own, knows his share in its accomplishments:

"Let them go over us all I say with the thunder of
  What's to be next in the world. It's we will be under
    it!"

With increased maturity comes a deepening sense of kinship with his fellow men. Feelings strengthen. Even love becomes something more than the intimate emotion between two people; no longer tender and fragile, it "hardens into hate" and develops into the strong force that binds man to man in a common purpose.

This feeling of identity with his fellows is amplified in "Speech to those who say Comrade." They are brothers who have shared experiences; indeed, only experiences that have been shared have validity:

84

"The solitary and unshared experience
Dies of itself like the violation of love
Or lives on as the dead live eerily."

The question that had beset MacLeish in his more youthful days arises. With the years this, too, undergoes modification. Still the question of man's relation to the universe, it now has, besides its metaphysical aspect, economic and political aspects. "Whence was the word to come?" he asks in "Speech to a crowd." But no longer is he doubtful about the source of the answer. The answer comes from within; not from the individual, however, but from the mass:

"No one knows if you dont:

. . . . . . .

You have your eyes and what your eyes see is."

With this knowledge, should come action:

"Tell yourselves the earth is yours to take!

Waiting for messages out of the dark you were poor.
The world was always yours: you would not take it."

Prior to the publication of *Common Speech,* Mac-Leish had shown his sensitivity to existing economic conditions. Moreover, he had expressed his interest in a literary form other than that of pure poetry. *Panic,* a play in verse, had three performances and then appeared in book form in 1935. In the introduction to that volume, MacLeish states some of his philosophy of writing. Art, he declares, is by nature dynamic; refusing to be frozen and crystallized, it must find methods suitable for the time for which it is intended. So, the poet says, he experimented with verse forms for this play until he found one "capable of catching and carrying the rhythm of the spoken language of his time and place." Then, as if to emphasize that break with the past which, in his own case, had created peculiar verse patterns, he adds, "Verse, after all, is not an arrangement upon the page: it is a pattern in the ear."

*Panic* is the story of the ruin of a great financier. A chorus, used to express the many-voiced American people—not, as in classic drama, a single, unified viewpoint—suggests the poverty, the sickness, and the suffering of the great mass of people. But while there is explicit in the play the antagonism between poverty and wealth, between oppressed labor and finance, the drama does not lie in that conflict. It lies within the person of the financier, of McGafferty, himself, as he passes through the stages of the financial crisis and finally realizes his eventual defeat. The Blind Man, acting as spokesman for the oppressed, makes McGafferty realize the cause of his downfall:

> "It is not we who threaten you. Your ill is
> Time and there's no cure for time but dying!"

Far back in time lie the beginnings of wrong. With the inexorable march of time come the fateful consequences.

Time is the enemy; but time, alone, can be the rescuer. So the many Voices finally cry:

"Follow!

Give!
Go with the
Rushing of time in us!

Make of the
Silence of fate a trumpet!
Make of the time a drum!

March!

Shout!"

Consistent with his conception of art as a dynamic force are MacLeish's latest writings. In *The Fall of the City* and in *Air Raid,* he adapts his art to the radio so that he may enlarge his audience. In *The Land of the Free* he employs a technique suggested by moving pictures. This use of art forms designed primarily for great masses of people marks the final, the complete reaction from the first escapist attitude of the young romantic poet.

Radio, the poet feels, can well use poetry. "Over the radio," he writes in the introduction to *The Fall of the City,* "verse has no visual presence to compete with. Only the ear is engaged and the ear is already half poet. It believes at once: creates and believes." Furthermore, he recognizes in the Announcer, to whom the radio listener is accustomed, a useful addition to his cast of characters, one who adds depth to radio drama.

In *The Fall of the City,* a woman risen from the dead becomes an omen of disaster; thus she heralds impending doom:

> "The city of masterless men
> Will take a master."

The people are panic-stricken. They believe unquestioningly that the enemy will overthrow them, though who or what the enemy is they do not know. They are harangued by various factions: by the General, who bids them fight; by the Orator, who insists that force is useless, that truth is their only defense; by the priests, who urge them to turn to their gods.

The people, obsessed by fear, yield supinely to their terror. Convinced that defeat is inevitable, they declare:

> "There's no holding it!
> Let the conqueror have it! It's his!"

As they throw away their arms in a gesture of subjection, the Announcer takes up the narration. He describes how a huge figure has made his appearance, and has just opened the visor of his helmet to reveal himself. Then, in an awesome whisper, the Announcer proceeds:

> "There's no one!
> There's no one      at all! . . .

No one?

The helmet is hollow!

.    .    .    .    .    .    .

The people invent their oppressors: they wish to believe
  in them.
They wish to be free of their freedom: released from
  their liberty:—
The long labor of liberty ended!

The crowd hails their conqueror:
    The city of masterless men has found a master!
    The city has fallen!
    The city has fallen!"

The Voice of the Announcer picks up flatly the final
sentence and repeats:

  "The city has fallen. . . ."

It is that flat pronouncement that points the whole
drama: a people is indeed lost, when individuals cede
their rights and privileges. Those four words, simple,
direct, in the language and rhythm of common speech,
are weighty with poetic insight and philosophic import.

The destruction of a city, but in this case destruction from without not within, is the theme, too, of *Air
Raid*. The play, itself, has some of the wonder of
prophecy about it. It was written during the summer of
1938 and was in the hands of the broadcasting company several weeks before the Czecho-Slovakian crisis

of September of that year. Yet in pathos, in vividness, and in tenseness of situation, it depicts what has since proved to be the fate of many European villages and cities.

The Studio Director outlines briefly the general situation: the world is aware that a war ultimatum has been issued and that within the hour a decision has to be reached. Connection is to be made with the little town which will be the scene of the opening attack, an airplane bombardment. It is

"One of those old-time hill-towns where the papers
  Come tomorrow morning and the wars
  Come years ago or in some other country:"

Then the Announcer takes up the broadcast. He describes the early morning scene, the children playing, the women busy with their household tasks, gossiping, ridiculing the idea of war and men who think of war:

"Wasting their time on wars with the
Dishes to do and the children to chasten.

The wars!
As though to make the wars were something wonderful!
Millions of men have made the wars and talked."

.    .    .    .    .    .    .

"A woman's got no time to watch the wars—"

The happy, gentle, normal life is revealed. Suddenly it is broken off. The enemy planes are sighted. When the

Police Sergeant announces their arrival, the cries of the women are pitiful. This is something new, strange, fiendish; a war not between armed men, but a war on unarmed, peace-loving women. Amazed, as though their presence alone should drive off the enemy, the women cry

"It's us do you see."

The Announcer describes in detail the formation of the planes and their actions. One hears the cries of the women. The planes' guns are heard, now loudly, now faintly. Then there is quiet—the quiet of destruction. As the humming planes disappear into the distance, three sounds are heard: the call of a child; the plea of a young man to the woman he loves:

"Stay as you are: do not move:
Do not ever move."

and the agonizing scale sung by the Singing Woman. The rest is silence.

The impact of the play's ending is great. For by slight but extremely deft touches, MacLeish succeeds in building up the happy, sparkling life of a small community. He presents a number of distinct, if lightly drawn, characters. The implications of their annihilation are horrible.

*The Fall of the City* and *Air Raid,* produced on the radio, reached a large radio audience. *Land of the Free,* however, while employing modified moving picture technique has not been made into a moving picture. It has been published in book form; but it is a book that displays a reversal of usual and expected values. Instead of being a poem illustrated by pictures, it is a collection of pictures illustrated by a poem. The poem, like the sound-track of a talking picture, is used to explain and animate the visual images.

The pictures form a photographic American document. They tell the story of the search for real freedom by those who have been overwhelmed by poverty, by greed, and by exploitation. Once they were convinced that

"All you needed for freedom was being American."

As poverty overtakes them, they become less sure of their belief. As frontiers recede and disappear, taking from them hope of cheap, fertile land, they are less sure:

"Now that the grass is behind us: the measureless
        pasture
  Greening before the last frost left the ground:
  Yellow by middle summer: cured in autumn:
  Tawny: color of hide: windy as water:
  A mile up: big as a continent: clean with the
  Whole sky going over it:

        .       .       .       .       .       .       .

  Now that the land's behind us we get wondering

  We wonder if the liberty was land and the
  Land's gone: the liberty's back of us. . . ."

As industrial conditions oppress them, they grow more and more uncertain. Following the highways in their search for work, they wonder. "Men don't talk much standing by the roads." The final pictures are those of industrial workers in a May Day celebration of the end of a steel strike and of farmers emigrating from the dust bowl country to California for a new start in life. The final words are:

"We wonder if the liberty is done:
The dreaming is finished

We can't say

We aren't sure

Or if there's something different men can dream
Or if there's something different men can mean by

Liberty . . .

Or if there's liberty a man can mean that's
Men: not land

We wonder

We don't know

We're asking"

The poem does not end in a declaration. Doubtful, indecisive, it merely implies. But the implications are obvious: a need for group activity, a dire need for overcoming social and economic wrongs if the phrase "Life, liberty, and the pursuit of happiness" is to be more than mere words, is to have for vast numbers of Americans any real meaning at all.

Much more explicit is the message of *America Was Promises,* published in 1939. In a manner reminiscent of that of *Common Speech,* it sketches the development of America as the land of promise for the people. For the people, it is important to note:

"Whatever was truly built the People had built it.
Whatever was taken down they had taken down."

It cites the devastated countries of the world as testimony of what occurs when the people lose control of what is rightfully theirs.

"Listen! Brothers! Generation!
Listen! You have heard these words. Believe it!
Believe the promises are theirs who take them!

Believe unless we take them for ourselves
Others will take them for the use of others!
Believe unless we take them for ourselves
All of us: one here: another there:
Men not Man: people not the People:
Hands: mouths: arms: eyes: not syllables—
Believe unless we take them for ourselves
Others will take them: not for us! for others!

 .  .  .  .  .  .  .

Believe

America is promises to
Take!

America is promises to
Us
To take them
Brutally
With love but
Take them.

O believe this!"

These last two poems have great significance for an appreciation of MacLeish. One notes in them the search still for an ideal, the quest MacLeish has always pursued. But now he seeks it not for himself, but for all Americans. He seeks it, furthermore, not in an abstract realm, but in the material, physical, economic world, in man's harmonious relation with his fellow man.

As the field of MacLeish's poetic interest widened, he felt the desire and need for a growing audience; no writer, the poet himself said, wishes to be confined between the unopened covers of a book on a library table. This explains his sorties into the drama and the radio. It cannot be too strongly emphasized that in these new modes of expression he did not desert poetry for prose.

It is quite possible that MacLeish's verse will undergo modifications as he meets new problems. For the present, he has formulated a style suited to his needs. Its characteristics have already been indicated. Technical devices are merely means to an end, tools to be used in the creation of poetic beauty. Among the many poems in which such beauty lies are "L'an Trentiesme de Mon Eage," "Memorial Rain," "You, Andrew Marvell," "Immortal Autumn," "1892-19—," "The Late Meeting," "Reconciliation" and "Voyage":

> "Heap we these coppered hulls
> With headed poppies
> And garlic longed-for by the eager dead
>
> Keep we with sun caught sails
> The westward ocean
> Raise we that island on the sea at last
>
> Steep to the gull-less shore
> Across the ocean rush
> Trade we our cargoes with the dead for sleep."

MacLeish's practice of his art is no haphazard functioning of chance. He has a sure conception of the nature and function of poetry. Some of his theory he has expressed in verse: in "Certain Poets," for example, wherein words are compared to birds startled into flight, whether by "Pan or cur" is not known, but

> "save that t'was a prodigy
> A portent sure, and, with its passing by
> A new world dawned;"

and, again, in "Ars Poetica":

"A poem should not mean
But be."

A poem, that is, should exist for its own beauty. This is the ultimate expression of the esthetic tenet of art for art's sake, a reflection of MacLeish's earlier poetic spirit.

His esthetic views change, but always is he insistent on the value of poetry. In a number of articles in various magazines, he makes clear his views. "Poetry like any other art," he writes * in "An Anonymous Generation," "can only reach its highest level in a universe of which man is the center." Poetry, he insists, must concern itself with the "common spiritual experience of men." As science seemed to dethrone man from the universe, poetry suffered; man must be restored to a position of dignity before poetry can be at its greatest.

That to a tough-minded person might seem a putting of the cart before the horse, an unwonted emphasis upon poetry rather than upon man. Such a one might say that man is beset by so many problems today that poetry might well be ignored. In a world troubled sorely by social, political, and economic ills, is there any place for poetry at all?

This question MacLeish answers with an unequivocal affirmative. The failure of the world today is a failure of the spirit, he says,† and then proceeds: "This failure of the spirit is a failure from which only poetry

* *Saturday Review of Literature,* December 7, 1929.
† *Poetry,* July, 1938: "In Challenge, Not Defense."

can deliver us. In this incapacity of the people to imagine, this impotence of the people to imagine and believe, only poetry can be of service. For only poetry, of all those proud and clumsy instruments by which men explore this planet and themselves, *creates the thing it sees.* Only poetry, exploring the spirit of man, is capable of creating in a breathful of words the common good men have become incapable of imagining for themselves. Only poetry, moving among living men on the living earth, is capable of discovering that common world to which the minds of men do, inwardly, not knowing it, assent." Poetry, which draws the picture of "things that may possibly happen," the picture of the ideal, is a challenge to human possibility; it "alone imagines, and imagining creates, the world that men can wish to live in and make true."

What kind of world is that? Is it a world of Communism? When, in the spring of 1939, MacLeish was named by President Roosevelt for the position of Librarian of Congress (a position to which he was finally appointed) among the criticisms leveled against him was the charge of his being a member of the Communist party. Whatever may be his political affiliations as an individual, in his poetry he presents no clear-cut formula, no carefully packaged panacea. He avoids identification with any specific party. In "Invocation to the Social Muse," in fact, he insists that a poet must not align himself with any faction. The life of a poet is sufficiently difficult. "Is it just to demand of us also to bear arms?"

But does this imply a pusillanimous acceptance of things as they are? Such an attitude would scarcely be consistent with his belief in poetry as a constructive, forward-looking force. What, then, are the principles for which he stands, the principles which he as a poet, primarily and always as a poet, demands as requisites for existence?

As a poet he has "no stake in the existing economic order. *Qua* artist, we are perfectly unconcerned with the name by which the state is to be described, whether capitalistic or socialistic or communistic or Fascist." * The one thing in which as artist he is interested is freedom to pursue that art. "We cannot exist without that freedom to do our own work in our own way which is called, for lack of an accurate term, intellectual freedom."

These views he further enlarged in a talk in 1935 before the National Association of Book Publishers. An artist cannot accept fashionable esthetic dogma, he declared, whatever may be the source of fashion's authority or whatever may be the power that enforces it. "And the condition of any writer's success as an intelligence is the refusal to think as everyone about him thinks and the ceaseless effort to arrive at personal perceptions. In other words, a writer's real success is always founded in refusal to accept his time on its own terms." (To this, incidentally, he humorously added, "Quite commonly the time reciprocates.")

* *Saturday Review of Literature*, January 16, 1932: "To the Young Men of Wall Street."

So MacLeish cannot accept the ready-made code, the regimented thought of Fascism or Communism. He cannot blindly accept. He must be able to look on things from his own individual viewpoint, must be able to envision an ideal to which he as an individual can subscribe. That ability demands freedom of thought and freedom of expression: "What is necessary to the free man, what is above all necessary to the free writer is to consider *without reference to his enemies* the kind of world he himself would like to bring about. That world for all artists, for all men of spirit, is the democratic world, the world in which a man is free to do his own work, the world in which a man may think as he pleases, the world in which a man may with the complete responsibility of a mature individual, control his proper life." *

Whatever encroaches upon this freedom must be fought. In a stirring poem, delivered before the Columbia Phi Beta Kappa in 1937, MacLeish calls upon the scholars to rally to the cause of freedom. Old wars are physical wars, he says; new wars are intellectual wars in which "manuscripts are stretched"

"To make the drumhead to his drum."

So the scholar must fight:

"I say the guns are in your house:
I say there is no room for flight:

* *Forum,* April 19, 1934: "Preface to an American Manifest."

100

Arise O scholars from your peace!
Arise! Enlist! Take arms and fight!"

The scholars have a part to play. Years before in an article on liberal education * MacLeish had asserted that universities must "set before themselves the task of training men to feel themselves members of a race which, as a race, consciously in part, in part unconsciously, moves forward toward its final realization. They must postulate the regeneracy of the race, the hope of the race, God in us." But no less important is the part the poet plays. For it is the poet who establishes these postulates, who arouses and keeps alive these hopes.

However wide has become the circle of MacLeish's poetry, its center is still fixed. Its core is still the poet's intuitive sense. As the poet changes, however, that sense deepens and matures.

The intuitive was the impetus for MacLeish's earliest poetry. In those first years of writing, he was concerned only with his own individual problem of relationship to the universe. He sought—in vain—for a solution:

"What is it we cannot recall?"

The war was devastating, its effects not allayed by the peace. His flight to Europe was a flight, but not a successful escape. Pressure drove him within himself, immured him behind walls that let in no light. With his

* *Yale Review,* January, 1923: "Professional Schools of Liberal Education."

return to America, he gradually broke through the walls; he came to see his problem in the light of the problem of others, to project his feelings into the feelings of others. With increased maturity and more varied experience, he sought not to avoid the world but to participate in its activities. He no longer withdrew into self-contemplation but identified himself with mankind:

"It is this in life which of all things is tenderest—
To remember together with unknown men the days
Common also to them and perils ended."

But in this process of identification he did not lose sight of his own dignity, his own integrity of personality.

Some criticism has been leveled against MacLeish because he has failed to subscribe to any positive social platform, because he has contented himself with the exposition of wrongs that should be righted rather than with arguments for specific means of righting them. In short, he has been criticized not only because he does not indulge in propaganda, but because he does not indulge in propaganda of some specific economic group. That, MacLeish insists, is not the function of the poet. In so far as the poet serves as an instrument of propaganda for any one group, by just that much is he less the poet.

That attitude is, perhaps, the very basis of MacLeish's strength as a poet. There is need today for one who can look upon our time not from one or another limited angle, but can see it as a whole. MacLeish seems to have that wider viewpoint. He is no longer withdrawn into his remote ivory tower or—as so many poets may be—shut up in his dusty attic. Nor is his view limited by what can be seen from a coal pit or through factory windows. He knows economics as he knows poetry; he knows big business as he knows the pitiful meagerness of poverty. He is engaged in trying to understand the here and the now in its entirety. His position is of all perhaps the most difficult, that of a liberal thinker resisting the pressure of organized thought so that he may formulate his own beliefs. William Rose Benét says of him that he "is one of the very few American poets who are trying to get any perspective at all upon their own country."

With such a viewpoint there cannot fail to be an increase in his measure as a poet of America. He will acknowledge no master but himself, serve no cause but his art. For "the first and inescapable obligation of the poet is his obligation to his art."

### POETICAL WORKS

| | |
|---|---|
| THE TOWER OF IVORY | *Yale University Press* |
| THE HAPPY MARRIAGE | *Houghton Mifflin Co.* |
| THE POT OF EARTH | *Houghton Mifflin Co.* |
| STREETS IN THE MOON | *Houghton Mifflin Co.* |
| THE HAMLET OF A. MAC LEISH | |
| | *Houghton Mifflin Co.* |
| NEW FOUND LAND | *Houghton Mifflin Co.* |

103

## POETS OF OUR TIME

CONQUISTADOR                    *Houghton Mifflin Co.*

POEMS, 1924-1933               *Houghton Mifflin Co.*

PANIC, a Play in Verse         *Houghton Mifflin Co.*

PUBLIC SPEECH              *Farrar and Rinehart, Inc.*

THE FALL OF THE CITY, a Verse

  Play for Radio    *Farrar and Rinehart, Inc.*

LAND OF THE FREE          *Harcourt, Brace and Co.*

AIR RAID, a Verse Play for Radio

                              *Harcourt, Brace and Co.*

AMERICA WAS PROMISES

                          *Duell, Sloan and Pearce, Inc.*

*VACHEL  LINDSAY*

## VACHEL LINDSAY

"Yet we are drawn forever by desire,
  Hunting the Eden of the Bible days,
  Hunting the haunts of fays of nursery days,
  Hunting the ways of our fathers, the pioneers,
  Hunting the ancient world's lost lovely years."

MORE than anything else, it was this search for the past, for his own "lost lovely years" and those of the human race, that characterized the life of Vachel Lindsay and found expression in his poetry. He did not look back to the past with a defeated sense that all its splendors had forever departed. Rather he saw in it the virtues and ideas that would create a glorious future, a noble future which he was optimistically confident could and would appear, and to the speedy coming of which he dedicated himself.

With amazing distinctness one can see in Lindsay's childhood the forces that molded him as a man and the origins of his manhood's questings. Family inheritance, parental interests and training, his religion, the social and political background of his time, even the very geography of his birthplace—all these contributed to the making of Vachel Lindsay, the man and the poet.

The Lindsay family, of Kentucky, had been impoverished by the Civil War and its aftermaths. Slaves had been taken away; fertile farmlands had been lost in the Carpet-Bag era; and members of the family, accustomed to the riches and culture of the old leisurely South were reduced to a life of poverty and hardship. Vachel Thomas Lindsay, the poet's father, spurred by his own and his father's ambition, determined to overcome financial handicaps and be a doctor. A common school education enabled him to teach school during the day while he studied medicine at night. After an interrupted course at Miami Medical College, at Cincinnati, Ohio, he was graduated in 1869 and began practicing his profession in Cotton Hill, Illinois, a few miles from the city of Springfield. In 1875, he left Illinois for Europe, for further medical study in Vienna.

Among his fellow passengers on the boat were his own sister Eudora and her friend, Esther Catharine Frazee. Esther, of a family of doctors and lawyers originally settled in Virginia, was the daughter of Ephraim Samuel Frazee, whom fortune had carried to Indiana. While not unmindful of his Virginian background and tradition, Ephraim Frazee during the Civil War threw his sympathies wholeheartedly with the North and imbued his family with his own conviction of the inherent right and justice of the Northern cause. Nor was his influence confined to his family; as preacher, farmer, citizen, he was a dominating power in his community, who

"served a rigid Christ, but served him well—
And, for a lifetime, saved the countryside."

Much of her father's indomitable courage and energy
his daughter had inherited. In spite of a sunstroke at
the age of twelve which had resulted for a time in
almost total blindness and which made her constantly
susceptible to long attacks of nervousness, she had continued her formal education. In 1869, she had been
graduated as valedictorian from the Glendale Female
College. Then she had studied art and had become an
instructor of English and of art at Hocker College,
Lexington, Kentucky. The trip which she was now
taking with Eudora Lindsay was the realization of all
her longings and interests.

Soon it was apparent that a strong attachment existed between the young art instructor and the serious
young doctor. The romance, begun on shipboard, flourished still further when Esther became sick in Rome
and was cared for by Dr. Lindsay. The two became engaged and, upon their return to America, were married
on Thanksgiving Day. They made their home in Springfield, Illinois.

There on November 10, 1879, their second child,
their first—and only—son, was born, Nicholas Vachel
Lindsay. (The *Nicholas* in time came to be dropped
from the poet's name. As for *Vachel*, an old Lindsay
family name, "Vachel is pronounced to rhyme with
Rachel, and is spelt with one *l*. It does not rhyme with

satchel. The poet asked me to tell you that.") * In him was a mixed inheritance: Scotch through his father; and, through his mother, Scotch, English, Welsh, Spanish, and, according to Frazee tradition,

"There's just one drop of Indian blood in me."

There was, too, the mixed cultural background of the old South and the new Middle West, the former predominating in his father, the latter in his mother. "I am a Virginian, born in Springfield," the poet paradoxically, but aptly, described himself. Within him he felt the two forces never completely fused. "The inexplicable Mason and Dixon line, deep-dyed and awful, ran straight through our hearts."

But the home in which young Lindsay grew up, if it did show some diversity of opinions, was a unified one in its strict adherence to the social and religious ideals in which it believed. Dr. Lindsay, a thoroughly good man, devoted to his profession, was a prohibitionist, unalterably opposed to liquor, tobacco, dancing, and card playing. Mrs. Lindsay was an ardent temperance worker, a Sunday-School teacher, and the founder and first president of the Union of Women's Missionary Societies of all the churches of Springfield. They were both members of the Campbellite Church, sometimes called "Disciples of Christ," a church founded on the simple, fundamental elements of evangelical Christianity.

* Stephen Graham: *Tramping with a Poet in the Rockies,* D. Appleton & Co., New York.

There were other influences besides religious ones. Mrs. Lindsay had never relinquished her interest in art; she gave frequent lectures on European artists and writers. She, herself, wrote and produced two pageant-plays, in one of which, "Olympus," the poet, then a boy of six or seven, played the part of Cupid.

There was, too, a devotion to books and to learning. Vachel, a frail child, was not early sent to school, but was taught at home by his mother, learning first to read in Grimm's *Fairy Tales*. Other books soon presented their treasures to him: *Tom Sawyer* and *Huckleberry Finn, Heroes of Chivalry,* Poe's *Poems* in a blue covered volume that had come all the way from Kentucky, Rawlinson's *History of Egypt,* a *History of Japan in Monosyllables,* Stanley's *Darkest Africa*—its cover design a map of Africa with the Congo traced in gold—Dante's *Divine Comedy* illustrated by Doré, *Paradise Lost* by Milton, of whom Lindsay was later to say, "It was Milton made me a poet and blessed me and cursed me at nine years of age."

Lindsay's home, then, was one of education and culture, but obviously not of the New England culture that colored so much of America's literature. "In infancy I never heard of New England," wrote Lindsay. "I heard of Europe every day." The fantasy of Poe and the faerie of the Grimm brothers, the romance, color, and light of far places, the religious idiom of Dante and of Milton, the fundamental Biblical training of his own religion—these, reworked and developed, were later to appear in his poetry.

But these alone cannot explain Lindsay; to them must be added the potent influence of his birthplace. "The mystic Springfield in which I always live, wherever I may happen to be" was basic in Lindsay's soul. "Everything begins and ends there for me." It entered into the early, formative years of his boyhood. It was the nucleus of his life's philosophy. There, and there only in his later years, he found peace.

The very house in Springfield in which he had been born was rich in tradition. It had been owned by a sister of Abraham Lincoln's wife. The night before Lincoln left Springfield to be inaugurated President at Washington, he had been given a reception in the parlors of that house. He was said to have slept that last night in the room in which Lindsay was born. Small wonder that Lincoln came to be one of the boy's earliest heroes!

Four blocks away, next to the house of an uncle of Vachel's, was the Lincoln house, with its collection of Lincoln memorabilia. There Vachel and a cousin constantly played. They grew familiar with the exhibits of the house. Vachel became interested particularly in the collection of Lincoln cartoons, gathered by Mr. Oldroyd, the custodian, who, delighted by the interest of his young visitors, used to explain to them the treasures in his care. Through this contact, familiar if secondary, Lincoln became a real and living presence to the boy.

History was not something shut within the covers of school text-books. It was in the making about him. Political and economic repercussions struck him. Next to the Lindsay home was the Illinois Executive Mansion, where Vachel could see politicians entering and departing. At four he was taken to hear a presidential campaign speech made by James G. Blaine. He heard argued and discussed until they became a part of him such subjects as the tariff, the 1873 panic, the march of Coxey's army of unemployed, the anarchist outbreak in Chicago, the stand of Mayor Altgeld in the crisis. In the early decades after the Civil War, the newly united nation felt new strength. Political feelings ran high. Something of the national energy, the interests and vitality of the America of the 1880's, is suggested in the poem, "John L. Sullivan, the Strong Boy of Boston."

For Vachel the year 1890 was important. It was then that he formally joined the church of his parents. His religious feelings he expressed, possibly more ardently than poetically, in verses which Edgar Lee Masters quotes in his biography * of the poet:

"He that is weary come, refreshed,
  He that is thirsty come and drink,
  'I,' says the Savior, 'I am he
  I am that fountain clear and free.'

Come sinner, Come, Why longer delay?
Hear what the Master has to say;
I have been crucified for thee.
Why not come? now come to me.

* Edgar Lee Masters: *Vachel Lindsay,* Charles Scribner's Sons.

You may not live through the coming night,
Why do you waver this battle to fight?
The Master calls you with pitying voice
You'll choose Heaven, or Hell, which is your choice?

If you obey his voice and follow him today,
Then with a joyful heart he will say;
Come blessed servant, come to me,
Inherit the kingdom prepared for thee."

The same year was the one in which he began his formal schooling, at the Stuart Grammar School of Springfield. There he won two prizes for essays, one on the subject of "Labor and Learning," the other on "Advantages of Farm and City Life."

In the fall of 1893, he entered the Springfield High School. One of his teachers, Miss Susan E. Wilcox, became his staunch and lifelong friend, criticizing the poetry which he at that time began to write and encouraging him always in his work. Even then, however, his ambition was divided; in addition to his poetry he began to show a great interest in drawing.

Nor with his matriculation in college did there come any more clearly defined purpose. He had entered a Campbellite college at Hiram, Ohio, the Hiram Christian College, evidently with the intention of studying medicine. But his father's ambition for him, that he become a doctor, was one in which he, himself, did not share. His medical courses were failures, though he did well in his other work.

He enjoyed thoroughly the life at Hiram. He helped illustrate the college annuals. He was reading widely, in Kipling, Ruskin, Emerson, Lowell, Poe. He was indulging in introspection, in self-analysis, of which he kept a record in a series of notebooks, each one inscribed, "This book belongs to Christ." One notes a steadily developing humanitarianism and a desire growing stronger and stronger to devote himself to his fellow men. He was finally able to write, "At last I am attending my choice of a college. It is organized within myself—the college of the love of the people. . . . Tolstoy after my 31st year shall find me his literal follower. As he has consecrated the novel, so may I consecrate art." * He convinced himself that he should be allowed the "privilege of self-education" and of leaving college.

This decision could not have been made without some struggle. His father's wishes were being disregarded. His mother, while she sympathized with Vachel's desire to become an artist, still saw her husband's viewpoint, his fear that "you are throwing away a certainty of a very useful vocation for a very uncertain dream"; and felt, furthermore, that any training he might get at Hiram, every contact with his fellow students there, would help him in the practice of the work he had chosen, "Christian art," which he saw as made up of literature, speaking, and illustration, with particular emphasis on the last. In spite of parental objections and pleas, he left college in the spring of 1900.

* Quoted in Edgar Lee Masters: *Vachel Lindsay.*

January 1901 found him in Chicago, where he began the study of art. He attended classes at the Art Institute and spent hours in the Field Museum. His studies did not make him forget his dedication to humanity; he soon became identified with a church in Chicago and, within a month, was a teacher in its Sunday-School. His father, in spite of his disappointment, continued to support him. For only a few months Lindsay had a job in the toy department of Marshall Field and studied at night in the Institute. As soon as he found that his day work tired him and prevented him from doing his best work at night, he did not hesitate to give up his job and concentrate on his art studies. After four years in Chicago, he left for New York to study under Robert Henri, then an instructor in the Chase Art School.

"There is one consistent thread in my life," Lindsay said of himself. "From first to last I have been an Art Student." But while he was still in Chicago he was writing poems which magazine editors consistently and with marked unanimity of judgment rejected. In New York he continued to write. At last a poem was accepted for publication, "The Queen of Bubbles," appearing in the *New York Critic* in 1904. Significantly enough, this poem has a subheading, "Written for a Picture."

Possibly Dr. Lindsay now became less generous in the allowance he was sending to his son. Possibly it cost more to live in New York than it had cost in Chicago. Or even possibly Vachel Lindsay at last felt he should earn his own living. At all events, he now embarked on a quixotic adventure, that of selling copies of his own poems. From door to door up and down the West Side of New York he went, trying to peddle his verses for a few cents apiece. He thought of himself as an ancient troubadour making his way through the world by his songs. With a good deal of humor he describes his adventures in his diary.*

"Well, I tried a sleepy big shock headed baker first. I tried to give the poem to him. He considered the thing for some time as I explained it, but finally handed it back saying he had no use for it. I thought there was a touch of class pride and the resentment of my alms and irritated independence in his manner. So the next place I said to the proprietor, 'I will sell you this for two cents.' At once I saw the thing take. My customer smiled, and said, 'Newspapers cost only one cent, with lots more reading matter than this.' But he took two cents from his till all right. I said, 'You can see me the author; that is why I charge the other cent, and I made that myself.' He said, 'It looks like it,' and laughed, and we parted, I promising to come again sometime for another."

Candy stores, Chinese laundries—"I must land a Chinaman yet"—delicatessens, drug stores, fish markets, all were entered. For several nights he repeated his performances. The result was an enriching of his experiences and a strengthening of his conviction that "the people like poetry as well as the scholars, or better," but no very great improvement in his finances.

* Quoted in Edgar Lee Masters: *Vachel Lindsay.*

Much more fruitful financially was his work at the Y.M.C.A. He organized groups of young people to whom he lectured on art and whom he took on trips to the Metropolitan Museum. For this work he received ten dollars a week. For several years he continued lecturing, not only at the Y.M.C.A. but also at several New York settlement houses.

He seemed, however, to be beset by a fundamental restlessness, an inability to conform to any rigid requirements either for continuing his study of art or for applying his art to earning a livelihood. He apparently felt that commercial art would reduce him to a standardized unit in a huge industrial organization, a procedure against which he rebelled. Yet for his own pictures or verse there was no market. At last, yielding to his restlessness and, what is more important, hoping to find an audience for his message of art and life, the philosophy which he had been developing, he left New York for a walking trip through the South.

In March 1906, with a friend, he sailed from New York in a boat bound for Jacksonville, Florida. The two men, however, landed at Charleston. Their plan was to lecture on art and writing to whatever groups they might gather throughout the countryside. As a further means of making his way, Lindsay carried with him copies of "The Wings of the Morning or The Tree of Laughing Bells," a complicated, involved poem which he had written and which he planned to explain—and explanation was needed!—to those he might come upon in his walks, in exchange for food, lodging, or money.

After one lecture Lindsay's friend left him; and on March 11, he began to walk alone through Florida, Georgia, North Carolina, Tennessee, and Kentucky. This trip, together with a later trip through New Jersey and Pennsylvania, he recorded in *A Handy Guide for Beggars, Especially Those of the Poetic Fraternity*. Of the eight rules of the road that he formulated, concerned with where to travel, how to conduct himself, what to carry, when to ask for meals, the final one was "Preach the Gospel of Beauty."

From farmhouse to farmhouse, from cabin door to cabin door, this twentieth century troubadour trudged the highways, reading and elucidating his poem to those who would listen, gathering groups of people to whom he might talk on poetry and on the importance of poetry and of beauty in the building of good men and women. At one farmhouse he found a patriarchal old man who exerted his strongest efforts in gathering together an audience for the poet. With what results Lindsay tells in a description of the lecture, which was typical of the adventures of this trip.

"He sent his family about to announce my lecture in the schoolhouse on 'The Value of Poetry.' Enough applecheeked maidens, sad mothers, and wriggling, large-eyed urchins assembled to give an unconscious demonstration of the theme.

"The little lamp spluttered. The windows rattled. Two babies cried. Everybody assumed that lectures were delightful, miserable, and important. The woman on the back seat nursed her baby, reducing the noise one third. When I was through shouting, they passed the hat. I felt sure that I had carried my point. Poetry was eighty-three cents valuable, a good deal for that place. And the sons of the Patriarch were the main contributors, for before the event he had thunderously exhorted them to be generous. I should not have taken the money? But that was before I had a good grip on my rule."

This trip of the poet brought him in close touch with the men and women of the American country, those on poor, struggling farms, in small stores in isolated communities; it deepened his faith in them; and it confirmed in him his belief that America's art must find its beginning and gain its strength with just such people in just such towns. Something more, however, was needed before the poet became certain of the part that he must play in ordering his ideals for a beautiful and good America.

It was an entirely different kind of trip that brought him insight into himself. In June of the same year, he sailed with his parents for Europe on a conventional tour of England, Holland, Germany, Belgium, and France. He shared in the renewal of his parents' steadily maintained interest in European culture. But, even more important, as though his removal from the American scene enabled him to see himself more clearly, he discovered that "One cannot be completely one's self unless alone" and he began to realize the necessity, indeed the inevitability, of his being a native, an American poet. "Real poetry is not based on the verse one has read, but on the men and women one has met, and what one has seen them do. . . . In the end a man can expect to understand no land but his own. But having met its many phases he can meditate when he is far from it."

After his return from Europe, he resumed for a time his New York activities, took another short walking trip through New York, New Jersey, and Pennsylvania, and then went back to his family home in Springfield. By now his social philosophy had become fairly well formulated. He based it on a fundamental belief in democracy, beauty, and holiness.

"Of the Coming of Religion, Equality, and Beauty," he wrote, "the priest, the statesman, and the singer shall discern one another's work more perfectly and give thanks to God." He decried the greed, avarice, and ugliness, which he felt were inherent in industry and in cities. He saw the roots of his new order, his Utopia, springing from the country and small town, where boys and girls, instructed in arts—music, dancing, literature, painting, sculpture—would of necessity grow into strong and noble men and women and bring about a renaissance not only of art but of morality.

This gospel was one that had to be preached. Lindsay began his mission first by lecturing through central Illinois for the Anti-Saloon League. Then in lectures in Springfield, particularly at the Y.M.C.A., he pleaded for a new and more beautiful city, one that would absorb from each national group of immigrants the best that that nation had to offer. His mission became a campaign. He grew more militant in his attitude and issued a number of pamphlets under the title *Springfield War Bulletins,* in which he fought against greed for money, industrialism, conventional religion, institutionalized charity, conservatism in any form. He printed, too, his *Village Magazine,* which contained articles, pictures, poems—all created by himself—pointing to his ideals.

His propaganda, naturally enough, made him unpopular with established citizens and laid him open to criticism and ridicule. Springfield was not yet the Perfect City; indeed, it was not even hospitable to his ideas. So in May 1912, he left on another trip of exploration and of preaching, this time through the West.

On this trip he carried a book protected from the weather by an oilcloth cover. The book, a small portfolio, made for the entertainment and enlightenment of the farmerfolk he would meet on the way, contained a variety of pictures—portraits of Ruskin, Whistler, Poe, Tolstoy, Bryan, pictures of famous buildings like the Taj Mahal, the leaning tower of Pisa, Trinity Church in New York, Lincoln's home in Springfield; a copy of *The Village Magazine,* with his large, expositional drawing "The Village Improvement Parade"; a number of his poems, some of which, illustrated by himself, had been published in 1909 as *The Tramp's Excuse and Other Poems.* He had had printed several of his poems in a pamphlet with the self-explanatory title, *Rhymes to be Traded for Bread.* He carried, too, for distribution some leaflets, *The Gospel of Beauty,* a "one page formula for making America lovelier."

What was this Gospel of Beauty which Lindsay felt it his mission to preach? It had two tenets. One was a tenet of beauty: "After this let the denomination to which you now belong be called in your heart, 'the church of beauty' or 'the church of the open sky.' . . . The church of beauty has two sides: the love of beauty and the love of God." The other tenet was that of the New Localism: "The things most worth while are one's own hearth and neighborhood. We should make our own home and neighborhood the most democratic, the most beautiful and the holiest in the world." The three poems which he felt best expressed his gospel were "The Proud Farmer," "The Illinois Village," and "On the Building of Springfield." These are printed in his *Collected Poems* under the note: "I recited these three poems more than any others in my mendicant preaching tour through the West. Taken as a triad, they hold in solution my theory of American civilization." "The Proud Farmer" is the idealized portrait of his grandfather, religious, noble, the respected leader of his community. In "The Illinois Village," the "little prairie towns" are extolled as the home of liberty, beauty, learning, and true love of God, "The Artist's town of Bethlehem!" "On the Building of Springfield" presents a picture of the ideal city. It is a small town, "Where Music grows and Beauty is unchained," where Science, Machinery, and Trade build

"against our blatant, restless time
An unseen, skilful, medieval wall,"

a town created by the loyal devotion of generations:

"We must have many Lincoln-hearted men.
A city is not builded in a day.
And they must do their work, and come and go,
While countless generations pass away."

From his previous journeyings he had grown experienced. He knew now how best to approach people for food or for lodging. He recognized those who could be interested in his poetry. He knew how to get work on the farms and wheat fields when it was necessary either to earn money or to work his way.

"I am a tramp by the long trail's border,
Given to squalor, rags and disorder.
I nap and amble and yawn and look,
Write fool-thoughts in my grubby book,
Recite to the children, explore at my ease,
Work when I work, beg when I please,
Give crank-drawings, that make folks stare
To the half-grown boys in the sunset glare,
And get me a place to sleep in the hay
At the end of a live-and-let-live day."

Many were the adventures he had: working for a Mennonite farmer; introducing the poetry of Swinburne to a Kansas wheat stacker; meeting with a Mr.

McSweeny who said that he "was the goods and offered to pass the hat, but I would not permit." He relates them in letters which were later published as *Adventures While Preaching the Gospel of Beauty*. Humor colors his description of himself when he no longer looked genteel and so was asked to work for his meals: "My derby hat has been used for so many things,—to keep off a Noah's flood of rain, to catch cherries in, to fight bumblebees, to cover my face while asleep, and keep away the vague terrors of the night,—that it is still a hat, but not quite in the mode. My face is baked by the sun and my hands are fried and stewed. My trousers are creased not in one place, but all over. These things made me look like a person who, in the words of the conventional world, *'ought to work.'* "

Altogether delightful and tender is one of the final scenes in the book. After a day's walk, Lindsay came upon a building in a woods, an eating place for the woodsmen. The five children of the household were seated about a table, eating their evening meal of mush. The poet, welcomed for a night's food and rest, offered to entertain them by reciting some of his poems. "The last of the series recounted what Grandpa Mouse said to the Little Mice on the Moon question. I arranged the ketchup bottle on the edge of the table for Grandpa Mouse. I used the salts and peppers for the little mice in circle round. I used a black hat or so for the swooping, mouse-eating owls that came down from the moon. Having acted out the story first, I recited it, slowly, mind you." The poem he recited was one of his many moon poems, "What Grandpa Mouse Said."

From this trip came suggestions for later poems. But more valuable for Lindsay than such specific suggestions was the general effect of his wanderings upon his spirit, his feeling of close identity with the people with whom he had come in contact and with the farms he had seen. "I feel that in a certain mystical sense I have made myself part of the hundreds and hundreds of farms that lie between me and machine-made America." He had worked with men and felt the strength that came from work.

Nothing that he encountered on this trip caused Lindsay to modify the social beliefs that had started him on his journey. His original premises still held; his experiences served merely to confirm them. After the trip, he wrote and saw published several *Proclamations,* ringing assertions of the truth of his views. "The roots of some of our trees," he said, "are still in the earth. Our mountains need not to be moved from their places. Wherever there is tillable land, there is a budding and blooming of old-fashioned Americanism, which the farmer is making splendid for us against the better day."

Lindsay's message now reached a larger audience. *The American Magazine* published his "Gospel of Beauty" and "The Proud Farmer." Soon the fame of the itinerant preacher-poet was widespread—at least in the literary world. A first spark of literary interest, struck by Edward J. Wheeler, the editor of *Current*

*Literature,* who had been impressed by a copy of *The Village Magazine,* flamed brightly with the publication in the January 1913 issue of *Poetry* of "General William Booth Enters into Heaven." The poem is a tender glorification of General Booth of the Salvation Army; it is a reiteration of Lindsay's own faith in humanity and of his idealization of the leaders of mankind. Its subject matter, its simple but noble conception, its basic pulsating rhythm were fresh notes in a poetry that was just experiencing a new birth of vigor and a wider and deeper public interest. The poem attracted attention; it won the *Poetry* prize, and proved to be the real beginning of Lindsay's career as a poet.

With the publication in 1913 of a volume of poetry taking its title from the General Booth poem, it was apparent that a new voice was singing in America. The poet was independent, an adherent of none of the new schools that were springing up and formulating rules:

"To my own tunes I will chant my words."

He stood alone, quite untouched by literary movements or theories. His subjects were completely his own. One group, called "Fantasies and Whims," showed a delicate, at times wistful, imagination, reminiscent of the little boy reading Grimm's *Fairy Tales*. The other poems were, for the most part, an exposition of his social philosophy; exhortation to beauty and goodness, affirmation of faith in mankind, praise of the heroes and great men of the past. His methods were dictated only by himself and his subjects. Some of his meters were old and conventional. Many were the alternately rhyming quatrain, or some slight variation from it, that was closely related to the verse form of innumerable hymns in innumerable Sunday hymnals. Some few, however, were new—new, that is, in American poetry. They were written in a basic, emotional rhythm, that had some counterpart in political oratory, in religious preaching, and in group singing and activity.

This choice of method was no haphazard one. Lindsay felt the necessity of reaching with his poetry as many people as possible. He had come to modify his early belief in the readiness of people generally to accept conventional poetry; and so he had learned to employ the means best fitted to communicate thoughts and feelings to large groups. In a letter to Jessie B. Rittenhouse, in January 1914, he wrote: *

"The American people hate and abhor poetry. I am inventing a sort of ragtime manner that deceives them into thinking they are at a vaudeville show, and yet I try to keep it to a real art. I can put what might be called my prose essay self into it. In the end I shall go back to the Olympian gods and the muses, but I have been accused of being inhuman for seventeen years, and desire just a little respite, and revelry on paper, and companionship with my fellow creatures."

Embarked on what he called the "Higher Vaudeville," Lindsay toured the country, giving poetry re-

* Jessie B. Rittenhouse: "Vachel Lindsay," *South Atlantic Quarterly,* July 1933.

citals before college students, women's clubs, variously assorted groups. He became a platform celebrity. He recited his poems, elaborating and playing upon the subtle speech cadences (which sometimes escape the reader's ears), until the audience became infected by their vigor and joined with him in the creation of a communal chant.

Thousands throughout the country came to know him, a person half dreamer, half solid citizen—"a robust Puck, born in a middle western town," he has been described—with gray eyes, bulging forehead, and sandy hair. One can visualize him, as so many saw him, upon a lecture platform, balancing upon his toes, his face upturned, his eyes half-closed, intoning in his deep, vibrant voice the "Mumbo-Jumbo will hoo-doo you" of "The Congo"; exhorting the "Are you washed in the blood of the Lamb?" of "General William Booth"; or joyously proclaiming the "Hoot, toot, hoot, toot" of "The Kallyope Yell."

It was, indeed, the very popularity of these three poems, the entertaining qualities of Lindsay's perform-ances, that carried their own penalties and came, in time, to bring him bitterness instead of joy. During the period of his lecturing tours, he published several volumes of poetry, *The Congo and Other Poems*, 1914; *The Chinese Nightingale*, 1917; *The Golden Whales of California*, 1920; *Collected Poems*, 1923; *Going-to-the-Sun*, 1923. He sought to return to "the Olympian gods and the muses." But his audiences who knew him as "the Jazz Poet," a term he hated, came for amusement from his poetry rather than for instruction in the art of living and demanded from him again and again the recitation of his three popular poems. "They wanted to Barnumize me and take me all over America as a reciting freak," he complained. He rebelled against the hardships of lecture tours, the long railroad trips and dismal hotel rooms. Then, as the novelty of his lectures eventually wore off, he saw his audiences dwindle; he felt that his vogue was passing and despaired lest his poetic powers, too, had vanished.

But before he reached the lowest depth of his despair, he had had in 1920 a triumphant visit to England where, with his mother, he had been welcomed and fêted. On his return, his own city, his beloved Springfield, held a banquet in his honor. His pride was great.

It brought him joy, however, for only a short time. In 1922 his mother, to whom he had been closely attached, died. Through some family difficulties in the settling of her estate, he lost the Springfield home which had always meant so much to him. A short term as resident poet at Gulf Park College, Gulfport, Mississippi, was not completely successful. It was while he was there that he felt that possibly his life as a poet was over.

Despondent, he left the college in 1923 for Spokane, Washington. There he became part of the literary and musical life of the city. There he met again Miss Elizabeth Conner, whom he had first met in 1912 at Mills

College, a woman of sensitivity and understanding and, herself, a talented writer. He married her on May 19, 1925.

For a few years they lived in Spokane. But again Lindsay felt it impossible to conform, this time to what the Spokane citizens expected of him. Always, too, his heart turned longingly to Springfield. "I am certainly a citizen of Springfield," he wrote, "and will be till I die. I want to get back there as soon as possible, to my birthplace with my wife and children, and stay there forever." In 1929, a return to his old home was possible and he with his wife, son, and daughter left Spokane for the Illinois city of his birth, the center of all his dreamings, where, he felt, he, if not his work, was understood:

"If I should print new drawings in the Illinois State
    Register,
They would not gabble 'pen stroke,' 'swirl,' or 'pas-
    sion.'
They would merely grunt 'Again?' like honest, blunt
    he-men,
Would not assume to call me not in fashion."

At last he was among those who had known him since boyhood and with whom he felt at home. He had published several more books of verse: *Going-to-the-Sun*, 1923, a "sequel and a reply to a book (*Tramping with a Poet in the Rockies*) by Stephen Graham, explorer-poet, and Vernon Hill, artist"; *The Candle in the*

*Cabin,* 1926; *Going-to-the-Stars,* 1926; *Johnny Apple-seed,* 1928; and *Every Soul is a Circus,* 1929.

With his writing and a return to lecturing, Lindsay settled down to life in Springfield. With a growing family, his expenses increased. His health was poor. He was worn out. In February 1931, away from home on one of his lecture tours, he wrote to his wife, "What I am really hungry for is my youth that will never return." One triumph that he had longed for in his youth he did live to enjoy. November 30, 1931, he lectured at the First Christian Church of Springfield. He was enthusiastically received and was able to say, "I feel that at last I have won Springfield." But the triumph was a short one. Five days later, on December 5, he was dead.

In death, Springfield honored him; churches, schools, the City Council paid him tribute. His funeral was impressive. His burial place, appropriately, was near the tomb of Lincoln. Vachel Lindsay had at last and for all time returned to his home.

If an inability to conform to the requirements of usual existence was a source of unhappiness for Lindsay, still he devoted himself unceasingly to what he felt was right. He realized that his ideas were not always those of most people, his ideals and purposes not theirs:

> "Often my lone contrary sword is bright
> When every other soldier's sword is rust."

132

But his sword he wielded in a cause which he felt was worthy.

What was that cause? One of his critics,* perhaps somewhat too simply, states it: "Fundamentally Mr. Lindsay wants us all to be good and to be good together in a nice, neighborly tuneful spirit." Yet it was just such simple, basic goodness that Lindsay sought.

Goodness to him was simple of definition, its achievement not too difficult of accomplishment. But Lindsay was not very critical. He was unable to grasp the complexities of modern civilization, the vast structure which man has built and which, in turn, has created man. One aspect of it he did see and deplore, machinery and industrialism. "In the East," he wrote in *Adventures While Preaching the Gospel of Beauty,* "the railroads and machinery choke the land to death and it was there I made my rule against them."

Because industrialism was strongest in the East, Lindsay believed that true good could not flourish there; it must come from the West, from the land and small villages. "I don't believe in class war," he told his friend Stephen Graham, "I believe in the war of the mountain and desert with the town. Only the deserts and mountains of America can break the business-hardened skulls of the East." With no less sincerity, but with humor and satire, he expressed the same idea in his poem, "So Much the Worse for Boston":

* Llewellyn Jones: *First Impressions,* "Vachel Lindsay, Millennialist," Alfred A. Knopf.

" 'There are such holy plains and streams, there are
      such sky-arched spaces,
There are life-long trails for private lives, and endless
      whispering places.
Range is so wide there is not room for lust and poison
      breath
And flesh may walk in Eden, forgetting shame and
      death.'

And then I contradicted him, in a manner firm and
      flat.
'I have never heard in Boston, of anything like that.'
*'Boston is peculiar.*

*Boston is mysterious.*

*You do not know your Boston,'* said the wise, fas-
      tidious cat,
And turned again to lick the skull of his prey, the
      mountain-rat!"

No, goodness could not be found in the cities:

"Arm me against great towns, strong spirits old!
    St. Francis keep me road-worn, music-fed."

Furthermore, unlike most moderns, he felt that science could help little in securing the goodness he sought.
He had no use for those who talked of the "machinery
in the butterfly" or who thought

      "If we could see the birdie
      That makes the chirping sound

> With psycho-analytic eyes,
> And Xray, scientific eyes,
> We could see the wheels go round."

With some variation, the same idea is expressed in "A Rhyme About an Electrical Advertising Sign." But this poem carries the poet a step further: an assurance that invention leads on to the "change beyond change," a faith in the ultimate goal, a goal to be reached by prayer. These are Lindsay's solutions to all problems of the complicated world about him—simple, religious faith and prayer.

> " 'The sun says his prayers,' says the fairy,
> 'Or else he would wither and die.' "

The faith that he learned in the Campbellite Church, the mystic absorption with God, this Lindsay expresses over and over again in his poems. His faith is a firmly established conviction:

"Back of the smoke is the promise of kindness again."

Accompanying this religious faith is an unwavering faith in mankind, a belief that man can and will achieve the ultimate good. This is an expression of democracy founded on the brotherhood of man. This fundamental certainty Lindsay expressed in such poems as "To Reformers in Despair," "Why I Voted the Socialist Ticket," and in "Sew the Flags Together," wherein youth with its "patchwork flag of brotherhood" is bidden to

"Highly establish
 In the name of God,
 The United States of Europe, Asia, and the world."

So staunch a believer in the brotherhood of man was
naturally aghast at the events of the World War of
1914-1918. With an almost uncanny prescience Lindsay had seemed to foretell its coming in "The Scissors
Grinder," a poem which he later subtitled "An Unconscious Prophecy Written in 1913." When the war finally
did break, his poems followed its course. One notes in
them a distinction made between the great masses of
people and the rulers and leaders of nations who thrust
their people into war. Throughout the poems is the plea
for peace, in poems like "Where is the Real Non-Re-
sistant," "The Merciful Hand," and the moving, lovely
"Abraham Lincoln Walks at Midnight" with its closing
stanzas:

"He cannot rest until a spirit-dawn
 Shall come;—the shining hope of Europe free:
 The league of sober folk, the Workers' Earth,
 Bringing long peace to Cornland, Alp and Sea.

 It breaks his heart that kings must murder still,
 That all his hours of travail here for men
 Seem yet in vain. And who will bring white peace
 That he may sleep upon his hill again?"

The peace that Lindsay envisaged was one he felt to
be possible, one he experienced later when he and

Stephen Graham on a walking trip through the Rockies found out "that a Britisher and a United Stateser can cross the Canadian-American line together and discover that it is hardly there; can discover that an international boundary can be genuine and eternal and yet friendly. If there is one thing on which Stephen and I will agree till the Judgment Day, it is that all the boundaries of the world should be as open, and as happy, as the Canadian-United States line."

The war of generals and of armies was not the only one that Lindsay condemned. He poured out his indignation against all forms of warfare, all forms of exploitation, avarice, and greed that debased men. Strongly he raised the cry against social injustice:

"Let not young souls be smothered out before
  They do quaint deeds and fully flaunt their pride.
It is the world's one crime its babes grow dull,
  Its poor are ox-like, limp and leaden-eyed.
Not that they starve, but starve so dreamlessly,
Not that they sow, but that they seldom reap,
Not that they serve, but have no gods to serve,
Not that they die but that they die like sheep."

Lindsay saw clearly the difficulties and disasters that overwhelm mankind. But his solution for overcoming and obviating them is, as has been suggested, a little too simple; it does not take into consideration the vast ramifications of the present-day social order. In its simplicity it is, indeed, almost childish—or else most mature! According to him the rules of childhood can govern mankind; life is a Christmas tree, or a circus, as in "The Kallyope Yell" wherein "Popcorn crowds shall rule the town." Or it can be governed by the simple regulations of a fundamental religion and of art:

"Let Beauty be the State,
　Let Peace be the State,
　Let Wisdom be the State,
　Let the Wonder and the Thunder of Great Music be
　　　the State,
　Let the Wonder and the Thunder of Great Singing be
　　　the State."

This is Lindsay's gospel of beauty, of which he writes, "Beauty is not directly pious, but does more civilizing in its proper hour than many sermons or laws." This is the motif of such poems as "In the Immaculate Conception Church," "The North Star," "The Dream of all the Springfield Writers," and of his trilogy, "The Proud Farmer," "The Illinois Village," "On the Building of Springfield."

That Springfield becomes the subject of so many poems is unquestionably no mere chance. Springfield was the geographical core of his existence. But more than that, Springfield signified for him the New Localism. The New City was to be the center of learning and of beauty. Through books and the arts, its citizens were to be noble and beautiful and good.

To proclaim the coming of that time and to prepare

men and women for it was the major element in Lindsay's conception of his role as poet. The reformer and the preacher were strong in him; family inheritance and his long attachment to his church nurtured his tendency. He used his poetry to preach. Such poems as "The City That Will Not Repent" and "On the Road to Nowhere" might almost be rhymed sermons of the fundamental, orthodox kind. Others, "Foreign Missions in Battle Array," for example, in subject and in manner are like the hymns sung by devout congregations throughout the land.

It is the nature of a hymn—whether patriotic or religious—that its thought and emotion are shared, participated in by those who sing it. Community of feeling is its basic element. This quality was fundamental to Lindsay's conception of poetry. For Lindsay, however, a ready-made congregation did not exist. He had to create his own; he had to gather together those who would first listen to his poetry and then share it. To do this he used the appeals he felt were strongest. He relied on oratory rather than logic, on emotions rather than thought; and his emotional appeal was based on the wide, the simple, the elemental. One can note a close connection between the method of many of Lindsay's poems and that of popular songs or of revival meetings.

In a number of poems, "The Congo," for example, "General Booth," "John Brown," "King Solomon and the Queen of Sheba," poems designed for reading aloud, the listeners are expected to play a vocal part in the rendition, marginal notes being presented with each poem suggesting how it is to be recited and when the audience-chorus is to play its part. The poem frequently becomes a theme, upon which improvisations are to be based. Consider the long preface to "Bob Taylor's Birthday," in which Lindsay emphasizes the fact that the poem was written to be recited to an outdoor audience and then goes on to say: "At natural intervals in the song, when finally given, let there be good tunes by a good picnic fiddler;—an old-fashioned, barn-dance, log cabin jig fiddler. At the proper moment solemn tunes, like 'Old Hundred,' and famous dances like 'Money-Musk!' Then, after a moment's pause, let the orator resume, paraphrasing and improving on the poem, as he gets the swing. Please let the production be understood by the crowd as oratorical, to be cheerfully filled with local allusions, in the spirit of Taylor's own political speeches, and improvisations on his own fiddle."

There was yet another manner in which others could take part in the creation of Lindsay's poems, and that was in the dance. At the Chicago Little Theatre, at the University of Chicago, and at the Lewis and Clark High School of Spokane, among other places, Lindsay worked out experiments in which to the chanting of his poetry were added musical background, pantomime, and dancing. As his experiments developed, Lindsay came to feel that the instrumental music should be omitted since it "blurs the English." So to the words of the poem, suitable actions were performed; and because "speaking generally, poetic ideas can be conveyed word by word, faster than musical feeling," repetitions of word phrases were introduced *ad libitum* so as "to keep the singing, the dancing and the ideas at one pace." For these "rhythmic picnics," Lindsay wrote a number of Poem Games, among them "The Mysterious Cat," "Mister Chipmunk," "The King of Yellow Butterflies," and the thoroughly delightful "The Potatoes' Dance":

" 'Down cellar,' said the cricket,
'Down cellar,' said the cricket,
'Down cellar,' said the cricket,
'I saw a ball last night,
In honor of a lady,
In honor of a lady,
In honor of a lady,
Whose wings were pearly white.
The breath of bitter weather,
The breath of bitter weather,
The breath of bitter weather,
Had smashed the cellar pane.
We entertained a drift of leaves,
We entertained a drift of leaves,
We entertained a drift of leaves,
And then of snow and rain.
But we were dressed for winter,
But we were dressed for winter,
But we were dressed for winter,
And loved to hear it blow

> In honor of the lady,
> In honor of the lady,
> In honor of the lady,
> Who makes potatoes grow,
> Our guest the Irish lady,
> The tiny Irish lady,
> The airy Irish lady,
> Who makes potatoes grow.' "

Lindsay suggests these poem games to amateurs, to be developed on their own initiative. Dancing, he felt, vivified and socialized poetry. "It becomes," he says, "writing in the air."

This "writing in the air" is closely akin to that other interest of Lindsay's which he sought to exemplify in some of his poems. He was an eager student of Egyptian hieroglyphics, a subject that linked closely to his youthful ambition to practice Christian Art, a desired merging of word and picture. He believed that hieroglyphics provided what he called a "higher symbolism"; that word-pictures revealed an inner meaning not completely suggested by words alone. In a chapter on hieroglyphics in his book *The Art of the Moving Picture,* Lindsay says, "Literary style and mere penmanship and brushwork are to be conceived as inseparable." Much earlier, in one of his college notebooks, he had written, "Seldom put down a poem until it is clearly to be illustrated or cartooned." The Art Student insisted upon expressing himself. Adhering to this theory, Lindsay wrote a number of picture-poems, which appeal through the "imagination of the inner eye." Such poems make up the larger number of those in *Going-to-the-Sun,* of which he warned the critics, "This book is drawn and not written. I serve notice on the critics—the verses are most incidental, merely to explain the pictures." *The Candle in the Cabin* also contains examples of this method, of which "The Musical Butterfly" is typical:

> "The musical
> Butterfly
> Whose wings are a harp,
> And the dots
> Are the notes
> Of the tunes
> That he plays."

This poem, of itself, does present a picture and does evoke some emotional response. But most of the poems of this type are—what the author intended them to be —merely illustrations of his drawings and so, one might object, not even to be considered in a study of Lindsay as a poet. So closely connected in his mind, however, were the various arts, that it seems proper not to omit them completely. This much should be said. Art forms and pictures may possess a certain universality that words lack. But the very universality leads to vagueness. One can never be certain that the meaning derived is the one which the creator wished to convey. The interpretation of the symbol varies according to the experiences and associations of the interpreters. So, of many of Lindsay's pictures even when accompanied by his illustrative poems, and certainly of many of the picture-poems themselves, the meaning is completely elusive.

It is quite apparent that Vachel Lindsay's chief concern was with the world outside himself. It was not his own soul-development, his inner self, that he wished to express. So he was not essentially a lyric, subjective poet. This does not, by any means, imply that he wrote no lyrics. There are several love poems, delicate and tender, among them "The Writhing, Imperfect Earth," "My Lady Is Compared to a Young Tree," "The Spice Tree," and "To a Golden-Haired Girl in a Louisiana Town":

"You are a sunrise,
If a star should rise instead of the sun.
You are a moonrise,
If a star should come, in the place of the moon.
You are the Spring,
If a face should bloom,
Instead of an apple-bough.
You are my love
If your heart is as kind
As your young eyes now."

In addition to his emotions, a poet calls upon his own experiences and associated ideas to provide the background for his poems. Lindsay's longing for the past reflects itself in his choice of material; his childhood could be re-created almost in entirety from his poems. There appears the political interest in "Bryan, Bryan, Bryan, Bryan" and in "The Eagle That is Forgotten." His whole political creed seems to center about great men. Lincoln, his early hero, not only becomes the subject of an entire poem as in "Abraham Lincoln Walks at Midnight," but is used as an allusion, a heroic yardstick, in a number of poems: in "King Arthur's Men Have Come Again," for example, wherein King Arthur, Cromwell, and Lincoln are joined in a common cause. President Theodore Roosevelt, too, seems to have evoked Lindsay's wholehearted enthusiasm, which he expressed in poems like "Roosevelt" and "In Which Roosevelt is Compared to Saul."

The Biblical knowledge suggested in the title of this last-named poem forms another large part of Lindsay's imaginative background. Campbellite services and prayer in the Lindsay home had an abiding influence. Religious feeling permeates poems like "Two Easter Hymns" and "How I Walked Alone in the Jungle of Heaven." Biblical phraseology, allusions, and ideology color poem after poem: "Lucifer," "King Solomon and the Queen of Sheba," "John Brown."

The Holy Land, created by Biblical imagery, became very real to him. Through similar means, through his mother's missionary interests and his own youthful reading, other lands took on color and form and reality. They were delicate, perhaps, and a little tenuous; but they were real. The color and spirit of China glow in

"The Chinese Nightingale" and in "Shantung"; the gorgeous lushness of Africa runs like a secret menace through "The Congo"; the mystery and beauty of the East pervade "A Doll's 'Arabian Nights' "; the fairy quality of all foreign lands lies in "Aladdin and the Jinn":

> "A palace of foam and of opal,
> Pure moonlight without and within."

That is what Aladdin asked for and the Jinn built for him; that is what Lindsay yearned for and built for himself with poetry.

As an expression of the special fascination the moon held for Lindsay was a whole series of moon pictures, some humorous, some whimsical, some grave:

> "A mirror on fair Heaven's wall,
> We find there what we bring."

So to the little girl, the moon is a cookie baked by the South Wind and nibbled away by the North Wind; to the snake, it is a prairie-dog; to the old horse in the city, a peck of corn; to the forester,

> "The moon is but a candle-glow
> That flickers thro' the gloom:
> The starry space, a castle hall:
> And Earth, the children's room,
> Where all night long the old trees stand
> To watch the streams asleep:

146

    Grandmothers guarding trundle-beds:
    Good shepherds guarding sheep."

These poems, in the delicacy and humor of their imagination, the simplicity and vividness of their comparisons, have a childlike quality. The desire for his own childhood Lindsay caught and distilled in many of his poems, in "The Little Turtle," "Crickets on a Strike," "The Visit to Mab," "The Song of the Sturdy Snails." Sometimes these child poems become trivial, as do "An Explanation of the Grasshopper" and "The Dangerous Little Boy Fairies." But in others is suggested the essence of Lindsay's philosophy, the return to the simple as the solution of life's problem. This is epitomized in the wholly satisfying poem "Euclid." Euclid by means of diagrams drawn on the sand is demonstrating his theories to a group of gray-bearded mathematicians. A child stands by entranced because "they drew such charming round pictures of the moon." One infers that Lindsay believed that the child arrives at quite as much truth as do the geometrists and arrives at it more directly.

The moon, butterflies, dragon-flies, snails, crickets, mice, these are the nature symbols that recur throughout his poetry. These, with his circus and Christmas-tree figures, proclaim him essentially a child at heart.

The small things in nature interest him. But Lindsay is not a nature poet. His concern is with man. So one finds no theory, no philosophy of nature. One does find, however, keen observation of natural objects, a delight in recording brief, vivid pictures: "bee-stung apples," "frost-wrapped spring," "flowers burst like bombs," "snow-born waterfalls."

This aptness of phrase quickens much of his poetry. Edgar Allan Poe is the "wizard in the street"; Michelangelo possesses a "whirlwind soul"; Bryan is a "gigantic troubadour speaking like a siege gun"; Biloxi is a "filagree city of fogs and mystery"; words are "sky-rocket and star-spangled words, round sunflower words."

Such ability to choose unerringly the right word, exemplified at its best in the opening stanza of "General William Booth," is the mark of a poet's fancy and imagination. It must be instinct within him; training may develop it, but can never produce it. So it can scarcely be called a literary device or technique. For such technical devices as Lindsay does employ, there seem to be two apparent sources: one, the less important, derived from study of other poets, from literary sources; the other derived from the life about him.

Of those who may have been Lindsay's literary ancestors, Poe seems to have had the strongest influence. Quite in the mood and tone of Poe are such lines as:

> "I saw him by the wall
> When I scarce had written the line,
> In the enemy's colors dressed
> And the serpent-standard of wine
> Writhing its withered length
> From his ghostly hands o'er the ground."

More specifically, Lindsay inherited from the earlier poet the use of refrain and repetend, the latter the repetition of phrase or line with slight variations. Altogether unmistakable in their resemblance to Poe's methods are the refrains of "The Congo":

"Then I saw the Congo, creeping through the black
   Cutting through the forest with a golden track."

and the repetends:

"In that strange curling of her lips,
   That happy curling of her lips."
and
"I hear a thousand chimes,
   I hear ten thousand chimes,
   I hear a million chimes
   In Heaven."

Slight, indeed, is Lindsay's debt to literature. He owed most to the life he observed, to the beliefs he held. These, of themselves, suggested a technique which he found suitable for his purpose. The source of his rhythm is to be found in his religious and political interests. His frequent use of hymn-rhythm can be directly traced to the former. From the latter, with its bands and marching men, come his march rhythms. From the double source, the oratorical display of both pulpit and platform, derives the chant. It should not be imagined that Lindsay confines himself to such rhythms; but he is most distinctly himself when these are the ones he uses. Such lines as

> "Onward the line advances,
> Shaking the hills with power,
> Slaying the hidden demons,
> The lions that devour.
> No bloodshed in the wrestling,—
> But souls new-born arise—
> The nation's growing kinder,
> The child-hearts growing wise."

reflect innumerable pages of Sabbath day hymn books. So faithful to the rhythm of exhortatory preaching that they might be pure examples of Negro pulpit oratory are "The Booker Washington Trilogy," leading its hearers to active participation, and "When Peter Jackson Preached in the Old Church," running from loud insistent

> "Arise, arise,
> Cry out your eyes."

to the peace of the benediction

> "Blessed Jesus,
> Blessed Jesus."

Closely patterned to parade echoes, the rhythm of marching feet and booming drums, are such poems as "General William Booth" and "Bryan, Bryan, Bryan, Bryan." The chant, wherein, as the poet himself says, "one-third of the music must be added by the instinct of the reader," is exemplified in such poems as "John L. Sullivan, the Strong Boy of Boston," or "In Praise of Johnny Appleseed":

> "In the days of President Washington,
>     The glory of the nations,
>     Dust and ashes,
>     Snow and sleet,
>     And hay and oats and wheat
>     Blew west."

When one desires quickly to arouse emotions, one does not always wait for the delicate choice of the nice, the elegant phrase. Often, indeed, to achieve one's desire, a surprising injection of a coarse, vulgar expression is effective. In his appeal to basic emotions, Lindsay does not hesitate to employ such means. So one finds in his poetry—and this is true of some of his best poems—expressions like the following: "scoot for the sea," "whoop that their souls are free," "bawling flannel-mouth," "beat the cheapskate," "on a toot."

There is no question that such expressions, rightly used, add color. The life and fire present in the sources of Lindsay's inspirations are present in his own creations. Even the moon poems and the child poems, which might be expected to be pale, far from being colorless, are suffused with delicate iridescence. As for the more vibrant of his poems, one finds the color of sound, as in the lines from "The Santa-Fé Trail":

"Listen to the iron-horns, ripping, racking,
 Listen to the *wise*-horn, desperate-to-*advise* horn,
 Listen to the *fast*-horn, *kill*-horn, *blast*-horn."

and the gleaming color of light as in "The Congo":

"Just then from the doorway, as fat as shotes,
 Came the cake-walk princes in their long red coats,
 Canes with a brilliant lacquer shine,
 And tall silk hats that were red as wine.
 And they pranced with their butterfly partners there,
 Coal-black maidens with pearls in their hair,
 Knee-skirts trimmed with the jassamine sweet,
 And bells on their ankles and little black feet."

The play upon the emotions becomes an interacting one; as Lindsay uses devices to stir the emotions of his readers, his own become stronger. His language grows more and more picturesque. He is carried away by his own feelings. The moon metaphors and the extended metaphors of poems like "An Indian Summer Day on the Prairie" lead to exaggerations, startling, stimulating, such as might be told by a child, or by a naive, imagination-driven person. Trees become so tall that "the crows are dizzy flying to their nests at the top." A sea serpent in the "Sea Serpent Chanty" "cracks the ribs of the ships with his teeth of stone." The shops of Buffalo glow "with garnets, sapphires, pearls, rubies, emeralds." The first section of "In Praise of Johnny Appleseed"—"Over the Appalachian Barricade"—

teems with these intense exaggerations, indulged in here with a sure sense of humor. Majesty, too, may be present:

"The mountains with storms for war-bonnets,
 The mountains with earthquakes for ponies,
 Ride on through the hundreds of millions of years,
 Talking and laughing through rain, wind and tears."

   Lindsay's reliance upon the emotional dulled his own critical sense. His poems harbor such weaknesses, such manifestations of careless technique as:

   "For she is there in armor clad, today,
     All the young poets of the wide world say."

or

   "We have seen them fly up Mount McKinley
    From the deep of the valley to where
    The peak lifts tremendous snowstorms,
    And throws them like flowers through the air."

His exuberance often degenerates into easy rhetoric, as in "The Fireman's Ball" or "A Rhymed Address to all Renegade Campbellites." His fancy may result in triviality, as in "A Dirge for a Righteous Kitten." His seriousness and intentness of purpose too frequently become sermonizing, as in "The Drunkard's Funeral," and "On the Road to Nowhere." That he lacked critical selectivity is apparent from the fact that in his *Col-*

*lected Poems,* the good and the bad are indiscriminately included.

When Lindsay does exercise restraint, when material and method are appropriately united, he writes unforgettable poems. His "General William Booth," "The Congo," "Bryan, Bryan, Bryan, Bryan," "John Brown" have an insistent, permanent appeal. Other poems, those that transcend the "higher vaudeville," are no less sure and fine. The fanciful moon poems, "The Ghosts of the Buffaloes," the stately "The Eagle That is Forgotten," the tender "Abraham Lincoln Walks at Midnight," "Shantung," and his own favorite among the longer poems, "The Chinese Nightingale," these must endure.

Nor should there be omitted from this grouping "A Net to Snare the Moonlight," that poem wherein more subtly, more poetically, perhaps, than in most, he outlines his hopes for mankind, his desire that all might have

"A place of toil by day time,
Of dreams when toil is done."

or "The Traveller-Heart":

"I would be one with the dark, dark earth:—
Follow the plow with a yokel tread.
I would be part of the Indian corn,
Walking the rows with the plumes o'erhead.

. . . . . . .

I would be one with the sacred earth
On to the end, till I sleep with the dead."

In death, as in life, Lindsay wished a return to that with which he closely identified himself, the earth, his home. But the subject of death concerned Lindsay very little; it is the theme of a bare handful of his poems. It was life that interested him, life to be more abundantly lived in his own country. "The Soul of the U.S.A.: —that is my life-quest."

His Americanism could never be called into question. Essentially he is an American poet. His manner is American, direct, straightforward, simple, colorful. The humor, which permeates much of his writing, is American, humor which varies from the wistfulness of "The Chinese Nightingale," the satire of "So Much the Worse for Boston," to the understanding of "Elizabeth Barrett Browning" and to the sheer joyousness of "Two Old Crows." The whole tone of his poetry is characteristically American, that individual, distinctive blending of political-religious manner with political-religious ideology. His social ideal is simplified and presented with a religious ardor. The faith that believes in the possibility of establishing his ideal is religious—and American. It is symbolized by the American Indian, Pocahontas:

> "Tomorrow's hopes, an April flood
> Come roaring in. The newest race
> Is born of her resilient grace."

It was faith that sustained Lindsay. His search for his own "lost lovely years" was not successful. His gospel of beauty, preached so insistently, he knew could not be put into practice within his own lifetime. Yet it was his conviction that ultimately the new order would be established; and in that conviction, he could sing, with no suggestion of discouragement or despair, his own "Epilogue—One More Song":

"All I can bring is one more song,
   Though I have brought you a thousand and one.
   So it will be till my life is done.
   I would set right the old world's wrong;
   I would outbuild New York and Rome.
   But all
   I can bring home
   Is one
   More
   Song."

POETICAL WORKS

GENERAL WILLIAM BOOTH ENTERS INTO
   HEAVEN AND OTHER POEMS   *Mitchell Kennerley*
THE CONGO AND OTHER POEMS   *The Macmillan Co.*
THE CHINESE NIGHTINGALE AND OTHER
   POEMS                    *The Macmillan Co.*
THE GOLDEN WHALES OF CALIFORNIA
   AND OTHER RHYMES IN THE
   AMERICAN LANGUAGE         *The Macmillan Co.*
COLLECTED POEMS             *The Macmillan Co.*

## VACHEL LINDSAY

| | |
|---|---|
| GOING-TO-THE-SUN | *D. Appleton and Co.* |
| GOING-TO-THE-STARS | *D. Appleton and Co.* |
| THE CANDLE IN THE CABIN | *D. Appleton and Co.* |
| JOHNNY APPLESEED AND OTHER POEMS | *The Macmillan Co.* |
| EVERY SOUL IS A CIRCUS | *The Macmillan Co.* |

*THOMAS STEARNS ELIOT*

## THOMAS STEARNS ELIOT

IN 1933, at Columbia University, T. S. Eliot was thus presented for the honorary degree of Doctor of Letters: "sprung from well-known American stock and given the best preparation for a life of letters that Harvard, the Sorbonne, and Oxford could afford; a poet, essayist and critic who refuses to write without thinking; a noteworthy survival of classicism in a generation that falls off so easily into practical romanticism; one who has been hailed as the most important single influence in the English poetry of our time." This description, balanced and precise and wholly adequate in suggesting the outstanding characteristics of a candidate for a degree, still needs elaboration and, most certainly, additional biographical details for those who desire some understanding of Eliot, the man and the poet.

When one critic * endeavored to supply this information under the heading of "The Man Behind the Poetry," he did so by quoting the skeletonic biography of *Who's Who,* to which he added, "These things constitute everything about the man behind the poetry that it is necessary to know or mannerly to inquire." Mind-

* Hugh Ross Williamson: *The Poetry of T. S. Eliot,* G. P. Putnam's Sons.

ful of one's manners, one may yet feel even this to be inadequate.

Against one usually fruitful source of biographical material, the seeker is warned by Eliot, himself, who urges caution in trying to reconstruct his life from his writings. He suggests how he has been the victim of misinterpretation:

"I admit that my own experience as a minor poet may have jaundiced my outlook; that I am used to having cosmic significance, which I never suspected, extracted from my work (such as it is) by enthusiastic persons at a distance; and to being informed that something which I meant seriously is *vers de société;* and to having my personal biography reconstructed from passages which I got out of books, or which I invented out of nothing because they sounded well; and to having my biography invariably ignored in what I *did* write from personal experience."

What, then, may one, without being accused of mannerless prying, know of Eliot's life? A paradox characterizes it. Born and brought up in the Mid-West, in St. Louis, Missouri, for many years a resident of Europe, and finally a naturalized British subject, Eliot, only a few years ago, declared: "I speak as a New Englander." It is, indeed, essentially as a New Englander that Eliot writes; and, at that, as a Puritan New Englander, one engrossed in religious questioning and in concern over the state and ultimate salvation of his soul. However far removed in geographic space, in spirit he is close to his New England heritage, which came to him through both his parents.

On the paternal side, Eliot traces his descent from Andrew Eliot, who settled in Massachusetts in 1670 and became the founder of the distinguished Eliot family. His own branch of the family, noted for its merchants and ministers, remained identified with New England until his grandfather, William Greenleaf Eliot, after his graduation from Harvard Divinity School early in the nineteenth century, left Massachusetts for a ministry in St. Louis. He became a leader in that young and growing community. He was an active opponent of slavery. He helped found Washington University, of which he became Chancellor in 1872. Of his four sons, three entered professions; but his second son, Henry Ware Eliot, the poet's father, chose business as his career.

The New England background was further strengthened through the poet's mother, Charlotte Chauncey Stearns, who was the daughter of a Boston commission merchant. Through her, even more immediately, came an interest in writing; her own ability expressed itself in a biography of her father-in-law and in a dramatic poem based on the life of Savonarola, which was published in 1926 and to which her poet son contributed an introduction.

It was on September 26, 1888, in St. Louis that this son, Thomas Stearns Eliot, was born. His formal education was begun at St. Louis. He attended Smith Academy there, a department of Washington University, until he left for the East, for a year of preparatory school at Milton Academy. In the autumn of 1906, he entered Harvard.

Eliot entered college with an interest in poetry already developed. It had first been aroused when he was a little boy and then, as is so likely to happen, had died out completely. But in his early teens, he came upon a copy of Fitzgerald's translation of the *Rubaiyat* of Omar Khayyam. Thereupon, a new world of emotional experience was opened to him; and from that time on, he became an avid reader of poetry, particularly of Byron, Shelley, Keats, Rossetti, and Swinburne.

This interest in poetry, however, did not determine his course of study at Harvard. He majored, not in English, but in philosophy and religion, manifesting thus early a concern with the bewildering problem of man's place in the universe. A good student, he decided in his sophomore year that he would complete his undergraduate work in three years and spend the fourth year in getting a master's degree. This resolution he carried out, being graduated with the degree of B.A. in 1909, and receiving his M.A. in 1910.

Life for the college student, however, was not composed exclusively of courses. There were summer vacations which he spent with his family on the Massachusetts coast at East Gloucester. There, the Western-born young man enjoyed that part of a New England inheritance which will not be denied, a love of the sea. He became at home on the water and learned to handle a sailboat expertly. He grew to know and to absorb into a background of existence, that was later to give color and imagery to his poetry, wind, waves, and sand, and that unreal, romance-stirring quality of water that is symbolized by mermaids:

"I have seen them riding seaward on the waves
   Combing the white hair of the waves blown back
When the wind blows the water white and black."

Even during the school year, there were interests beyond those of the classrooms. Eliot took part in extra-curricular activities. He belonged to social and to literary clubs. He was chosen Class Poet and he was a member of the editorial board of *The Harvard Advocate,* recognitions, both, of his literary ability.

For the delight in poetry that had first been passively satisfied by reading sought active expression. As early as his freshman year, in May 1907, he contributed a poem to the *Advocate,* "Song":

"When we came home across the hill
   No leaves were fallen from the trees;
   The gentle fingers of the breeze
Had torn no quivering cobwebs down.

The hedgerow bloomed with flowers still,
   No withered petals lay beneath;
   But the wild roses in your wreath
Were faded and the leaves were brown."

Fading flowers and their message of the swift passage of time appear again in a poem published the following month. According to a note made by the poet's mother, this is a revision of what is believed to be the first poem Eliot ever wrote; of its two stanzas, however, the second retains its original form:

"The flowers I sent thee when the dew
    Was trembling on the vine
Were withered ere the wild bee flew
    To suck the eglantine.
But let us haste to pluck anew
    Nor mourn to see them pine,
And though the flowers of life be few
    Yet let them be divine."

These poems, conventional, even trite—however well constructed—gave little evidence of the new literary movement that was then making itself felt and that numbered Eliot among its admirers. Through it, restrictions on poetic form and subject matter were breaking down; a new freedom was entering poetry. Eliot had discovered the French symbolist poets, who had given the impetus to this new trend, and the writers of *vers libre*, the "free verse" that acknowledged restraints of neither rhyme nor formal meter. In his enthusiasm, he introduced fellow students to his discoveries. Under this liberalizing influence, he, himself, wrote poems, which, however, did not appear in print until a number of years later.

To get in closer touch with the leaders of this literary movement and to continue his studies for a Ph.D.,

Eliot planned to go to Europe. Which of the two reasons was the more important in Eliot's mind, or whether somehow the two became fused, one cannot know. At all events, Eliot found no need to justify his decision to his family; for always he received their loyal encouragement in his desire to study and to write. So he went to France and for the year of 1910-1911 studied at the Sorbonne.

With his return to America in the autumn of 1911, there followed a period of further graduate work at Harvard, where he studied metaphysics, logic, psychology, and oriental philosophy. During the 1913-1914 academic year, he was an Assistant in Philosophy and then was awarded a traveling fellowship. He chose to study in Germany, and was there at the outbreak of the World War of 1914-1918. He was prevented by the war from returning home to submit his dissertation for his doctorate, "Experience and the Objects of Knowledge in the Philosophy of F. H. Bradley." Instead, he spent the 1914-1915 school year at Merton College, Oxford, reading in Greek Philosophy.

This may seem peculiar preparation, indeed, for one who was to become a poet; but it was training that gave him a solid background for his critical writing and for his poetry. He felt himself part of the great stream of learning, a receiver from the past who was to fulfill his function by giving to the present, a link in that tradition which he insists is an essential element in literature. The erudite references and snatches of foreign languages which, to readers without similar scholarship, are frequently unintelligible and smack of intellectual snobbishness, are not extraneous affectation for Eliot, but integrated parts of his knowledge.

That knowledge soon was turned toward teaching. In the spring of 1915, Eliot married Miss Vivienne Haigh-Wood of London. Thereafter, he was confronted with the problem of earning a livelihood. He became a teacher in the Highgate School near London, where he taught almost every subject from Latin to mathematics and from drawing to history, with swimming as an extra. After a period of teaching, he became a bank clerk in Lloyd's Bank.

Though teaching and banking were ways of earning a living, neither in practice absorbed all of Eliot's activity. The interest in writing that had been stirred in his college years and fostered by his residence in Paris became still more keen. The very period was one to stimulate any interest, let alone one so well grounded as Eliot's. For the new, free movement in the arts, both graphic and literary, was becoming known generally and was the subject of ardent discussions and bitter partisanships. In London, one literary group centered in Ezra Pound, the expatriated American poet, who formulated for the new poetry tenets which eager enthusiasts accepted. Eliot was one of those who came under Pound's influence. How great this influence was Eliot acknowledges in a review * he wrote in 1928 of Pound's book of poems, *Personae:* "I have in recent years cursed

* T. S. Eliot: *The Dial,* January 1928, "Isolated Superiority."

168

Mr. Pound often enough, for I am never sure that I can call my verse my own; just when I am most pleased with myself, I find that I have only caught up some echo from a verse of Pound's."

Eliot's approach, then, to this lively literary interest was from two directions: the critical, seeing and examining all writing in perspective against the culture of the past, which he knew so well; and the creative, writing poetry of his own. So, even at those times when school or bank made demands upon him, he was acting as assistant editor of the magazine, *The Egoist,* and contributing to others. One of the magazines of this period, one that was pre-eminent in its sponsorship of the new poetry and its introduction of young poets to enthusiastic readers, was the American *Poetry.* In 1915, *Poetry* published a number of Eliot's poems: "The Love Song of J. Alfred Prufrock" in its June issue; and, in the October number, "The Boston Evening Transcript," "Aunt Helen," and "Cousin Nancy." These had all been written while he was in Boston; but, unlike the poems in the *Harvard Advocate,* these were not conventional in manner. They had no fixed verse form; they discarded rhyme completely, or else used it occasionally and without regular pattern.

These four poems and a number of others in a "mss. typed neatly by a machine which specialized in italics" had been offered for publication in book form as early as 1914. It was not until 1917 that they were finally accepted and published, in England, under the title of *Prufrock and Other Observations.*

In April of that year, the United States entered the war. Eliot wished to serve in the Navy but his efforts to do so failed because of his poor health.

This potential interruption to his literary career was averted. Still another threat had to be met, the demands upon his time and energy made by his bank position. He found that without more leisure he was unable to create what within him demanded expression. His selection as editor of *The Criterion,* a magazine first subsidized by Lady Rothermere, enabled him to leave his bank clerkship to devote himself to literature. One result of the increased leisure which he thus acquired was "The Waste Land," that poem which has been called "the most discussed and least understood poem of our day"; the poem which has, on the one hand, been hailed as a new poetic revelation and, on the other, been denounced as a hoax. Parts of it appeared in English publications. It was printed in its entirety in *The Dial* for November 1922, and was awarded the Dial prize for the year, an award that instigated probably more controversy than any similar award has ever stirred.

Before 1922, Eliot had published a second volume of poetry, called simply *Poems.* Since then he has written a small number of poems, appearing in slender volumes: *The Hollow Men,* 1925; *Journey of the Magi,* 1927; *Ash Wednesday,* 1930; *Collected Poems,* 1936; *Old Possum's Book of Practical Cats,* 1939; and three poetic dramas, *The Rock,* 1934; *Murder in the Cathedral,* 1935; and *The Family Reunion,* 1939.

More voluminous than his creative writing has been

his critical work. He has written a large number of essays on philosophical and literary subjects, particularly on the Elizabethan dramatists, the metaphysical poets of the seventeenth century, and on Dante. He has spread his views, moreover, beyond the readers of his books through lectures both in England and in this country. In 1926 he was Clark Lecturer at Trinity College, Cambridge. In 1932 he was appointed Charles Eliot Norton Professor of Poetry at Harvard and, in the same year, gave a series of lectures at the University of Virginia. (His arrival here to take up these duties was, incidentally, his first return in eighteen years to the country of his birth.)

His contributions to literary and educational life have brought him honorary degrees, not only from Columbia, but also from the Universities of Cambridge, Bristol, and Edinburgh. A most distinctive honor was the dedication to him of the entire number of the *Harvard Advocate* of December 1938. The issue was made up of messages of appreciation, critical articles on his work, reprints of some of his earlier poems, and brief college recollections of him as a "personality from a remote and limited period, especially of one who was then as shy and reticent as he is probably still."

During these years of writing, Eliot had made a momentous decision. Like so many Americans of the postwar period, faced with changing standards of thought and action, Eliot had found European ways of life congenial. He decided that England provided him with a more sympathetic milieu than did the United States.

So, in 1927, he renounced his American citizenship and became a British subject. It was at just about this time that he described himself and his point of view as "classicist in literature, royalist in politics, and Anglo-Catholic in religion." He went on to explain, "I am quite aware that the first term is completely vague, and easily lends itself to clap-trap; I am aware that the second term is at present without definition, and easily lends itself to what is almost worse than clap-trap, I mean temperate conservatism; the third term does not rest with me to define."

This statement opened the way to misconceptions. In an address to the Anglo-Catholic Summer School of Sociology held at Oxford in the summer of 1933, he showed one of the likelihoods of error:

"But I am the more careful in the matter, because some years ago I made, wisely or unwisely, a brief announcement of faith religious, political, and literary which became too easily quotable. It may have given some critics the impression that for me all these three were inextricable and *of equal importance*."

All three faiths do stem from the same root, a reliance on authority and an instinct for tradition and for fixed and accepted codes of principles. It is the religious faith, however, that is central for Eliot, the one of which the other two are offshoots. Not only has he become identified with religious movements, with those like the 1933 School and like the 1937 International Congress of the Council of Christian Life and Work held at Oxford; but, one realizes, he is in his poetry concerned primarily with a religious problem, the problem of the soul of man. To find an answer to that problem, the Puritans left England and, according to popular conception, denounced all forms of art; their descendant, on the same quest, returned to England and made the art of poetry his medium of expression.

What sort of person is this religiously minded individual? One whose other-worldly interests destroy all mundane humor and joy? Not at all. "Those who know Tom Eliot best," writes R. E. Gordon George,* "know a very shrewd observer of life with an untiring sense of humour; he has a comic sense at once so droll and so acute that in all practical affairs he is one of the most prudent advisers that could be imagined, just as in the troubles of life he is one of the most sympathetic."

This is an illuminating and heart-warming glimpse of the man. Eliot, however, would be the first to disclaim its importance for his poetry. For, according to him, poetry has for its purpose neither the expression nor the satisfaction of individual personality. "The end of the enjoyment of poetry," he says in "The Perfect Critic," "is a pure contemplation from which all the accidents of personal emotion are removed." Even from the art of creating poetry, these same accidents of personality should be absent. Only when personal experience has been detached from the person and become objective and emotion-free, only then, he insists, does

* R. E. Gordon George: *The Bookman,* September 1932, "The Return of the Native."

it become a proper part of the poet's material. The poet must yield himself wholly to the art of creation which Eliot sees as a constant surrender of the poet's self to something infinitely greater. "The progress of an artist is a continued self-sacrifice, a continued extinction of personality." No poet, furthermore, stands alone or has full meaning in and by himself. He must be himself conscious of the past, and he must be judged by the past— the long progression of developing culture which is behind him and of which he is a present part. "By losing tradition, we lose our hold on the present."

This insistence upon the unisolated position of the individual poet is a manifestation of Eliot's adherence to the idea of tradition in literature. He feels himself the inheritor of all that has made English literature what it is, of the contributions that Greece and Rome and the Middle Ages made to the civilization that is called Anglo-Saxon. His own studies in the literatures and philosophies of the past, evidence of this feeling, have but served to strengthen it. One must, then, according to this view, judge a writer in the light of the culture of which he is but one exponent. Eliot deplores the tendency to praise a poet for those qualities which are merely peculiar to him, wherein he differs from those who have preceded him. "Whereas, if we approach a poet without this prejudice," he declares, "we shall often find that not only the best, but the most individual parts of his work may be those in which the dead poets, his ancestors, assert their immortality most vigorously."

What elements in Eliot's poetry carry on the voice of the past? That characteristic concern with the basic religious questions of man's place in the universe and of his relation to a divinity is one that has troubled the soul of the artist from time immemorial; the resulting sense of frustration and bitter disillusionment which overwhelmed Eliot is no less deep-rooted in the past. In method of approach, too, there is the influence of the past; the sophisticated point of view is a reflection of the highly intellectualized manner of the seventeenth century metaphysical poets. Finally, there is the influence of those who had early aroused his poetic enthusiasm, the French poets of the late nineteenth and early twentieth centuries; it is manifested in the use of symbolism, the method of suggestion implicit rather than explicit, that method which, when carried to the extreme of privacy of emblems, results in unintelligibility to the uninitiate.

In poetry the development of basic ideas and the expression of points of view depend upon poetic technique, which Eliot has defined as "excellent words in excellent arrangement and excellent meter." However startling is his use of some technical devices, he has not rejected completely the well-tried methods—conventional meters, rhyme, figures of speech—of the poets of the past; but—and this must be made immediately emphatic—these he modifies to his needs.

One of the conventional verse forms which he uses frequently is the quatrain, iambic tetrameter lines rhyming alternately. Its effect, however, is not conventional when, as in "A Cooking Egg," he injects between two four-line stanzas a single line,

"Where are the eagles and the trumpets?"

Occasionally he employs, with or without rhyme, a line longer than the usual English poetic line, a six-foot line derived from the French alexandrine:

"The October night comes down; returning as before
  Except for a slight sensation of being ill at ease
  I mount the stairs and turn the handle of the door
  And feel as if I had mounted on my hands and knees."

By far the greater part of Eliot's poetry does not have such regular meter. With long lines opposed to shorter ones, whether rhyme is present or absent, the effect is much more usually that of free verse. That indefinite form shows a masterly handling, a subtle variation of lengths of lines, of heavy and light syllables, of differently placed rests:

"Stone, bronze, stone, steel, stone, oakleaves, horses'
    heels
  Over the paving
  And the flags. And the trumpets. And so many eagles."

Yet, even in free verse, Eliot feels at liberty to break one of the very few restrictions that form sets. It is one of its generally accepted tenets that line length should bear a close basic relation to thought length. In violation of this rule, there are many lines in Eliot's poetry that end with words or phrases which logically should begin new lines. Rule or no rule, the result is one of amazing emphasis:

> "Follow the dance
> Of the goldfinch at noon. Leave to chance
> The Blackburnian warbler, the shy one. Hail
> With shrill whistle the note of the quail, the bob-white
> Dodging by bay-bush."

Another, but quite different, instance of an unwillingness to be restricted is shown in "Hysteria." Come upon in a volume of poetry, this immediately attracts the reader's eye; for it looks like a prose paragraph. Yet it is not quite prose. Its plane is a poetic plane; its figures of speech are poetic; its rhythm is not the rhythm of ordinary prose. What is the distinction between the two forms? Eliot declares it to be but a tenuous one. In the preface to his translation of St. J. Perse's *Anabasis,* this is how he expresses it: "It would be convenient if poetry were always verse—either accented, alliterative, or quantitative; but that is not true. Poetry may occur, within a definite limit on one side, at any point along a line of which the formal limits are 'verse' and 'prose.' "

Equally free from fixed rules is Eliot's use of rhyme. When unrhymed verse best serves his purpose, lines are without rhyme; when rhymed verse seems preferable, rhyme is used, when and as he wills. In a single stanza, lines may rhyme alternately, in couplets, or without any fixed pattern, as they do in:

"Well! and what if she should die some afternoon,
　Afternoon grey and smoky, evening yellow and rose;
　Should die and leave me sitting pen in hand
　With the smoke coming down above the housetops;
　Doubtful, for a while
　Not knowing what to feel or if I understand
　Or whether wise or foolish, tardy or too soon. . . .
　Would she not have the advantage, after all?
　This music is successful with a 'dying fall'
　Now that we talk of dying—
　And should I have the right to smile?"

How differently is rhyme handled in the following lines, wherein the *ide* and *ay* sounds are delicately interwoven as terminal and internal rhymes:

"O Thomas my Lord do not fight the intractable tide,
　Do not sail the irresistible wind; in the storm,
　Should we not wait for the sea to subside, in the night
　Abide the coming of day, when the traveller may find
　　his way,
　The sailor lay course by the sun?"

The skillful handling of vowel sounds, suggested by these lines, is revealed—without rhyme—in such passages as:

178

"The cold spring now is the time
   For the ache in the moving root
   The agony in the dark
   The slow flow throbbing the trunk
   The pain of the aching bud."

and

"What seas what shores what grey rocks and what
      islands
   What water lapping the bow
   And scent of pine and the woodthrush singing through
      the fog
   What images return
   O my daughter."

   That stanza, the opening one of the lovely "Marina,"
is varied to form the closing lines of the poem:

"What seas what shores what granite islands towards
      my timbers
   And woodthrush calling through the fog
   My daughter."

This modified repetition, haunting, reminiscent, is a
device which Eliot frequently uses. So, too, is exact
repetition. In the second stanza of the same poem, for
example, the words "meaning Death" are used over and
over with an insistence that cannot be denied. Sometimes, words and phrases are caught up and repeated
as though spoken by one under some strange compulsion:

"Because I do not hope to turn again
Because I do not hope
Because I do not hope to turn"

or again:

"All this was a long time ago. I remember,
And I would do it again, but set down
This set down
This."

Meter, rhyme, repetition—all these may be considered part of the excellent arrangement demanded by Eliot's definition of poetic technique. What of the other half of the definition, that concerned with excellent words? Using "words" in its literal sense, one is first amazed by Eliot's vocabulary. Aware of his many years devoted to abstruse studies, one need not be surprised at the number of words which, while intelligible to the highly educated, are, nevertheless, somewhat unfamiliar to the average person and certainly most unusual in poetry. From the point of view of thought, there is no quarrel with the poet's medium of thinking. But from the point of view of poetry! What value for poetry can there possibly be in such words as "protozoic slime," "polyphiloprogenitive," or "anfractuous rock"? Sometimes, indeed, it would seem as if Eliot is carried away by the mere sound of words, as are the French dadaist poets who make verse out of nonsense syllables. It might be satire on the empty ranting of a political orator in "Difficulties of a Statesman"; but the voice is so typically Eliot's own that one feels it is the poet, himself, speaking in the following line:

"If the mactations, immolations, oblations, impetrations."

When not indulging himself in such verbal pyrotechnics, the poet manifests an unerring instinct for the vivid, exact phrase, for the precise choice of specific, illuminating detail. Sharp and clear cut he draws his pictures, as he does in these contrasting scenes in "Journey of the Magi":

"And the camels galled, sore-footed, refractory,
  Lying down in the melting snow"

and

"Then at dawn we came down to a temperate valley,
  Wet, below the snow-line, smelling of vegetation;
  With a running stream and a water-mill beating the
      darkness,
  And three trees on the low sky,
  And an old white horse galloped away in the meadow."

Just as vividly are characters presented. Some outstanding feature may be seized upon and made to serve as identifying tag, as does the "meagre, blue-nailed, phthisic hand" for Princess Volupine. Or conversation may be used with wicked skill to reveal the inner person, as it does in "Portrait of a Lady."

This sharp feeling for detail enables the poet to

crystallize a mood or an impression in some sudden phrase. He describes a landscape:

"Since golden October declined into sombre November
And the apples were gathered and stored, and the land
    became brown sharp points of death in a waste
    of water and mud."

In the phrase, "brown sharp points of death," what might have been a gently melancholy scene is instantly revealed as bleak and desolate. With the same economy of expression, the extreme of futility, of continuous but empty social engagements, is conveyed by "I have measured out my life with coffee spoons." Wry humor colors the no less succinct and vivid "damp souls of housemaids." That fact must be recognized, that humor —sometimes gentle, more often sardonic—frequently colors these brief, vivid revelations, as it does in the picture of the real estate clerk

        "on whom assurance sits
    As a silk hat on a Bradford millionaire."

What is or is not humor each individual can decide only for himself; so completely is it a matter of personal point of view. But along with the acknowledged humor in Eliot's verse there is such an element of smartness that one feels that the poet frequently lays himself open to the charge of choosing expressions chiefly for their ability to startle the reader. Of such a nature is the promise of "pneumatic bliss" held out by the full-bosomed Grishkin. So, too, is the line

"To spit out all the butt-end of my days and ways."

In "The Love Song of J. Alfred Prufrock," the poem in which that occurs, the figure in the opening lines

"When the evening is spread out against the sky
Like a patient etherised upon a table,"

is so completely unexpected a comparison that it makes the reader wonder how the relationship had ever been established in the author's mind.

This fantastic juxtaposition of seemingly unrelated ideas is a distinctive characteristic of Eliot's poetry. The relationship between the thoughts, the moods, the objects has no obvious logical basis; it springs from some emotional association private to Eliot. When he writes

"Midnight shakes the memory
As a madman shakes a dead geranium,"

one feels that the dead geranium has some specific connotations for him. The basis for selection is purely personal.

"The memory throws up high and dry
A crowd of twisted things."

These "twisted things" gathered together produce the effect of a surrealist painting, the painstakingly drawn picture of a number of objects connected somehow in the artist's unconscious, and only there. The method adapted to poetry results in swift changes and sharp contrasts. It may in a single stanza change the setting from romantic myth to stark realism:

> "Morning stirs the feet and hands
> (Nausicaa and Polypheme)
> Gesture of orang-outang
> Rises from the sheets in steam."

It may, as in the fifth section of "The Hollow Men," jump piteously from a nursery jingle rhythm and patter to an expression of religious despair. Or it may, as in "The Waste Land," provide breath-taking, rapidly succeeding impressions. A reference to the ancient rites of the worship of Adonis follows immediately a brief picture of London. A line reminiscent of Shakespeare breaks into a syncopated rhythm:

> "I remember
> Those are pearls that were his eyes.
> 'Are you alive, or not? Is there nothing in your head?'
>
> But
>
> O O O O that Shakespeherian Rag—
> It's so elegant
> So intelligent."

Just as Eliot's mind takes sudden turns and darts, peculiarly his own, so there are motifs throughout the poems that have meaning primarily for him. Converted into symbols, they are used to evoke memories and to represent compactly a whole body of emotions. Seagulls and fog are recurring images in his poems. Lilacs appear as a symbol of spring, of life born out of death. Hyacinths, too, seem to have private significance for him; the perfume of the flowers revives for him memories of desired things; the "hyacinth girl" appears to be a memory from his youth. One of the symbols, created by him, readily shares its meaning, however, with his readers. Apeneck Sweeney who appears in "Sweeney Erect," "Mr. Eliot's Sunday Morning Service," in "Sweeney Among the Nightingales," and briefly in "Sweeney Agonistes," comes to embody the ordinary man-in-the-street, presented just a little patronizingly as a vulgar and materialistic product of present-day civilization.

Still another characteristic distinguishes Eliot's poetry. This is a reflection not so much of his inner emotional life as it is of his studies, the broad education on which his thinking is based. His verse rings with echoes from his reading. He borrows phrases as he desires, from the Bible, Shakespeare, Dante, a practice which he thus defends: "One of the surest of tests is the way in which a poet borrows. Immature poets imitate, mature poets steal; bad poets deface what they take, and good poets make it into something better, or at least something different." He refers often, if at times somewhat cryptically, to Donne, to Marlowe, to the Elizabethan dramatists. He alludes to anthropological and philosophical studies. He does not hesitate to incorporate into his poems lines or passages in foreign languages: Italian, French (in which he wrote four complete poems), Greek, Latin, and German. These are all integrated parts of his intellectual background, it is true; but unless his reader has had the same scholarly experience, or unless he has some wise and patient guide, he is very likely to find himself mentally bewildered and lost.

These characteristic qualities of Eliot's poetry were not a slow development. They were present in his first book, *Prufrock*. His second volume, *Poems,* carried on the methods. For two things particularly this second book should be noted: one having to do with subject matter, the other with manner. One sees in this book that besetting concept of Eliot's, the superiority of the past over the present. In the Sweeney poems and in "Burbank with a Baedeker: Bleistein with a Cigar," one finds the comparison drawn between the two periods, always to the implied detriment of the later one. From the point of view of method, it is to "Gerontion," the opening poem of the book, that attention is specifically called. For "Gerontion" illustrates the loose construction of Eliot's longer poems, the method that was to become identified with him; neither chronological narrative, nor the orderly sequence of ideas, the poem is the free musing of "an old man in a dry month," disconnected—almost inchoate.

Carried to its extreme, this becomes the method of "The Waste Land." That poem can be compared to a crazy quilt of which each piece has some ready association for the sewer and is put into its position with relation to other pieces because of a contrast in material pattern or because of some memory link. Whatever may be the sense of design that the quilter has, the person looking at the quilt sees only a vast kaleidoscope of color and, unless he is told, does not know the significance of each piece of cloth. Just so with this poem. Comparatively short—it consists of 433 lines—it contains quotations from some thirty-odd sources, ranging from the Bible to popular songs; passages in six languages; and even, in its fourth part, a reworking and translation of one of Eliot's own earlier French poems, "Dans le Restaurant." Notes provided by the poet serve to identify the sources of his material. It is as though the quilter were to say, "This piece is from a dress I had when I was ten; and this is an old neck-tie; and this is from my grandmother's wedding gown." Yet for the average reader the notes fail to throw great light on the poem as a whole.

In spite of this, the poem has served as a poetic milestone to many poets; its method of free association, of hazily expressed thoughts, has been a model for their own writing. In that respect, one can understand why for literary influence it has been compared * to the *Lyrical Ballads* of Wordsworth and Coleridge. It has been called by some writers the most significant poem of our times. Yet to many readers, even those who diligently follow Eliot's notes and provide themselves with a running commentary, it still remains unintel-

* Hugh Ross Williamson: *The Poetry of T. S. Eliot*, G. P. Putnam's Sons.

ligible. It cannot, however, be lightly dismissed. Particularly because Eliot, himself, considers that it sums up one phase of his work, it might be well to consider it in some detail.

In an essay on Dante, Eliot writes, "It is a test (a positive test. I do not assert that it is always valid negatively) that genuine poetry can communicate before it is understood." Assayed in this fashion, "The Waste Land" is poetry, genuine poetry. For though one may not, even after countless readings, understand with the mind the full meaning of the poem and its parts, one does sense—and a single reading suffices for this—the strong emotion underlying it, despair, overwhelming grief over the futility of existence; and one does retain the memory of vivid passages.

The poem—its title and much of its symbolism—was suggested by a book, *From Ritual to Romance* by Jessie L. Weston. This book is a detailed study of the stories of the search for the Holy Grail as they have appeared in different languages; through a psychological and anthropological approach, it analyzes these Christian legends, tracing their descent from still more ancient nature myths. In addition to this book, Eliot acknowledges his debt to Frazer's *The Golden Bough,* that exhaustive study of folk-ways and folk-lore. The symbols that are used in the poem are symbols that these books explain. The Waste Land, itself, a land in which the senility of the king typifies the desolate and lifeless character of the country, becomes the symbol for decaying European civilization. Fire is used in its symbolic form as a force of destruction and, through destruction, of purification. Its antithesis is water, the symbol of life. Another life-symbol is the Fisher-king. The symbols are numerous and not always clear to the uninitiate. A further complication arises from the fact that various symbols may represent the same thing. Thus, the Phoenician sailor of the first part of the poem, Mr. Eugenides of the third, and Phebus of the fourth, are essentially one and the same person.

It is, however, chiefly through this use of symbols that whatever continuity exists is achieved among the five component parts of the poem. The repetition of lines or of words provides another slight connecting device. "Those are pearls that were his eyes," for example, is found in both the first and second parts.

> "Unreal City
> Under the brown fog,"

used to open a passage in the third part, sends the mind back to the same lines used in the same way in the first section. The nightingale that in part two sings its song of "Jug Jug" repeats it in the third section.

Just as the connection among the five divisions of the poem is tenuous, so each section of itself fails to produce a unified and coherent whole. Impression follows impression for no readily apparent reason. Transitions are abrupt. Meter changes rapidly. The very variety suggests instability and impermanence. Religion and paganism, past and present, romance and realism, city and country, high society and low, beauty and ugliness pile one upon the other in a helter-skelter mass. The effect is one of discord and of chaos.

The poem, just because of its multiplicity of elements, becomes the expression of reaction to the whole of existence. Not one aspect of life is its subject, but all aspects of life. Its theme is the despair of the individual confronted with a realization of the futility of life; but it is the futility not merely of the individual's life but of all life, of the life of mankind.

"What are the roots that clutch, what branches grow
  Out of this stony rubbish? Son of man,
  You cannot say, or guess, for you know only
  A heap of broken images, where the sun beats,
  And the dead tree gives no shelter, the cricket no relief,
  And the dry stone no sound of water."

  In the face of such extreme desolation, there is but one hope for the individual, but one solution. It is the answer of the mystic: greed and hate must disappear before the soul can enter real life.

"Datta. Dayadhvam. Damyata.
  Shantih shantih shantih."

These are the mysterious-sounding closing lines of the poem. From an old Buddhist sermon comes the alliterative, "Datta. Dayadhvam. Damyata," which is translated as "Give. Sympathize. Control." Giving, it is explained, is a human quality; sympathy is an aspect of the angelic order; control—of one's own life; and, in its highest form, reached by only a few, of the lives of others—is a manifestation of the divine. By a proper exercise of these powers and only so does one achieve "Shantih"—a word from Hindu holy writings which can be liberally translated as "The Peace which passeth understanding."

If the poem is difficult to interpret, one passage may serve as solace to the bewildered.

> "I have heard the key
> Turn in the door once and turn once only
> We think of the key, each in his prison
> Thinking of the key, each confirms a prison."

In explanation of those lines, Eliot quotes from *Appearance and Reality,* a book by the philosopher, F. H. Bradley: "My external sensations are no less private to myself than are my thoughts or my feelings. . . . In brief, regarded as an existence which appears in a soul, the whole world for each is peculiar and private to that soul." It is that very private world of his own which Eliot seeks to express in "The Waste Land"; if he fails to express it in its entirety to the reader, if he fails to make it wholly clear and intelligible, it is because the task by its very nature is impossible.

There was one more return to the disjointed manner of "The Waste Land" in the unfinished poem, "Sweeney Agonistes"; and in "The Hollow Men," published in 1925, there is an echo of the manner. But except for these, Eliot's later poems are more conventional in form. *Ash Wednesday*, a series of six lyrics published in 1930, sings in a new measured rhythm, with an effective use of repetition and of irregularly placed rhymes:

"Who walked between the violet and the violet
Who walked between
The various ranks of varied green."

The symbolism employed may still be elusive, as in the "three white leopards" of the second poem; but it is not quite so bewildering as the symbolism in the earlier poems. The imagery, while varied and provocative, is, nevertheless, more restrained and less grotesque; it is in the subdued tones of a medieval tapestry rather than in the flamboyant colors of a cheap print:

"Will the veiled sister pray for
   Those who walk in darkness, who chose thee and oppose thee,
   Those who are torn on the horn between season and season, time and time, between
   Hour and hour, word and word, power and power, those who wait
In darkness?"

In "Ariel Poems" and that group gathered under the heading of "Minor Poems," are poems which no longer shriek out their mannerisms. Allusions may not always be obvious, but they do not clamor for attention. Meters are varied even within a poem, but the changes are not startlingly abrupt. Rhyme is a flexible tool, to be used as need dictates. "New Hampshire" exemplifies this manner adapted to a lighter use:

> "Children's voices in the orchard
>   Between the blossom- and the fruit-time:
> Golden head, crimson head,
>   Between the green tip and the root.
> Black wing, brown wing, hover over;
> Twenty years and the spring is over;
> Today grieves, tomorrow grieves,
> Cover me over, light-in-leaves;
> Golden head, black wing,
> Cling, swing,
> Spring, sing,
> Swing up into the apple-tree."

In addition to lyric poetry, Eliot's interest has turned toward poetic drama. He has long recognized the fact that "the majority, perhaps, certainly a large number of poets hanker for the stage; and second, that a not negligible public appears to want verse plays." In response to this two-fold demand, Eliot has written *The Rock*, a religious pageant play for the Church Fund of the Diocese of London, a play in which the choruses are in verse; *Murder in the Cathedral*, a play based on the murder of Thomas Becket; and *The Family Reunion*, a psychological story of today told in the somewhat elevated spirit of old Greek tragedies.

*The Rock* was produced in the spring of 1934. Its choruses are cadenced with a rhythm that is Biblical:

"Though you forget the way to the Temple,
 There is one who remembers the way to your door:
 Life you may evade, but Death you shall not.
 You shall not deny the Stranger."

Its message is filled with the religious fervor of service to God.

The religious theme is continued in *Murder in the Cathedral,* produced originally at the Canterbury Festival in England in June 1935. It has received effective stage production in this country. Viewed as drama, it has its effective scenes but it seems a little too loosely constructed. Viewed as poetry, it is musical and exalted.

*The Family Reunion,* published in 1939, has not yet had a stage presentation. One wonders, indeed, whether it can be effectively produced; whether the combination of realistic material and far from realistic manner can appear successfully on the public stage. What, for example, would be the effect of the uncles and aunts of Harry, Lord Monchensey, the protagonist, standing in modern clothes and saying in unison, like a Greek chorus:

"Why do we feel embarrassed, impatient, fretful, ill at
     ease,
  Assembled like amateur actors who have not been as-
     signed their parts?"

The theme of the play is the psychological effect upon Harry of his murder of his wife. His release comes through the efforts of his Aunt Agatha who had loved his father and who loved Harry as her own child. She tells him that his own father had plotted the murder of Harry's mother and had been thwarted in his plans only by Agatha herself.

This is subject matter fitting for a Greek tragedy. But it is posed against a background of present-day England, which serves to present the English upper class in a most satiric vein. Opposed to this stark satire is a bewildering atmosphere of the weird and super-natural, best typified by one of Agatha's numerous incantatory speeches:

> "This way the pilgrimage
> Of expiation
> Round and round the circle
> Completing the charm
> So the knot be unknotted
> The crossed be uncrossed
> The crooked be made straight
> And the curse be ended."

In its poetry, *The Family Reunion* adds little to Eliot's reputation. It is interesting, though, for its revelation that Eliot is still concerned with a religious question, this time the question of an individual's struggle with his conscience. Two other subjects that have long occupied Eliot's thoughts are touched upon. One is that of the flow of time, the interdependence of past and future:

> "How can we be concerned with the past
> And not the future? or with the future
> And not with the past?"

The other is that of the overwhelming sense of frustration, futility, and despair.

> "What you call the normal
> Is merely the unreal and the unimportant.
> I was like that in a way, so long as I could think
> Even of my own life as an isolated ruin,
> A casual bit of waste in an orderly universe.
> But it begins to seem just part of some huge disaster,
> Some monstrous mistake and aberration
> Of all men, of the world, which I cannot put in order."

*The Family Reunion* is basically a psychological study. Through all of Eliot's poetry, the approach has been through modern psychology. He has probed into his own unconscious, into his underlying fears and failures, and he has assumed that what is typical of him is typical of the race. His attitude toward his findings is the attitude of modern psychology:

> "Success is relative:
> It is what we can make of the mess we have made of
>   things,

It is what he can make, not what you would make for
   him."

Eliot is obsessed by the "mess we have made of
things." One of a generation that through the World
War of 1914-1918 and the succeeding years saw its
orderly scheme of things disorganized, its standards up-
rooted, its ideals destroyed, he became oppressed by the
thought of the futility of existence. Yet he is far from
being the advocate of a philosophy of futility. Above
all he has desired passionately something to believe in;
his supreme despair has arisen when futility alone presented itself.

In the early years, when the present appeared unbearable, his recourse was to a glorification of the past.
Burbank "meditating on Time's ruins" is merely Eliot
decrying his present. But while he continued to express
a nostalgia for the past, he came to sense, as he does in
"The Waste Land," that that mood may be a roman-
ticizing of the unknown and the unfamiliar; that past
glamor may not be very different from present vulgarity. How far apart in spirit, he suggests, were Elizabeth and Leicester on a royal Thames barge and an
ordinary holiday couple in a canoe at Richmond?

So insistent is this revelation that time becomes compressed. Past and present become interwoven, as they
do in "Triumphal March." A Roman triumph and a
victory of modern war are telescoped into a single
event; descriptive details of one mingle with those of
the other:

"Those are the golf club Captains, these the Scouts,
And now the *société gymnastique de Poissy*
And now come the Mayor and the Liverymen.

.    .    .    .    .    .    .

Now they go up to the temple. Then the sacrifice.
Now come the virgins bearing urns."

Elsewhere, he writes:

"Time present and time past
Are both perhaps present in time future,
And time future contained in time past.

.    .    .    .    .    .    .

What might have been and what has been
Point to one end, which is always present."

The inescapability of the past, the interweaving of the
three tenses is a recurring note in Eliot's work.

Time appalls him because somehow the present is
unbearable. The idea of life as something to be lived
richly fails him. It is significant, indeed, that it was a
very youthful Eliot who wrote "The Love Song of J.
Alfred Prufrock," the poem of an aging man who,
though desiring to conform to the conventional, is deterred by a fear of appearing ridiculous:

"I have seen the moment of my greatness flicker,
And I have seen the eternal Footman hold my coat,
and snicker,
And in short, I was afraid."

Mr. Prufrock's indecision, his incapacity for action, seems to be something more than the humorous inability of an elderly man to make a proposal of marriage that may be refused. It takes on something of a more general nature and becomes typical of the bewildering despair of any—of every—individual who tries to find his place in life but lacks the courage or the wisdom to take some definite action to achieve it.

The particular deterrent from life, in the case of Eliot, appears to be a fear of vulgarity and of tawdriness. Yet the fear is accompanied by a certain amount of fascination. Apeneck Sweeney is the epitome of vulgarity; he, nevertheless, cannot escape Eliot's attention and, one suspects, admiration. "Faint stale smells of beer," "broken blinds and chimney-pots," "a broken spring in a factory yard"—details like these force themselves into his observation. Yet, like Prufrock, he insists upon going

> "through certain half-deserted streets,
> The muttering retreats
> Of restless nights in one-night cheap hotels
> And sawdust restaurants with oyster-shells."

These are the unlovely aspects of city existence. It is from the city, much more than from the country, that Eliot draws his imagery. But, unlike so many of his contemporaries, he does not glorify the city or the city's ways. For him, there is no beauty in the city. Its crudities are "the last twist of the knife."

His protest against these things is merely an esthetic protest. There is no crying indignation against a social system that makes them possible. There is no rebellion against economic or industrial conditions. There is merely the statement that such things exist and so man should be pitied.

> " 'Issues from the hand of God, the simple soul'
> To a flat world of changing lights and noise,
> To light, dark, dry or damp, chilly or warm;
>
> .    .    .    .    .    .    .
>
> Pray for us now and at the hour of birth."

There is, then, little suggestion in Eliot's poetry of the political, social, or industrial activity of man. Of primary concern is man's religious aspect; more accurately, indeed, it is Eliot's own relation to the universe, the state of his own inner being, which is the chief motif of his poetry. In his first volume, in "The Love Song of J. Alfred Prufrock" and "Portrait of a Lady," the sense of the futility of existence already overwhelms him. In his second book of poems, as Gerontion, he is still seeking the answer to the question of what is human life and has succeeded in reaching only this conclusion: that thought, feeling, life itself are useless, "the giving famishes the craving." This mood pervades "The Waste Land"; but in that book becomes generalized into a despair not only for individual man but for all present-day civilization. Could anything be more devastating than this? Yes, unbelievable though it might seem. For in "The Hollow Men" man is presented as so insignificant that he no longer is the focus for emotions, whether of sympathy or of pity; he is so valueless that he is not even damned:

> "Remember us—if at all—not as lost
> Violent souls, but only
> As the hollow men
> The stuffed men."

Surely, it is the very depths of black despair that provokes the piteous cry of ineffectiveness, the plaint that the world ends

> "Not with a bang but a whimper."

However, in the poems following "The Hollow Men," one finds a new note. In the "Ariel Poems" there is suggested a sense of direction for the search for understanding, a hope of some salvation. In "Animula," man's indecision and inability to act are still stressed, it is true; but present in the poem is a plea for pity, an implication that man is not wholly unworthy. In "Journey of the Magi" and "A Song for Simeon," there is a definite turning toward religion, toward an Almighty Providence as a source of salvation. The liberation of his soul from perplexity and fear and destruction may not be certain; the "ultimate vision" may not be vouchsafed him; but that there is a vision he knows, as the Magi know that

> "There was a Birth, certainly,
> We had evidence and no doubt."

The first resolution of perplexity comes in "Ash Wednesday." Though the symbolism of the poem is sufficiently confusing to prevent a complete intellectual comprehension of all its lines, one is, nevertheless, aware of a feeling of repose, of ease, a new sense of security. It arises from humility of spirit; out of self-abnegation, out of the disavowal of struggling reason, out of faith has come peace.

> "And I pray that I may forget
> These matters that with myself I too much discuss
> Too much explain
> Because I do not hope to turn again
> Let these words answer
> For what is done, not to be done again
> May the judgement not be too heavy upon us
>
> Because these wings are no longer wings to fly
> But merely vans to beat the air"

An acknowledgment of limitations brings acceptance. The poem ends with a confession of unworthiness:

> "Lord, I am not worthy
> Lord, I am not worthy
>                         but speak the word only."

So strong is the religious fervor of the poem, so certain the belief, that one is sure of Eliot's conviction that the word will be spoken.

This avowal of religious faith, satisfying as it must be for the poet, is wholly and exclusively personal to him. How is it to be achieved by others? Eliot does not say. It seems to be the result of a mystical experience, an essentially religious experience, with which some people are blessed but which cannot be shared. It cannot be gained from cold, logical reason. In an address on "Catholicism and International Order" delivered in 1933 at Oxford, Eliot said, "And human wisdom, I add finally, cannot be separated from divine wisdom without tending to become merely worldly wisdom, as vain as folly itself." The source of this divine wisdom Eliot finds in established religion, in the church.

His attitude toward formal religion has developed and changed greatly from his denunciation of the True Church in the early poem "The Hippopotamus," in which he draws a scathing picture of it "wrapt in the old miasmal mist." The seeming failure of the formal church, however, did not cause him to accept the substitute that other disillusioned contemporaries accepted, that of a political economy. "If people don't take their religion in the usual proper way," he makes Ethelbert say in *The Rock*, "they'll take it in other ways, such as politics, and then they get into a 'ell of a muddle." Nor is a purely ethical philosophy sufficient. He criticizes "talking of right relations of men, but not of relations of men to God." The relation of men to God is the field of religion: and it is in religion and, very specifically, in religion as expressed in the Anglo-Catholic Church that Eliot has found the goal of his soul's questing.

It was a painful search, one is sure; as he declares in his most recently published poem, "East Coker," "You must go by a way wherein there is no ecstasy." If Eliot has advanced from alternation "between futile speculation and unconsidered action" to a state of security, the progress must unquestionably have been a soul-searing process. Like the poet Donne, he "knew the anguish of the marrow." That it was also a lonely search, one feels certain. Eliot seems to have pursued it alone, cut off from others. Just as he did not share the experience of the search, so he seems unable to share the result of it with others. He appears isolated from his fellow men; his truth, personal to him. It is not, one must hasten to add, that he does not wish others to accept that truth; it is that he fails to show them how they can sincerely accept it.

For dwelling thus on the religious content of Eliot's poetry, there need be no apology. The poet insists that literary criticism should be supplemented by criticism from an ethical and theological point of view. On the grounds of theology one may differ violently from Eliot. So, too, one may see man's place in the universe as something quite different from Eliot's concept of it; one may see man as a more active agent, as a many-sided constructive force rather than a humble accepter of things as they are. Eliot, himself, proceeds from accepted premises which he holds to be indisputable. "For poetry," he says, "is not the assertion that something is true, but the making that truth more fully real to us." This is an attitude consistent with his firm adherence to tradition and authority, for it is tradition and authority that discover and affirm his truth for him.

His purpose as a poet is not to argue or to persuade. Nor is it merely to express his personality on paper, to lay bare his emotions and to reveal his inner fears and hopes. His purpose is rather through his experiences and thoughts to throw a revealing light on the truth which he has decided has validity for him.

## POETICAL WORKS

PRUFROCK AND OTHER OBSERVATIONS
*The Egoist, Ltd.*

POEMS *Alfred A. Knopf, Inc.*

THE WASTE LAND *Boni and Liveright*

THE ROCK (A Pageant Play)
*Harcourt, Brace and Co.*

MURDER IN THE CATHEDRAL (A Play)
*Harcourt, Brace and Co.*

COLLECTED POEMS *Harcourt, Brace and Co.*

THE FAMILY REUNION (A Play)
*Harcourt, Brace and Co.*

OLD POSSUM'S BOOK OF PRACTICAL CATS
*Harcourt, Brace and Co.*

*SARA TEASDALE*

SHAFTESBURY

## SARA TEASDALE

OUT of the happiness, the joy, the sorrow, the "soul's distress and body's pain" of a sensitive woman, Sara Teasdale made seven volumes of verse, delicately but firmly wrought, simply but authoritatively stated. In them can be traced the record of a developing personality. Yet it is not a thoroughly complete personality that is therein expressed; for in spite of the sincerity and frankness with which are revealed some of the most intimate emotions possible to experience, there is also present a strong spirit of reticence surrounding what the poet says and, consequently, restricting what the reader may know.

> "Unmeaning phrase and wordless measure,
> That unencumbered loveliness
> Which is a poet's secret treasure
> Sings in me now, and sings no less
> That even for your lenient eyes
> It will not live in written guise."

The same reticence marked Sara Teasdale's life. Few biographical facts are available. Few, indeed, are necessary; for, in the creation of poetry like hers, feelings are more important than dates, thoughts more important than events. Yet there can be sketched the life which formed a background for her work.

She was born August 8, 1884, in St. Louis, Missouri, the youngest child of John Warren Teasdale and Mary Elizabeth Willard. Both on her father's and her mother's side, her family was old American. About the middle of the nineteenth century, both grandfathers left the eastern seaboard for the Middle West. They must have carried with them and handed down to their granddaughter a love of the sea; for though born in an inland city, she still could feelingly say

> "Tho I am inland far, I hear and know,
> For I was born the sea's eternal thrall."

As a youngster she evinced a marked enjoyment of poetry. In later life she declared that her mother told "incredible tales" of the extremely early age at which she recited Mother Goose jingles. Since almost every mother has similar tales of children's precocity, this, in itself, is no means for distinguishing an embryonic poet. But very soon after the "See-Saw," "Little Boy Blue" and "Ride-a-Cock-Horse" stage, the little girl was introduced to real poetry and of the poems she heard, Christina Rossetti's "Christmas Carol," beginning, "In the bleak midwinter, frosty winds made moan," soon became her favorite. "I think I liked it better than other poems," she once said, "partly because snow is mentioned in it. I used to stand at the window during a snow-storm literally enchanted by the music of the lines."

Sensitive, delicate, never strong, she was educated first at home, then at a private school for girls in St. Louis, where she first began her writing. She translated Heine and other German poets. She wrote some original verse. This was childish, unskillful, marked by an ineptitude of rhyme and manner which, she confessed, rose to haunt her in maturity.

But the girl persisted. After graduation from school in 1903, she continued her writing, disciplining and training herself in poetic technique. She and some friends brought out a monthly magazine, *The Potter's Wheel*, each issue consisting of a single copy, in manuscript, with original illustrations. This amateur magazine continued its existence for several years.

Shortly after her graduation, too, Sara Teasdale began to travel. Her journeyings through the western and southwestern parts of the United States are recalled in her poetry, as in "Night in Arizona," with its local color touches of coyotes and crouching mountains. But the poems inspired by these and by her European travels give little indication of any intellectual curiosity on her part concerning the places visited, or of sympathy, or contact even, with people she must have seen. For the most part, new countries and new cities seemed merely to provide settings for her own highly personal feelings.

During her first trip abroad, which she began in 1905 and which took her to southern Europe, Greece, the Near East, Egypt, and the Holy Land, she wrote steadily. Upon her return in 1907 she received the first public acknowledgment of her ability. William Marion Reedy, who must be credited with innumerable literary discoveries, published in his *Reedy's Mirror* her poem, "Guenevere," a blank verse monologue of Arthur's Queen, "branded for a single fault."

"But none will pity me, nor pity him
Whom Love so lashed, and with such cruel thongs."

The same year saw the publication of her first volume, *Sonnets to Duse and Other Poems*, dedicated to her father and her mother. The adolescent phenomenon of the "crush" here found expression in verse. The book was the outpouring of a young girl's fancy and day-dreaming, undirected and untrained. The object of adoration was far off and, indeed, unknown; for Eleonora Duse, the Italian actress of the rich voice and dark, haunting eyes, was familiar to Sara Teasdale only in pictures, as she appeared in *The Dead City* or in the title role of *Francesca da Rimini*. The poems were equally far removed from a sense of reality. They were filled with personifications of Pain and of Delight, with Sicilian shepherds, Orphean lays, and lotus blossoms. They were marked by wild, if strongly felt, extravagance:

"Alone as all the chosen are alone,
Yet one with all the beauty of the past."

Included, too, were several poems addressed to another idol, removed in time as well as in place, to

Sappho, the Greek poetess; and a few most trivial lyrics. One may note in these poems a sense of form, facility particularly with the sonnet form, that held promise for future work. For the most part, however, the poems were such as might have been written by any well-brought-up young woman, well-read, thoughtful, and with a flair for writing.

The well-brought-up girl of that period, particularly one with any intellectual claims at all, felt that the immediate expression of emotions was not in good taste. On the other hand, it was impossible completely to repress all feelings. Sara Teasdale, caught with her contemporaries in the dilemma, found a way out. The feelings which she, herself, was experiencing she expressed in monologues as the thoughts of others and of them in 1911 made her next book of poems, *Helen of Troy and Other Poems.*

"Guenevere," her first published poem, was included in this volume. In addition to the early British queen, other heroines became the mouthpiece for the poet's own deepest feelings: Sappho, Helen of Troy, Dante's love, Beatrice, to name but a few. Blank verse was the chosen meter for the poems, but used lightly, lyrically. Sappho sings:

"Twilight has veiled the little flower face
 Here on my heart, but still the night is kind,
 And leans her warm sweet weight against my heart."

and Marianna Alcoforando, a Portuguese nun of the late seventeenth and early eighteenth century, in lines prophetic almost of Sara Teasdale's own later life, speaks in the same flowing meter:

> "And then I knew that Love is worth its pain
> And that my heart was richer for his sake,
> Since lack of love is bitterest of all."

But a large part of the book was made up of something much more personal, intimate, and subjective than the longer poems in blank verse. The poet overcame some of the diffidence of the self-controlled young woman and spoke, at last, in her own person. A woman's attitude toward love—her desire for fulfillment through it, fear lest it pass her by or find her unprepared, humility at its coming—this became the theme of the second volume of verse. To express it, Sara Teasdale was perfecting her technique, the writing of direct simple lyrics in clear-cut quatrains of simple meters. However deeply felt the matter, the manner was restrained and so the more effective. Typical of this method, a simplicity of form and of statement that implies much more than is openly said, is the completely characteristic poem, "The Song for Colin":

> "I sang a song at dusking time
>    Beneath the evening star,
> And Terence left his latest rhyme
>    To answer from afar.
>
> Pierrot laid down his lute to weep,
>    And sighed, 'She sings for me,'

But Colin slept a careless sleep
Beneath an apple tree."

The summer of 1912 the poet spent in Italy and Switzerland. In Italy, in particular, she found inspiration for a group of poems which, as "Vignettes Overseas," appeared in her next volume. Except for this European trip and for two or three winters spent in New York, she lived with her parents in St. Louis until her marriage in 1914 to Ernst B. Filsinger, an importer and authority on international trade. Shortly her husband's business carried the couple to New York. For a while they were whole-heartedly happy together; but soon they found their lives diverging. Their separate interests, needs, and temperaments made different demands. Her increasingly poor health made her more and more of a recluse; his business necessitated frequent absences in Europe. Finally, in September 1929, they were divorced. The woman for whom love meant so much, for whom it gave meaning and direction to life, was able to relinquish it sharply and clearly.

In 1915, another volume of poems, *Rivers to the Sea,* was published. From that time on, the poet's external life was uneventful, marked only by her travels, in England in 1923 and in France in 1924, and by the publication of her various books. Of these two were anthologies: *The Answering Voice* and *Rainbow Gold,* the latter a collection of poems for children which included her own childhood favorite, the Rossetti poem. Her other books were all volumes of poetry. The publication in 1917 of *Love Songs* brought her great recognition, popularity with the public, and the acclaim of critics. Harriet Monroe in her magazine *Poetry* said of it that it "contains a few poems which may be ranked among the finest woman's love songs in the language, and the whole book reveals with singular clarity and precision a beautiful bright spirit of rare vividness and charm." A committee composed of William Marion Reedy, Bliss Perry, and Jessie B. Rittenhouse chose it for the prize presented by Columbia University for the "best book of poetry published last year in the country by a citizen of the United States." It won for its author a second prize, this from The Poetry Society of America. The three following books, *Flame and Shadow* in 1920, *Dark of the Moon*, 1926, and the posthumous *Strange Victory*, 1933, served only to strengthen the now firmly established reputation of the poet.

Was it possible that the desire to be a poet was born when the little girl first learned to love Christina Rossetti's "Christmas Carol"? At all events she became intensely interested in its author and planned to write a biography of that earlier woman poet. In June 1932, she went to London to undertake some research for the contemplated book. There she was stricken with pneumonia. Greatly weakened, she returned to New York and suffered a nervous breakdown. On the morning of January 29, 1933, she was found dead.

The unswerving devotion to poetry that marked her life she projected beyond death. Her last wishes, as recorded in her will, were concerned with poetry. She directed that after the death of her former husband and of a friend, her residuary estate be given to Wellesley College to provide an annual award for poetic achievement to an American who has had published at least one volume of verse. Jealous pride in her own work dictated her request that no previously unpublished poem of hers be published "unless written sanction for such publication appear thereon."

One further wish she did express. As a young woman, confronted with the thought of eventual fate, she had written:

"How can they leave me in that dark alone,
  Who loved the joys of light and warmth so much,
  And thrilled so with the sense of sound and touch—
  How can they shut me underneath a stone?"

As though to avoid that final shutting in, she asked that her body be cremated. Her final wish was granted and her ashes were buried in the family cemetery plot in St. Louis.

The gentle woman with the oval face, the red-gold hair parted in the middle, wide-set eyes and large sensitive mouth, was no more. The quiet voice that frequently startled with bright unexpected flashes of wit was forever stilled. The reticence which Sara Teasdale chose as her prerogative was complete.

Once, indeed, the poet broke her usual public silence to explain her theory of poetry and its creation. To

Marguerite Wilkinson's *New Voices*,* she contributed
a brief article on "How Poems Are Made." Poetry, she
insisted, is the result of emotions produced by experience, either real or imaginary, and is written so that the
poet may be relieved of his emotional burden. "Out of
the fog of emotional restlessness from which a poem
springs," she wrote, "the basic idea emerges sometimes
slowly, sometimes in a flash. This idea is known at once
to be the light toward which the poet was groping. He
now walks round and round it, so to speak, looking
at it from all sides, trying to see which aspect of it is
the most vivid. When he has hit upon what he believes
is his peculiar angle of vision, the poem is fairly begun.
The first line comes floating toward him with a charming definiteness of color and music. In my own case the
rhythm of a poem usually follows, in a general way, the
rhythm of the first line. The form of the poem should
be a clear window-pane through which you see the
poet's heart. The form, as form, should be engrossing
neither to the poet nor to the reader. The reader should
be barely conscious of the form, the rhymes or the
rhythm. He should be conscious of emotions given him,
and unconscious of the medium by which they are trans-
mitted." To achieve this end, she urged simplicity of
diction and expression lest verbal tricks and complicated mannerisms distract the reader from the emotional content of the poem. "The poet should try to
give his poem the quiet swiftness of flame, so that the

* Marguerite Wilkinson: *New Voices*, The Macmillan Co.

reader will feel and not think while he is reading. But the thinking will come afterwards."

A brief record is this, and a fragmentary one, of a poet's life and personality. For the rest, for the thoughts, and feelings, the moods, the longings, and the desires that made the woman and poet, one must look to the poems, themselves.

The poems are those of a thoughtful woman, not of one yielding herself to an abandon of emotions. But however aware one is of the mind behind the poems, one realizes that the initial poetic impulse is always in the feelings, not in thought.

"For my mind is proud and strong enough to be silent,
    It is my heart that makes my songs, not I."

And the feelings are, for the most part, grounded in her own personal, intimate experiences rather than in her contacts with an external world of beauty or of confusion.

Occasionally there are songs of places, of New York, and of foreign cities, as in the "Vignettes Overseas" in *Rivers to the Sea.* A poem like "Dawn" paints the picture of a worn, sleeping city, in which "dreams wear thin" and men tossing upon their beds "hear the milk-cart jangle by alone." Or the mood of a place may be caught, as in the vivid reconstruction of winter-bound, deserted Coney Island:

"With foams of icy lace
        The sea creeps up the sand,

The wind is like a hand
That strikes us in the face.
Doors that June set a-swing
Are bolted long ago;
We try them uselessly—
Alas, there cannot be
For us a second spring.
                Come, let us go."

But the changing scene, American or European, city, countryside, or ocean, assumes importance chiefly as a shifting background for her feelings. Gibraltar is for her a "delicate despair"; Stresa fills her heart with beauty until "it can hold no more"; the Metropolitan Museum in New York City evokes the glories of the past

"till you stooped
To find the present with a kiss."

Not only are the physical characteristics of the outer world of little significance to her, but there is revealed in her poetry scarcely any concern with the world of people, with a social system rightly or wrongly developed. It would have been impossible, of course, for her to have completely escaped the influence of city-life, one of the manifestations of present-day civilization; and so there are poems of the city: "The Metropolitan Tower," in her early book, *Helen of Troy and Other Poems*, "Broadway," "May Day," "In a Subway Station" in *Rivers to the Sea*, "A November Night" in

*Love Songs.* There is a recognition that there are other
men and women who live their lives, suffer or are glad.
"From the Woolworth Tower" presents a tapestry of
these human beings:

"We feel the millions of humanity beneath us,—
  The warm millions, moving under the roofs,
  Consumed by their own desires;
  Preparing food,
  Sobbing alone in a garret,
  With burning eyes bending over a needle,
  Aimlessly reading the evening paper,
  Dancing in the naked light of the café,
  Laying out the dead,
  Bringing a child to birth—
  The sorrow, the torpor, the bitterness, the frail joy
  Come up to us
  Like a cold fog wrapping us round."

But the realization of their struggling existence rouses
in her no indignation, no vehement protestation, no
crying out against man's lot. There is scarcely even
identification with those beneath her tower vantage
point. For herself, the poet is concerned with the love
that has come to her and set her triumphantly apart;
the answer to the problem of what she sees before her
is the exultant

          "Beloved,
            Tho' sorrow, futility, defeat
            Surround us,

They cannot bear us down.
Here on the abyss of eternity
Love has crowned us
For a moment
Victor."

It was in the emotion of personal love that she felt her strongest link to other people. When others were happy in their love, she rejoiced with them; when they suffered grief through love, her heart went out to them. So for her the World War of 1914-1918, because it meant the breaking of tender ties, the cruel separation of loved ones, was a very real and devastating experience. She could understand the loss of love and her sympathy welled up for

"The woman over the sea
Waiting at dusk for one who is dead!"

All the tenderness of her feelings pours forth in the poignant "Spring in War Time":

"Under the boughs where lovers walked
    The apple-blooms will shed their breath—
But what of all the lovers now
    Parted by death,
        Gray Death?"

That is the province which Sara Teasdale chose for herself and her poetry, the realm of the intensely personal. Political, scientific, industrial changes may sweep and modify the world; but ever there is present for each individual his concern with the fundamentals of life—the identity of self, love, sorrow, death. This concern at its most personal—more specifically, her concern with these fundamentals—is the material of her poems. She professed to speak, not for the great mass of mankind, but only for herself. "Most poets," she wrote, "find it easier to write about themselves than about anything else because they know more about themselves than about anything else." Sara Teasdale wrote about herself; and because she wrote honestly and sincerely, she touches a responsive chord in all those who ever felt or thought as she did.

Above all others, love was the basic motif of her poetry. Very occasionally she treated it in a coquettish fashion. The oft-quoted poems, "The Song for Colin," "The Look," "Pierrot," are typical of this mood. But the mood is not completely typical of the poet. Love had other, many other, sides; these were her subject. Delicately, with no false sense of shame, she poured out her feelings. Her viewpoint was essentially feminine; it is a woman's attitude that she expressed.

Like a growing, deepening theme, one can trace in the poems the development of a young woman's love. The first desires for some unknown fulfillment; the cry

> "Oh, beauty, are you not enough?
> Why am I crying after love?"

the fear lest life pass without love:

"The air is blue and sweet,
    The few first stars are white,—
Oh let me like the birds
    Sing before night."

these are quieted by its coming. With its coming, the poet yields to a very ecstasy of emotion.

"Now at last I can live!"

she cries. All perplexities are resolved; vague questings, answered:

"It is enough to feel his love
    Blow by like music over me."

These lyrics are unquestionably the love songs of a woman. Love is an all-embracing passion, not simply a single manifestation of existence; to it the poet—the woman—grants complete submission:

"I would beat with your heart as it beats, I would
    follow your soul as it leads."

This desire for complete absorption by love may appear slightly crinolined to the young people of today who see in love, as in other emotions, an opportunity for reciprocal relations. Yet Sara Teasdale was modern in her viewpoint. For, in spite of this longing, in spite of her desire that it might be otherwise, she realized the actual, the essential loneliness of the soul in love who knows the utter impossibility, not only of a complete merging of lover and beloved, but even of a complete understanding:

> "I am alone, in spite of love,
> In spite of all I take and give."

Indeed, she knew still more; she knew the "hard and precious stone" of truth, which she set forth so understandingly, so pointedly, in "Advice to a Young Girl":

> "No one worth possessing
> Can be quite possessed."

It is the clear-eyed realization and acceptance not only of the joys and delights, but of all the various stresses and strains of love, the possibilities of change and of cessation that make Sara Teasdale's viewpoint a modern one. Her own sensitivity, her own experience, taught her that love may not endure in its original form:

> "Our love is dying like the grass;
> And we who kissed grow coldly kind,
> Half glad to see our old love pass
> Like leaves along the wind."

Sometimes, too, one may continue to love where love is not returned. That is the theme of the very moving poem, "It Will Not Change." Surmounting the vicissitudes of life, of death itself, the poet declares her love "will live on"; "in all my songs for you," it will persist.

It would seem, indeed, as if the emotion itself were

more important than the object of devotion. Love, of itself, despite the pain and sorrow it may bring, is to be embraced. If it is the cause of some of life's sorrows, it is as well the solvent of its problems. It is the key to life:

"Only by love is life made real."

To beauty, too, it is the key. Color, movement, music—

"The night thou badst Love fly away,
He hid them all from thee."

One becomes aware, however, of a developing attitude toward beauty. Beauty becomes a thing apart, something to be pursued for its own sake, the epitome of the ideal. Again and again the note is repeated: beauty is the solace for grief; beauty is the weapon against mortality. Others may die, she says; but surely must there not be some "shining strange escape" for her

"Who sought in Beauty the bright wine
Of Immortality"?

The search for beauty, the poet maintained, is the search that motivates the human race. Out of the past the message comes to her. As the result of change, of "mutation on mutation," her "loving thoughts" spring from those who have gone before;

"I hear them cry, 'Forever
Seek for Beauty, she only
Fights with man against Death!'"

It was through her poetry that Sara Teasdale sought beauty. Sorrow and pain—for joy sings itself—she was able to transform into song; they became the material out of which beauty sprang and brought comfort. The "spirit's gray defeat," physical weakness, lost hopes—over all of these, she could rise superior:

> "For with my singing, I can make
> A refuge for my spirit's sake."

The clue to that indomitable power lies in the last line of that most beautiful poem, "On the Sussex Downs":

> "It was myself that sang in me."

Song, the power to feel and to express poetry, was the very essence of Sara Teasdale's being; and it was to that being, to her own sense of identity, to the individual she felt herself to be, that she clung. In herself she found her own refuge, her comfort, and her strength.

Nature gave her no lasting comfort. Its beauty brought her joy, it is true, and an enrichment of self. But Nature, she realized, is completely heedless of the individual; its concern is only with the race, with vast forces. What matters it to Nature that one human being suffers?

> "Earth takes her children's many sorrows calmly
> And stills herself to sleep."

What would it matter, indeed, should all mankind not simply suffer, but be wiped out?

> "Not one would mind, neither bird nor tree
> If mankind perished utterly;
> And Spring herself, when she woke at dawn,
> Would scarcely know that we were gone."

Nature is supremely indifferent; it withdraws from—rather, it is completely unaware of—the cares of mankind.

One's only importance is to one's self. This is the realization which Sara Teasdale reached through her life's experience. Love came and departed; something remained. Nature smiled but withdrew, cold and aloof; something persisted. That something is one's sense of self, one's will to be and to do. Again and again the call to self-reliance, to self-dependence, to self-sufficiency is cried; clearer and clearer it sounds with the passing of the years. An entire section of *Flame and Shadow*, for example, is called "Songs for Myself." These are poems, not of egotism or of narcissistic indulgence, but of strength and of courage. Again, in *Dark of the Moon*, the same note is struck. "The Solitary" declares that she, who is now "self-complete as a flower or a stone," has little need of others. "Day's Ending" in the same volume repeats that self, not love, is the key to life:

> " 'Only yourself can heal you,
> Only yourself can lead you,

The road is heavy going
And ends where no man knows;
Take love when love is given,
But never think to find it
A sure escape from sorrow
Or a complete repose.' "

Finally, in *Strange Victory,* her last volume, the summation of her life and growth is expressed in the sonnet "Wisdom":

"Oh to relinquish, with no more of sound
Than the bent bough's when the bright apples fall;
Oh to let go, without a cry or call
That can be heard by any above ground;
Let the dead know, but not the living see—
The dead who loved me will not suffer, knowing
It is all one, the coming or the going,
If I have kept the last, essential me.
If that is safe, then I am safe indeed,
It is my citadel, my church, my home,
My mother and my child, my constant friend;
It is my music, making for my need
A paean like the cymbals of the foam,
Or silence, level, spacious, without end."

One must not imagine that this attitude of maturity was a contradiction of the views of youth. It was a development and a growth, not a denial. If love was not the end-all and be-all youth thought it to be, it was, nevertheless, to be accepted—nay sought—joyously and freely. If life brought sorrow, it was still to be lived eagerly, fully.

> " 'I found more joy in sorrow
> Than you could find in joy.' "

Whatever life had to offer, that must be experienced and incorporated into one's very being. That made for an enriching and ennobling of self:

> "How can I quarrel with fate
> Since I can see
> I am a debtor to life
> Not life to me?"

And what was the poet's ultimate reaction to this life? She had experienced its bitter and its sweet, its pain and joy, its sorrow and its happiness. Out of the experience, deep if not broad, she was able to say sincerely, with conviction:

> "And on the whole, I think life good."

This attitude of unwavering acceptance is not the simple faith of our fathers, of those who found in some force outside themselves—in God, in Nature, in Law—the eternal and unchanging to which they could give their full loyalty. It is a modern attitude, cognizant of change and impermanence but undaunted by them. It faced and accepted the implications of mortal, changing love. So, in the poet's later life, it met the challenge of the impermanent physical; and realizing all that is meant by illness, by loss of physical strength, and by the inevitable, steady approach of death, still acknowledged reality and was not crushed.

Throughout the poet's later books there is made evident her preoccupation with change. There are yearning cries for youth that is no more. There is a wistful desire for joys and beauties that are past. There is regret for the inability to feel again the raptures that once she knew. But, in the face of change, in the realization that

"The rest of the way will be only going down,"

there is present a strong determination to live the latter days beautifully:

"Moon, worn thin to the width of a quill,
    In the dawn clouds flying,
  How good to go, light into light, and still
    Giving light, dying."

The poet's growing concern with death, the ultimate change, is marked by a developing attitude. The early reaction is fear, but one most closely associated with the fear of missing the beauties of earth:

"I am alone, the old terror takes me,
    Evenings will come like this when I am gone."

Such hopes that a belief in immortality holds out are vague and tenuous besides the known certainty of the losses death inevitably brings. It is no orthodox immortality that is suggested by two poems, "If Death is Kind" and "On the Dunes"; if there be a life after death, these poems say, then there may be some return of the dead to the places they loved in life.

But suppose there be no immortality? The poet does not even profess to give an answer. Her first angry rebellion at the idea of death, however, yields in time to acquiescence and acceptance until, indeed, death is declared a friend "save when he comes too late." She reaches a final triumph of spirit; she is able to welcome death while still glorying in life:

> "You only knew me, tell them I was glad
> For every hour since my hour of birth,
> And that I ceased to fear, as once I feared,
> The last complete reunion with the earth."

There can be no question that this is a modern attitude. Reality is unflinchingly faced. Life is not wholly sweet; nor is death. One cannot blithely reject the one for the other. Nor can one cling to a compromise in the form of a wished-for immortality. Whatever comes must be accepted, and accepted bravely. Meanwhile, there is the ever present insistence upon the self. Unless one learns, the poet says, to ask no help, to bear grief courageously, and to enjoy pleasure fearlessly,

> "Unless I learn these things on earth,
> Why was I ever given birth?"

Except for a scattering handful of poems, there is no suggestion of the debonair or of the flippant in the exposition of the poet's views. Nor is there any of the cynicism that was the mark of many of her contemporaries. What she felt she felt deeply and expressed sincerely. She resorted to no subterfuge, no assumption of one mood to conceal another. While there is no concealment of innermost feelings, the reader who shares the poet's intimacies does not feel that he has been forced to violate any sense of privacy. He is saved from that embarrassment by a delicate reticence and restraint that are characteristic of her poetry.

> "You thought to see me cry, but oh
> My tears were hidden in my heart."

Emotions are vivid; but there are few details of description or of exposition. That very absence serves only to intensify the feelings. No one has known another's heartbreak, the poet says in "Snowfall"; so she cannot answer directly the question whether some other woman is unhappy. But "she seems hushed to me," the poet continues. And by the use of that word *hushed,* she draws a complete picture of a woman subdued by a quietly borne unhappiness. By that same word she suggests her own life and poems.

This temperamental restraint manifested itself in a similar restraint of poetic manner, an extreme simplicity of method. The elaboration, the highly wrought imagery and diction of her first two books, the poet quickly abandoned for a compressed simple medium, similar to that of Housman. "Twilight," "The Long Hill," for example, and, very particularly, "The Look" suggest the manner of *A Shropshire Lad*. This telling economy of method is at its best in such a poem as "Sand Drift," with its unadorned but starkly beautiful last stanza:

"Nothing has changed; with the same hollow thunder
   The waves die in their everlasting snow—
Only the place we sat is drifted over,
   Lost in the blowing sand, long, long ago."

The danger inherent in such simplicity is the temptation to write the easy and the obvious. There results an occasional utterly trivial poem, like "The Return." Rarely—but most rarely—the ease degenerates into a poem like "February Twilight" wherein one objects not so much to the manner as to the simplicity of idea, a vagueness of thought and meaning.

But, properly used, this method is the poet's strength. The highest art lies, possibly, in the concealment of art. So the care and effort required for the production of such unaffected poems are not apparent; the reader is aware only of their unadorned worthiness. In their ease and flow, the poems are essentially musical, lyric, lending themselves to singing.

Sara Teasdale molded to her lyric use a variety of meters. She experimented with free verse, using it in such poems as "From the Woolworth Tower," "When I am Not With You," "The Lighted Window":

"In the winter dusk
 When the pavements were gleaming in the rain,
 I walked through a dingy street
 Hurried, harassed,
 Thinking of all my problems that never are solved."

But by far the largest number of her poems are written in some more highly formalized rhythm. These are, however, all marked by the singing flow of her words. Even the blank verse of her very earliest poems, as has been noted, bears this lyric quality. The same is true of the sonnet, which was the form used in her first book of poems and used, again, so unerringly in her last volume, in "Ashes" and in "Return to a Country House." Still another verse form that she made her own is the one called the Sapphic stanza. It is the form in which has come down the one fragment of poetry of the early Greek Sappho, who was, it will be remembered, one of Sara Teasdale's girlhood heroines. Surely nothing could be more lovely, more tender, than her poem in this meter, "The Lamp":

"If I can bear your love like a lamp before me,
  When I go down the long steep Road of Darkness,
  I shall not fear the everlasting shadows,
    Nor cry in terror.

If I can find out God, then I shall find Him,
 If none can find Him, then I shall sleep soundly,
 Knowing how well on earth your love sufficed me,
    A lamp in darkness."

But the more usual form in which her poems are cast is the quatrain, iambic tetrameter alternating with iambic trimeter, with the second and fourth lines rhyming. There are, of course, numerous variations within that form; for beauty and strength, lines are lengthened or shortened, stresses are shifted. Consider, for example, the effect of the shifted stress in the word *warm* in the lines:

> "My room is like a bit of June,
> Warm and close-curtained fold on fold."

or that on *sank* in the stanza:

> "The stately tragedy of dusk
> Drew to its perfect close,
> The original white evening star
> Sank, and the red moon rose."

While this familiar ballad stanza is the one most frequently used, it is noticeable that with increasing maturity and increasing concern with more somber subjects, the poet came to employ a longer and slower meter. For four and three stress lines are substituted five and six stress ones; "At Tintagel," in *Dark of the Moon,* to cite one instance, a hexameter alternates with a pentameter in a four-line stanza. So, too, instead of the short iambic foot, the longer dactyl or anapest is used, as in "August Night" in the same volume. The effect of subdued seriousness created by this use of a more slowly timed measure is illustrated by these lines:

"But if you remember, then turn away forever
  To the plains and the prairies where pools are far
    apart,
There you will not come at dusk on closing water
    lilies,
  And the shadow of mountains will not fall on your
    heart."

Something quite different, defying all fixed rules of
meter analysis, is the poem, "Let It Be Forgotten":

"Let it be forgotten, as a flower is forgotten,
  Forgotten as a fire that once was singing gold,
Let it be forgotten for ever and ever,
  Time is a kind friend, he will make us old.

If anyone asks, say it was forgotten
  Long and long ago,
As a flower, as a fire, as a hushed footfall
  In a long forgotten snow."

Under the dexterity that introduced such metrical
variations lay the firm certainty of control over the
simple meters. It is this simplicity of verse form of
which the reader is first aware. Then it is apparent that
this is combined with fundamental simplicity of word
and of expression. A slight tendency toward gawdiness
which was suggested in the first tentative volumes was
quickly overcome. The early habit of personification,
which starred *Sonnets to Duse* with capital letters, was
soon abandoned. So, too, was the rather distressing

habit of over-identification with nature. "I am the pool!", "I am the still rain falling," "I am a river," "I am a cloud," and other similar expressions followed each other in such rapid succession that the protean changes were breathtaking and ineffective! But once these habits were discarded—and they were rapidly out-grown—the poet wrote with a sure and compelling manner.

Throughout the poems there is evidence of the knowledge of words and feeling for their value that produce vivid, inevitable pictures. "Nimble sandpipers run twinkling by." Sounds are "shimmering"; shadows, "naked." Things are forgotten as a "hushed footfall" in a "long forgotten snow." Simple figures of speech add their beauty. Softness, warmth, and drowsiness are suggested by a "quilt of snow." Or, again, she writes:

> "Even the lights are cold;
> They have put shawls of fog around them, see!"

or again:

> "But all my life was like an autumn day,
> Full of gray quiet and a happy peace."

Sometimes, indeed, a figure is expanded and used throughout an entire poem. In "Deep in the Night," for example, in such a sustained figure, love is compared to a swallow crying in the night; in "Tides," it is similarly compared to the incoming and outgoing tides. In several poems, in which a figure is used throughout, the meaning is never definitely stated, merely implied; but it is none the less impressive. Indeed it is all the more so because it is only suggested. An illustration of this method is "The Long Hill" in which life is implicitly compared to a walk up a hill—and down; and in which all the weariness—and relief, too—of old age are movingly suggested by the last line:

"The rest of the way will be only going down."

If Sara Teasdale knew when to use a figure of speech, she knew equally well when not to use one. Consider, for example, this stanza from the poem "November":

"The world is tired, the year is old,
    The fading leaves are glad to die,
The wind goes shivering with cold
    Where the brown reeds are dry."

How very effective that last unadorned line is simply because it follows three lines which do contain figures of speech! A poem like "After Death," completely without figurative or "poetical" language, is movingly satisfying. "I Have Seen the Spring" contains two slight figures; for the rest, it is the choice of details and the suffusion of feeling that make it memorable.

That is, indeed, the secret of Sara Teasdale's poetry. It is marked by force of feeling rather than by obvious technical showmanship. Figures that are used are never extravagant or strained. Suggestive of associations within the reader's own experience, they are easy to accept. They never become highly intellectualized, cleverly elaborated "conceits."

One intellectual play, however, the poet does permit herself—a building up of suspense until the last stanza or, more frequently, last line; or a sudden twist of idea in the last line that produces a surprising contrast in mood or thought to that for which the preceding lines have prepared. "Buried Love," as an illustration, proclaims the carefree attitude of one who has seen love depart, but ends

> "I shall stay all day in the sun
> Where the wide winds blow,—
> But oh, I shall cry at night
> When none will know."

"Pierrot," in lighter mood, shows the same technique in sharper, still more incisive fashion.

It is quite evident that there is little of the intellectualized in Sara Teasdale's poetry. It is poetry of sentiment, of feeling. Its mood, if one can generalize, is that of "gentle despair." The early poems are filled with twilight, April rains, November nights, tender melancholy. In the later poems there is a steadily increasing sense of the passing of things. Life and earth are beautiful, she insists; regret that things change is only natural. But in her regret she is sustained by pride of mind. Behind her feelings, the mind, seeing and directing, creates poetry that is emotionally honest and strong.

She makes no discoveries, yields no new revelations.

She seems, indeed, unaware of much in the world about her, the complexity of civilization, its wrongs, the discontent of people. But within the sphere that she has chosen, she does give a modern answer to timeless feelings and questionings. The beauties of life and of nature, the beauty of love and the pain of love lost, sorrow at the transitoriness of all things, courage in the face of death—these are her province; and the feelings aroused by their contemplation she expresses honestly and sincerely, as a woman faithful to her own emotions and convictions. Because of her honesty and strength, she gives authority to emotions generally felt. Each one must make his adjustment to life, to love, and to death; this is the goal of human seeking. Sara Teasdale made her adjustment. She loved life whole-heartedly; calmly and bravely she accepted the phenomenon of death. The attainment of her own "inviolate quest" she declares in her last poem:

### THERE WILL BE REST

"There will be rest, and sure stars shining
    Over the roof-tops crowned with snow,
A reign of rest, serene forgetting,
    The music of stillness holy and low.

I will make this world of my devising
    Out of a dream in my lonely mind,
I shall find the crystal of peace,—above me
    Stars I shall find."

## POETICAL WORKS

SONNETS TO DUSE AND OTHER POEMS
*Poet Lore Company*

HELEN OF TROY AND OTHER POEMS
(Revised 1922)        *The Macmillan Co.*

RIVERS TO THE SEA        *The Macmillan Co.*

LOVE SONGS        *The Macmillan Co.*

FLAME AND SHADOW        *The Macmillan Co.*

DARK OF THE MOON        *The Macmillan Co.*

STARS TONIGHT        *The Macmillan Co.*

STRANGE VICTORY        *The Macmillan Co.*

COLLECTED POEMS        *The Macmillan Co.*

*WYSTAN  HUGH  AUDEN*

## WYSTAN HUGH AUDEN

"I have a handsome profile
I've been to a great public school
I've a little money invested
Then why do I feel such a fool
As if I owned a world that had had its day?"

THESE lines, which are closer to doggerel than
to great poetry, and which fail utterly to suggest the force and depth of W. H. Auden's best
verse, still in some ways very aptly epitomize the poet
and his work. Briefly they indicate the sort of person
the writer is, his background and training. They touch
upon the subject which is the theme of so many of his
poems, the disintegration of our present-day civilization. More than that, they reveal his typical manner of
writing, the juxtaposition of personal and impersonal,
of details of private existence and those of public politics and economics.

Auden writes—he, himself, says it—as "an intellectual of the middle classes." His point of view in his
poetry is not that of an introspective soul, anxious to
lay bare the inner world of his own emotions; it is that
of a liberal thinker who looks with pity and terror upon
a world of men and women, a world that is harsh and

cruel, that has been made so by human wills perverted, and that is destined to collapse unless there is individual and mass moral regeneration. In this respect, Auden performs the peculiar function of acting as poetic spokesman for innumerable fellow-thinkers who, without him, would never suspect that their thoughts and feelings are legitimate material for poetry. He writes, furthermore, neither as one of the oppressed workers nor as one whose lot is so far removed from theirs that he is unaware of their existence.

His background is one of financial and educational solidity. The poet's father, George Augustus Auden, was one of the seven children of a Church of England clergyman, of a family which had been

> "all Midland yeomen
> Till royalties from coal mines did them good."

He chose medicine as his profession; and it was as a rising young doctor that he met, fell in love with, and married Constance Rosalie Bricknell, a nurse, who by coincidence was, herself, the daughter of a clergyman and one of seven children. Their third son, the poet, Wystan Hugh Auden, was born in York on February 21, 1907.

The Auden home was one of love and kindliness. As a child, even with two older brothers—traditional sources of torment—the poet seems not to have suffered from those emotional difficulties or those wrongs, fancied or real, that so frequently beset a sensitive youngster. Besides affection, there were stimulating intellectual interests. The house at Solihull, where the young family grew up, had a well-stocked library in which the boys were encouraged to read. The elder Auden, furthermore, had a very real knowledge of Norse history and literature and a lively enthusiasm for them which he was able to transmit to his youngest son. As a result, anything pertaining to the Scandinavian countries stirred Auden's imagination. His favorite story as a boy was Hans Christian Andersen's "Ice Maiden." When he grew older, northern folk-lore and mythology were more familiar to him than Greek or Roman, the more customary background for English children's literary learning. This interest must have motivated, in part at least, the trip to Iceland which he was to take some years later. Unquestionably, it influenced the manner and form of some of his poetry.

Auden's more formal education was obtained at Gresham's School in Holt. His early school years coincided with those of the World War of 1914-1918. Whatever indirect effects the war and England's war atmosphere may have had on the little boy, the chief direct effect upon him, he came later to believe, was in the quality of his school instruction. For there were frequent changes in teachers as men were called from the school-rooms to military service; and always it seemed that those who left were the best men.

The breaks in school routine and the procession of new masters must have required many adjustments of the young pupil. Yet those were made calmly enough

247

and school and its requirements engaged only their proper share of his time and his attention. Between school sessions there were happy holidays with his mother "in furnished rooms on mountain, moor, and fen." Always there was the ceaseless activity of an alert boy—photography as a hobby, rides on a motorcycle of his own, an absorption in machinery:

"Those beautiful machines that never talked
 But let the small boy worship them and learn
 All their long names whose hardness made him proud."

His interests, centered on things mechanical, determined his youthful ambition to become a mining engineer.

When he was sixteen, this ambition suddenly changed. As he tells the story, he was walking with a friend who asked him whether he had ever written any poetry. He answered that he never had. But from the moment the question was asked, he knew in his heart that that was the one thing beyond all others that he wanted to do. With this burning desire, he entered Christ Church College at Oxford. There, a "raw provincial," he found his literary tastes molded by college classical standards, set by patterns of the cold and austere and formal.

Though the college world might cling to rules laid down in the past, the world outside college precincts had been subjected to new, overwhelming forces that required fresh and enlightened outlooks and values. Ten or fifteen years before, men, sensitive and intelligent, confronted by the complexities and indignities of existence, felt their own inadequacy and formulated a philosophy of futility and despair. Not so Auden. It was into a world of economic depression, of social and political unrest that Auden entered after leaving Oxford, into a world that challenged but did not crush him. He went to the continent and spent some time in Berlin, where, through some friends, he became interested in contemporary political doctrines. Masses of people were suffering. How could their suffering be alleviated? They were in want. How could their needs be supplied? They were oppressed. How could they gain freedom? As Auden saw this problem in the light of his own literary ambition, the important thing was not the question of his ability or inability to fit into a heartless world, but of making that world a less heartless place for people generally; furthermore, humanity rather than rules of esthetics or requirements of literary technique became the starting point of his writing.

He was able to carry out his desire to write poetry at the same time that he was carrying on his profession. With his return to England from Germany, he taught in a school near Malvern; the choice of teaching as a means of earning a living gave him opportunity to write. The influence of his teaching, in fact, is marked in his poetry. School and its activities—"prize giving afternoons," for example—provide him with an idiom of speech. School experience forms the basis of poems like "To Edward Upward, Schoolmaster," and, as in *The Orators,* a point of departure for a whole book. But, more than that, his teaching has strengthened in him a conviction that the hope of mankind lies in the young, in those who can be newly trained, in the schoolboy virtues that aging generations have discarded.

This is the attitude expressed in his first volume, *Poems,* published in 1930. Concerned with the threatened collapse of modern civilization, the book points out the dangers inherent in the contemporary economic system. *Poems* was followed by *Paid on Both Sides,* called by Auden "a charade," a bitter if somewhat baffling indictment of men's murderous hate, a hate that may be interpreted either as the enmity of nationalist conflicts or that of class wars. With *The Orators,* a jumble of prose, verse, diagrams, and notes, published in 1932, Auden's point of view, originally mildly liberal, becomes more and more left-wing. The book, suffering from a lack of organization, is divided into three parts: "The Initiates," "Journal of an Airman," and "Six Odes." After warning against individual and mass degeneracy and suggesting that a romantic attitude, as typified by the aviator hero, must fail in the solution of contemporary problems, it calls upon the young generation of schoolboys to establish a new and better world order by eradicating fear, wrath, and greed from private and from public life. *The Dance of Death,* a play published in 1934 and produced in London at the Westminster Theatre and in New York at the Adelphi Theatre by Alfred Kreymborg as part of the project of the Federal Poetic Theatre, is a satiric presentation of the decline and final collapse of the capitalist system. In its scathing—if, at times, amusing—denunciation of capitalism, it might seem the pronouncement of an avowed economic Communist, were it not for the fact that its ending—the appearance of Karl Marx and two young Communists and the curtain-lowering speech, "The instruments of production have been too much for him. He is liquidated"—has the same quality of satire and burlesque that marks the rest of the play and so fails to suggest with any degree of conviction that Marxian dogma is the panacea for human ills.

Auden's interest in the dramatic form had further opportunity for development in 1935, when he spent six months with his friend, Christopher Isherwood, in work with moving pictures. This experience was not without influence in the loosely episodic quality of the play which the two men wrote in collaboration, a play with the fascinating and—strange as it must seem—explicable title of *The Dog Beneath the Skin or Where is Francis.*

The year that saw the publication of this play saw, too, Auden's marriage to Erica Mann, the daughter of Thomas Mann, the distinguished German writer and thinker who had left his native land in protesting disapproval of its political regime. Poems inspired by his love and marriage are among those in Auden's next volume of verse, published in 1936 in England under the title of *Look, Stranger!* and, in the United States, as *On This Island.* Even these poems are not the idyllic rhapsodies of a lyric poet, interested primarily in the expression of his private and intimate emotions; they are rather the poems of a modern person who finds his love for another caught in the complexity of a distraught world.

"We ride a turning globe, we stand on a star;
It has thrust us up together; it is stronger than we."

In 1936, a second play written with Christopher Isherwood, *The Ascent of F 6,* appeared.

In the summer of that year, Auden and a friend, Louis Macneice, went to Iceland. For Auden, the assignment from his publishers to write a travel book was the fulfillment of his childhood interest in the Norse countries. The result was *Letters from Iceland,* a collaboration of the two men, a volume made up of letters written home; notes on their travels; photographs made by Auden; the jointly written "Their Last Will and Testament," a satiric verse criticism of the times; and Auden's long poem, "Letter to Lord Byron." Auden writes to his wife telling her the origin of this idea to use a letter to the dead English poet as a vehicle for his views on any subject that might engage his fancy:

"In the bus today, I had a bright idea about this travel book. I brought a Byron with me to Iceland and I suddenly thought I might write him a chatty letter in light verse about anything I could think of, Europe, literature, myself. He's the right person I think, because he was a townee, a European, and disliked Wordsworth and that kind of approach to nature, and I find that very sympathetic."

The flexibility of his plan permitted him to include

252

with his opinions on life and literature such revealing sketches of himself as these:

"My passport says I'm five feet and eleven,
  With hazel eyes and fair (it's tow-like) hair,
That I was born in York in 1907,
  With no distinctive markings anywhere.
  Which isn't quite correct. Conspicuous there
On my right cheek appears a large brown mole,
I think I don't dislike it, on the whole.

    .     .     .     .     .     .     .

In games which mark for beauty out of twenty
  I'm doing well if my friends give me eight.
(When played historically you still score plenty);
  My head looks like an egg upon a plate;
  My nose is not too bad, but isn't straight;
I have no proper eyebrows, and my eyes
Are far too close together to be nice."

The summer that Auden spent in Iceland was the summer in which civil war broke out in Spain. Miles away from the center of combat, Auden wondered how "things were really going in Spain." After his return to England, he answered that question for himself by going to the war-torn land to drive an ambulance for the Loyalist forces. His poem, "Spain," was further evidence of his sympathies.

The Spanish experience produced no book. But shortly, his publishers sent him together with his friend and early collaborator, Isherwood, to another troubled corner of the world. In January 1938, the two men left England for China and arrived in Hongkong on February 28. They traveled throughout China, visited the war front, saw important personages and reported on their adventures, somewhat superficially and lightly, in *Journey to a War*. But if the prose account of their visit sounds like a holiday jaunt, Auden's poems included in the volume strike a more profound and somber note. The war in China he saw not as an isolated phenomenon, but as a local outbreak of a tremendous struggle in which all the people of the earth "in all their living are profoundly implicated."

"This is one sector and one movement of the general war
  Between the dead and the unborn, the Real and the Pretended."

How deeply he was moved by what he saw is suggested by his sonnet, "Far from the heart of culture he was used." A Chinese soldier, poor, illiterate, and dull lies dead:

"He neither knew nor chose the Good, but taught us,
  And added meaning like a comma, when
  He turned to dust in China that our daughters

Be fit to love the earth, and not again
  Disgraced before the dogs; that, where are waters,
  Mountains and houses, may be also men."

254

# WYSTAN HUGH AUDEN

War with all its passions and all its futility is the theme of Auden's next book, a play written with Isherwood, and called *On the Frontier*. In it, the mythical realms of Osnia and Westland war against each other, duplicating each other's tactics; their inhabitants experience the same emotions and reap the same reward —meaningless death.

Before Auden's next book appeared, war—and not between any mythical lands—had broken out. *Another Time*, published in 1940, is colored by the tragedy of the Second World War, by the onrush of events leading to it, when "matters are settled by gas and bomb." But, concerned not exclusively with that subject, it contains, too, poems about places Auden remembers, about people who have influenced him, about events that have moved him. The poems vary greatly in quality. Some suggest that the poet has, indeed, passed

> "the time, dear,
> Till I see you, writing
> Down whatever nonsense
> Comes into my head."

Some, borrowing the flippant manner of music hall ballads, reveal the despair of the victims of modern civilization. So, in "Refugee Blues," the refugees sing:

"Once we had a country and we thought it fair,
  Look in the atlas and you'll find it there:
  We cannot go there now, my dear, we cannot go there
    now."

Others, like "In Memory of Sigmund Freud" and "Musée des Beaux Arts," reach the height of the poetic, justly balancing thought and feeling and expressing them in appropriate poetic form.

*Another Time* gives further proof of Auden's versatility and suggests that his poetry is still too flexible to be rigidly pigeon-holed. From a consideration of that poetry, one may omit the plays both on the ground of their not being exclusively his and on that of their being primarily prose. They do contain, however, some choruses in poetry, some interpolated poems, and some poetic passages. Some of these Auden has identified as his by including them in an English edition called *Selected Poems*.

Auden as a poet has been variously received; he has been the center of needlessly extravagant praise as well as of needlessly sharp criticism. He has, however, received the awards of acknowledged critical judgments. In 1937, he received the Guarantors Prize of the magazine *Poetry* for two poems that had appeared in its January number: "Journey to Iceland," and

> "O who can ever praise enough
>     The world of his belief?"

Somewhat more surprisingly—in view of the reputation for radicalism which he had acquired—he was awarded in the same year the King's Gold Medal for the best poetry of the year and to receive it was presented to George VI by the poet, John Masefield.

As one of the outstanding poetic spokesmen of our times, he was welcomed in 1939 to the United States, where he has since been writing and lecturing. In his poetry Auden, without question, does act as spokesman for others as well as for himself. He manifests no tendency to withdraw from his fellow men, to retire into the isolation of self-sufficiency, and create poems out of his own tender feelings and intuitions. His place is in the world of today, the world of machinery and industry, of wars—national and economic—of intolerance and of persecution, the world of living men and women. His thoughts and feelings have been concerned with the perplexing problems that beset this disordered world; of them he has made his poetry, a poetry of mighty protest.

Today, a poet of protest finds his task different from what it would have been some twenty-five years—less than a full generation—ago. He need no longer fight to have the bounds of poetic subject matter widened. Nor need he rebel against fixed requirements of poetic technique. His immediate predecessors fought those fights for him and won them. Sometimes, it is true, their interest was more in the combat than in the poetry. Nevertheless, they did succeed in breaking down restrictions and in freeing poetry for poetry. As a result, it is not necessary for the poet today to protest against limited subject or manner; or to experiment merely for the sake of experimenting. He need only write, on what subjects he chooses, in old forms—rigidly adhered to or freely modified—or in new forms, as he deems most suitable.

Such freedom has inherent dangers; removal of restrictions may lead to laxity. Auden, heir to this freedom, did not escape its pitfalls. He frequently, and very conspicuously in *The Orators,* shows the need for closer organization of material. He often does not exercise sufficient discrimination to exclude such baffling obscurities as:

> "A neutralizing peace
> And an average disgrace
> Are honour to discover
> For later other."

or to prevent poetry from degenerating into doggerel:

> "The dogs are barking, the crops are growing,
> But nobody knows how the wind is blowing;
> Gosh, to look at we're no great catch;
> History seems to have struck a bad patch."

Far more important, however, are the advantages of poetic freedom, among them the variety of form permitted the poet. Auden avails himself of this to the utmost. His poetry shows influences ranging from the heavily accented and alliterated line of old English poetry to the free association and free verse of Ezra Pound and T. S. Eliot. Just as for the "Letter to Lord Byron," he chooses a form

"that's large enough to swim in
And talk on any subject that I choose,"

so, throughout his poetry, he exercises the same latitude
of choice. When old forms suit his purpose, he uses
them: rime royal, as in the "Letter," with its seven-
line stanza and rhyming scheme of a b a b b c c; the
sestina, a large form of six stanzas of six lines each
and a concluding three-line stanza, which, instead of
rhyme, uses throughout its stanzas the same terminal
words, but in varying order—a form more easily illustrated, perhaps, than explained.

"Hearing of harvests rotting in the valleys,
  Seeing at end of street the barren mountains,
  Round corners coming suddenly on water,
  Knowing them shipwrecked who were launched for
      islands,
  We honour founders of these starving cities,
  Whose honour is the image of our sorrows.

  Which cannot see its likeness in their sorrow
  That brought them desperate to the brink of valleys;
  Dreaming of evening walks through learned cities,
  They reined their violent horses on the mountains,
  Those fields like ships to castaways on islands,
  Visions of green to them that craved for water."

The final stanza of this poem, No. VII from *On This
Island* (Auden rarely gives titles to his poems), uses
within its three lines the same terminal words:

"It is the sorrow; shall it meet? Ah, water
  Would gush, flush, green these mountains and these
    valleys
  And we rebuild our cities, not dream of islands."

When he feels, however, that an established form needs modification, he shows no hesitation in modifying it. The rigid sonnet becomes less rigid when it is cast in hexameters rather than the traditional pentameters; when lines within a single stanza vary in length; when the sestet is thus revolutionary, but effective:

    "But ideas can be true although men die,
      And we can watch a thousand faces
      Made active by one lie:

    And maps can really point to places
    Where life is evil now:
    Nanking; Dachau."

Nor does he restrict himself to a few forms. His meters vary all the way from the crisp

        "This lunar beauty
        Has no history"

to the long-lined

"Go there if you can and see the land you once were
    proud to own
  Though the roads have almost vanished and the ex-
    presses never run."

His verse ranges from the measured blank verse of

"To settle in the village of the heart"

to the satirically used popular song meter and rhyme:

"You were a great Cunarder, I
  Was only a fishing smack
  Once you passed across my bows
  And of course you did not look back
  It was only a single moment yet
  I watch the sea and sigh
  Because my heart can never forget
  The day you passed me by."

It is quite apparent, even from this parody, that Auden is fully aware of the value of conventional rhyme and able to handle it. But he is much more likely to use for his terminal vowel sounds either assonance or a tantalizing half-rhyme: hall, hill; strain, stone; confess, fuss.

Another marked characteristic of Auden's verse is the presence of alliteration. Typical of it are lines like "The day of his death was a dark cold day" and

"Watching through windows the wastes of evening,
  The flares of foundries at fall of year."

Its use becomes a *tour de force* in "The Airman's Alphabet" of *The Orators:*

"Ace—Pride of parents
       and photographed person
       and laughter in leather

o        •        •        •        •

Storm—Night from the north
        and numbness nearing
        and hail ahead"

This has the flavor of old English verse, in which alliteration took the place of rhyme. The effect, frequently
encountered in Auden's poetry, is heightened still more
by the presence of compound epithets: "exile-crowded
sea," "star-concealing dawn," and by a tendency to
omit articles:

"Though he reject you, join opposing team."

The basic strength and verve of poetry in its beginnings
are suggested by such lines as:

"What siren zooming is sounding our coming
Up frozen fjord forging from freedom
        What shepherd's call
        When stranded on hill
        With broken axle
        On track to exile?"

The omission of simple words like articles succeeds
at times in widening the implication of a statement, in
giving it an overtone of generalizing:

"But thinking so I came at once
Where solitary man sat weeping on a bench."

"Solitary man," thus used, takes on all the implications
of humanity at large. Sometimes, indeed, groups of

words may be omitted and the result is only a tightening of impression:

> "In legend all were simple,
>   And held the straitened spot;
>   But we in legend not,
>   Are not simple."

But when expression becomes so compressed that even necessary connecting thoughts are omitted, poems present insuperable difficulties. What is the meaning, for example, of the poem "Before this loved one?" or of "The silly fool, the silly fool" with its cryptic ending:

> "Simple to prove
>   That deeds indeed
>   In life succeed
>   But love in love
>   And tales in tales
>   Where no one fails."

Auden is aware of the bewilderment that is sometimes caused by his poetry and that of other modern writers. By his description of the contrasting poetry of Iceland, he implies it: "No 'modernist' poetry to puzzle the old ladies." Such difficulties as "old ladies" encounter in his verse arise from his failure to make clear the general meaning of the whole poem, not from recondite language or abstruse figures.

In fact, the individual parts are clear, clarified by the imagery which is, for the most part, intellectual and explanatory rather than sensory and purely decorative:

"And as foreign settlers to strange country come,
    By mispronunciation of native words
    And by intermarriage create a new race
    And a new language, so may the soul
    Be weaned at last to independent delight."

The fields from which his imagery chiefly derives are industry, "the furnace-crowded Midlands"; science; psychology, particularly the hazy realm between the known and the unknown, the dream world; and war.

"Tram lines and slagheaps, pieces of machinery
    That was, and still is, my ideal scenery."

So Auden writes in "Letter to Lord Byron"; and so, instead of flowers and birds and the forces of nature, one is much more likely to find in his poetry factory-whistles and motors, high-tension wires, and pylons. No less numerous are the references to man's intellectual studies, to his discoveries in the sciences of physics, and chemistry, bacteriology, biology. Test-tubes and porcelain filters form poetic background; so, too, do scientific theories, like that of evolution. Reflected in the poetry is Auden's interest in modern psychology, that half-science-half-art. That part of it concerned with the development of personality, the independence of the individual, provides some imagery. Much more comes from the sources of psychological findings, the unconscious, the partially-acknowledged, dreams. "Forms which I saw once in a dream" color his poems; comparisons are drawn between the real world and the dream world; the unconscious is used to explain the conscious:

"Lo, a dream met me in middle night, I saw in a vision
Life pass as a gull, as a spy, as a dog-hated dustman."

That brief quotation, by its use of the word "spy," suggests still another vein of Auden's thinking, the military. Almost any poem chosen at random will reveal how rich a resource this is for the poet. Maneuvers and tactics, personnel and armament, all are used to add color or meaning to the poetry:

"In my spine there was a base:
And I knew the general's face:
But they've severed all the wires,
And I can't tell what the general desires."

People are "intimate as war-time prisoners in an isolation camp." A lilac bush stands "like a conspirator." So frequently, indeed, does Auden draw upon soldiers and soldiery that one feels they must have for him some specific and cogent meaning, a privacy of value in which the reader does not completely share.

In this privacy lies a further clue to the obscurity present in so many of Auden's poems. Not only is there the omission, which has previously been mentioned, of essential connecting thoughts, but there is the inclusion of personal allusions and of references to facts known only to a few, of whom the reader is not one.

"O I hadn't meant to let the name out:
  To explain all that I shall have to go a long way back."

Frequently the way is too long or Auden is otherwise too engrossed to return and make things clear. A line like

"Heard a voice saying—'Wystan, Stephen,
  Christopher, all of you' "

has some meaning because the names are recognized as those of Auden, himself, and of his friends Stephen Spender and Christopher Isherwood. But in the following:

"Again in the room with the sofa hiding the grate
  Look down to the river where the rain is over,
  See him turn to the window, hearing our last
  Of Captain Ferguson"

the reference to Captain Ferguson is without meaning. The uninitiated reader is shut out from understanding. It is as though Auden were speaking to a small group of intimates who understand the allusions and share the point of view, as though he were both speaking to them and speaking for them.

This becomes most pronounced in those poems that deal with social problems. The attitude brings with it another difficulty, uncertainty as to exactly which social group Auden represents and to which he addresses his poetry.

"The important point to notice, though, is this:
    Each poet knew for whom he had to write."

But Auden so frequently shifts his viewpoint that the reader does not know. He knows, of course, that the poet's sympathies are with the oppressed; but in the poems dealing with their problems, who are the "we," the "you," and the "they"? "Brothers," he says to the workers coming out of factories, shops, and offices, "we know the fears that obsess you."

> "We cannot put on airs with you
>   The fears that hurt you hurt us too
>     Only we say
> That like all nightmares these are fake
> If you would help us we could make
>   Our eyes to open, and awake
>     Shall find night day."

Thus far it is quite clear that Auden is not one of the workers, but feels with them. Later in the same poem, however, he writes:

> "And you, the wise man, full of humour
>   To whom our misery's a rumour
>     And slightly funny;
> Proud of your nicely balanced view
> You say as if it were something new
>   The fuss we make is mostly due
>     To lack of money."

Obviously, the first person of this stanza is not the same as the first person of the earlier stanza. Who, then, is the "we" with whom Auden first identifies himself?

This confusion is typical of Auden's earlier poems. It is a confusion arising not so much from a careless use of pronouns as from a haziness in the poet's mind concerning his own position in a threatened economic society. The haziness gradually disappears in the later poems. It becomes increasingly apparent that Auden never completely identifies himself with "the workers." His sympathies, however, are with them and he denounces the wrongs that have come to them through the ineptitude or malice of what has been his own class. But the ruin that threatens them is calamitous because it threatens everyone. So he calls upon all—not to arise in a class war—but to work for a better society for all.

That, indeed, is the main motif of his poetry. It is concerned with the problems of the contemporary world, the world of

"Hitler and Mussolini in their wooing poses
  Churchill acknowledging the voter's greeting
  Roosevelt at the microphone, Von der Lubbe laughing
      And our first meeting."

So personal an emotion as the love hinted at in the last line is no refuge from these pressing problems. There is no escape from them:

      "Escaping cannot try;
        Must wait though it destroy."

From what specifically, then, is there no escape? From what Auden sees as the collapse of the capitalist economy, which he personifies as a world of invalids, of vapid sportsmen, and of cloistered intellectuals:

"The game is up for you and for the others,
    Who, thinking, pace in slippers on the lawns
    Of College Quad or Cathedral Close."

It is a sick world. "What do you think about England, this country of ours where nobody is well?" he asks in *The Orators.*

Throughout his poems broods the sense of impending doom, of threatened economic collapse. Factories will soon close, railroads lie unused; piers will rot.

"Soon through the dykes of our content
    The crumpling flood will force a rent,
        And, taller than a tree,
    Hold sudden death before our eyes
    Whose river-dreams long hid the size
        And vigours of the sea."

The forces of destruction, however vaguely identified, are symbolized by such terms as "the Adversary," "the supreme Antagonist." In spite of hazy symbolism, it is quite obvious that Auden believes that the ills of society come from the very class to which he by training, by inheritance, by background—by everything but interest and sympathy—belongs. The crime is the crime of the past, of generations who shut their eyes to the evil they created and refrained from announcing the truth when they found it, combining

> "Assertion and refuge
> In the common language of collective lying,
> In codes of a bureau, laboratory slang
> And diplomats' French."

Auden insists that the evils of the past must not be continued into the future. At this point he is confronted with the problem that confronts all liberals:

> "Here am I, here are you:
> But what does it mean? What are we going to do?"

There is nothing that should be done, that can be done to forestall the collapse of the present economic system. In *The Dance of Death,* with biting satire, he shows the vain efforts of such attempts as health cults, fascism, metaphysical systems of thought:

> "Who will be the one
> To teach us how to fly from the alone to the Alone?"

But though the capitalist regime as we know it seems inevitably doomed, those who might look for a Socialist or Communist answer to the problem cannot find it.

Auden is not a political Communist. It is true that some critics claim that he made his confession of political faith in the poem that appeared in *New Country,* a collection of the works of young writers of radical views, under the title of "A Communist to Others" and that began with the line

"Comrades, who when the sirens roar."

It is significant, however, that when the poem was included in his volume, *On This Island,* the revealing title was omitted and for the pass-word "Comrades" was substituted the more inclusive word "Brothers." The change would seem to indicate a divergence from the Communist party not so much in the ideals originally desired for individuals but in the method of achieving those ideals and in the philosophy underlying them. In Auden's poetry, there is no avowal of adherence to the Communist program of revolution and class war; nor is there any expression of belief in Communism as an instrument of government. On the contrary, Auden is opposed to any kind of totalitarian state, any kind of state that says

*"Man can have Unity if Man will give up Freedom*
*Leave Truth to the police and us; we know the Good."*

In thus refusing to accept the implications of a fixed political project, he may possibly lay himself open to the charge that he says his friends make against him, that of being "a selfish pink old Liberal to the last." His hope for the future lies not in the overpowering abstraction of the State, but emphatically in people as individuals.

"Only the free have disposition to be truthful,
  Only the truthful have the interest to be just,
  Only the just possess the well-known power to be free.
  For common justice can determine private freedom,
  As a clear sky can tempt men to astronomy
  Or a peninsula persuade them to be sailors."

"In America," he said in a recent interview,* "nationalism doesn't mean anything; there are only human beings! That's how the future must be."

It is in terms of human beings that he sees political issues and in terms of human values that he sees their solution. His first insistence is one that differentiates him sharply from the young intellectuals who were his immediate predecessors. His insistence is on a positive attitude of action. He deplores and detests the negative will, the will to inactivity, "the unbreakable habits of death," that afflicted the post-war generation. He grows ironical at the "Careful, careful; can we afford it?" attitude of the hesitant. Because he believes that the possibility of betterment lies within each human being, he believes that there, too, lies the responsibility for its achievement; and so he insists upon positive action:

"Act from thought should quickly follow:
  What is thinking for?"

This is a call for the revival of old—must one say "old-fashioned"?—personal virtues. It is a demand for sympathies no longer frozen, but now "awkward and

* *Time,* October 30, 1939.

alive"; for "disciplined love"; for steady effort in the face of disappointment; for determination to attempt the difficult and not "emigrate from weakness."

It may be too late for the present generation of men and women to revitalize qualities that have been allowed to atrophy or perish. So he looks to the young, to the school children. In the poem "To My Pupils," he asks:

"Are you in training?
Are you taking care of yourself? Are you sure of passing
   The endurance test?"

For the young he prays for the "long lost good" so that they "may never need our craft." In the young, he places his hope and his reliance.

Such reliance upon personal qualities is grounded in a moral conviction, in the belief in the value of human beings. It is not without significance that in *I Believe,* a collection of personal philosophies of men and women, Auden prefaces his credo with a quotation from the poet Blake, "Everything that lives is Holy."

Nor is it without significance that in the rhymed and witty "Last Will and Testament" of Auden and Macneice, to their poet friends Stephen Spender and Cecil Day Lewis are willed

> "Our minor talents to assist in the defense
>    Of the European tradition and to carry on
>    The Human heritage."

The talents, modestly designated "minor," which are thus bequeathed, are poetic talents. So the poet has a definite function in helping to create the world of the future and a place in that future world. Auden desires to create a world safe for poets, because such a world would be safe for all. The world which he sees as ideal is the one permitting the individual the greatest unconflicting freedom of action, the one allowing the individual the greatest opportunity for development. "A democracy," he writes in the introduction to *The Oxford Book of Light Verse,* "in which each citizen is as fully conscious and capable of making a rational choice, as in the past has been possible only for the wealthier few, is the only kind of society which in the future is likely to survive for long." To this he adds: "In such a society, and in such alone, will it be possible for the poet, without sacrificing any of his subtleties of sensibility or his integrity, to write poetry which is simple, clear, and gay. For poetry which is at the same time light and adult can only be written in a society which is both integrated and free."

Under such circumstances the poet is most free to write. But has the poet, then, no responsibility? The answer is suggested in a review that Auden wrote * of the English translation of the German poet Rilke: "If the writer is not to harm both others and himself, he must consider, and very much more humbly and patiently than he has been doing, what kind of person he

* *New Republic,* September 6, 1939.

is and what may be his real function." It is, then, incumbent upon him to perfect himself in so far as it lies within his powers to do so; and in his desire to communicate to others what he has perceived either "in the external world of sense or the internal world of feeling" to be sure that what he has to communicate has some value. It will have value, Auden insists, only if the poet refuses to isolate himself from the world.

Here, then, in Auden's philosophic belief, is a key to that quality that has been noted in his poetry—the close coupling of the private and public, the personal and the impersonal. The individual must be free "To shape, create and move, love and rejoice." The world must be remade to permit that freedom. Thus to remake the world, one must have an abiding faith in the value of individual human freedom and a determination to defend, at whatever cost, that value. The two are inextricably bound: the individual and the world, private existence and public politics and economics. One can not separate them either in poetry or in life.

In September 1939, war was declared in Europe. Auden, moved by the same feelings of horror and dismay as moved millions of others, wrote a poem which he called simply "September 1, 1939." Characteristically, he begins it with personal details:

> "I sit in one of the dives
> On Fifty-second Street
> Uncertain and afraid

As the clever hopes expire
Of a low dishonest decade."

He touches on the fears of his companions. He dwells on
international wrongs that have been committed. But
in spite of the evil, he knows that there is a good to be
worked for and the need for a positive faith in that
good.

"Defenceless under the night
Our world in stupor lies;
Yet, dotted everywhere,
Ironic points of light
Flash out wherever the Just
Exchange their messages:
May I, composed like them
Of Eros and of dust,
Beleaguered by the same
Negation and despair,
Show an affirming faith."

This, too, is characteristic.

### POETICAL WORKS

| | |
|---|---|
| POEMS | *Random House, Inc.* |
| ON THIS ISLAND (published in England as | |
| LOOK, STRANGER) | *Random House, Inc.* |
| SELECTED POEMS | *Faber and Faber* |
| ANOTHER TIME | *Random House, Inc.* |

276

### WYSTAN HUGH AUDEN

Poems are included in the following:

THE DOG BENEATH THE SKIN (with Christopher
  Isherwood)                *Random House, Inc.*

THE ASCENT OF F 6 (with Christopher Isherwood)
                            *Random House, Inc.*

LETTERS FROM ICELAND (with Louis Macneice)
                            *Random House, Inc.*

JOURNEY TO A WAR (with Christopher Isherwood)
                            *Random House, Inc.*

*STEPHEN SPENDER*

## STEPHEN SPENDER

IN the late nineteen-twenties, a seventeen-year-old boy living in a London suburb was using his hand printing press to earn money, by printing on it chemists' labels. Shortly, he made it serve another purpose: the printing of a pamphlet which, bound in green paper, was signed with the initials S. H. S. The boy was Stephen Spender; the initials were his own; and the pamphlet was *Nine Experiments,* his first book of poems. This biographical incident is significant as evidence of Spender's early determination to make articulate in verse his reactions to the world of which he found himself a part.

Few, indeed, are the other biographical details needed to suggest the external outline of Spender's life. He was born on February 28, 1909, the son of Violet Schuster and Edward Harold Spender, a journalist and lecturer. His early life was spent in London:

"The Hampstead
Incandescence burns behind windows
With talk and gold warmth.
Those brothers who we were lie wrapped in flannel,
And how like a vase looks my time then
Rounded with meals laid on by servants

With reading alone in a high room and looking down on
The pleasures of the spoiled pets in the garden—
A vase now broken into fragments,
Little walks which quickly reach their ends,
The islands in the traffic."

He received his schooling at University College School,
where he prepared for University College at Oxford.
Finding college life distasteful, he left to travel on the
continent; but he returned for one more trial of formal
education and stayed at Oxford until 1931.

Meanwhile, the literary career begun with *Nine Experiments* had been earnestly pursued. While still an
undergraduate, in 1930, Spender brought out his second
book, *Twenty Poems*. But even before that book made
its appearance in England, Spender had been introduced to American readers. Louis Untermeyer, the
American poet and critic, had met the young Englishman on a visit to England in 1928 and had been impressed by him and his writing. On his return to America, he had received from England what Spender in his
youthfulness described as some of his "later" manuscripts. Mr. Untermeyer found them to be "poems which
remarkably concealed his youth" and selected seven of
them for inclusion in the 1930 edition of his anthology,
*Modern British Poetry*. These poems, marked by deep
feeling, show a positive and active attitude toward life
and its problems:

"Let heart be done, shut close the whining eyes,
  And work, or drink, or sleep, till life defies

Minute, month, hour and day
Which are harrowed, and beaten, and scared away."

The problems which commanded Spender's attention
were the political and economic ones confronting a disorganized world. For their solution, Spender together
with a number of his contemporaries, eager, intelligent,
hopeful, looked toward an idealized form of Communism. He became one of a group of writers, called "liberal" by those who agreed with their views and branded
as "radical" by those who opposed them, who contributed to two volumes of prose and poetry: *New Sig-
natures* and *New Country*. Spender's poems appearing
in these collections were among those which made up
his next book, his first really recognized book of verse,
*Poems,* published in 1933.

This was followed, in 1934, by the publication of
*Vienna,* a long poem on the suppression of the Socialist
Revolution by the Dollfuss Government, a conflict
which Spender had witnessed during a visit to the
Austrian capital. The Vienna outbreak was but one evidence of the need which Spender saw more and more
clearly, a social order based on freedom and on peace.
In formulating his views, he made apparent that such
an order would gain his loyalty and active support for
two interwoven reasons: because it would give freedom
to humanity and because in that freedom there would
be place for a poet and a poet's art. In 1937, the year
in which he went as a delegate to the International
Writers' Congress in Spain and saw the havoc wrought

there by war, he published his political creed in *Forward from Liberalism*. This, together with his earlier book of literary criticism, *The Destructive Element*, serves as a background for his first book of poems and his later writing: a collection of short stories, *The Burning Cactus*, published in 1930; a verse play, *Trial of a Judge*, 1938, a bitter indictment of Naziism; two volumes of verse, *Poems for Spain* and *The Still Centre*, 1939.

Two more dates might be added to this brief chronology: 1936, the year in which Spender married Agnes Marie Pearn; and 1939, when he was awarded the Guarantors Prize by the magazine *Poetry*, for poems that had appeared in its May and its October issues.

Assuredly, this is not a richly detailed biography for the tall, slim man with the high forehead and the wavy hair whom Malcolm Cowley, the critic and his fellow traveler in Spain, described as "serious, subtle, generous, and full of charm"; or for the writer whom a large number of readers hail as the poet of a new and better social order. For some comprehension of this poet, however, more important than episodes and dates of private history is an awareness of the public history, of the period in time in which his life has been and is being lived. It is, perhaps, a biography of the twentieth century, from the beginning of its second decade to the years of the Second World War, that is needed—a biography that will detail the wars, the economic fluctuations, the rise of new political theories, the perfection of machinery, the steady progress of industrialism; for it is the influences that have affected mankind as a whole, fully as much as those intimate ones that may have affected Spender's individual life, that are reflected in his poetry.

Here one point must be made emphatic. If the Second World War has been set as the ending to such a biography, it is because those of Spender's poems which have thus far appeared in book form were written before its outbreak; before men in democracies, generally, altered their views to combat totalitarianism; before, very specifically, England's social and economic life underwent the upheaval and reorganization necessary to enable it to fight Germany. It is, then, to the years before 1939 that one must look for influences affecting Spender's poetry.

The World War of 1914-1918 colored the impressionable years of Spender's childhood:

> "Who live under the shadow of a war,
>   What can I do that matters?"

Whatever despair and dread and feeling of futility that war engendered have served but as faint patterns for the results of other wars waged in later years in various parts of the earth. So, the man of thirty, who had known throughout almost his entire life wars and their effects and hated them, could announce:

> "The guns spell money's ultimate reason
>   In letters of lead on the spring hillside"

and could ask:

"Was so much expenditure justified
On the death of one so young and so silly
Stretched under the olive trees, O world, O death?"

The twentieth century has been characterized not only by the persistence of this militaristic spirit, but by the continuous growth and application of machinery. Mechanical developments have reached a stage of perfection hitherto undreamed of; but as realities, not as dreams, they have become part and parcel of life. So radios and moving pictures, aeroplanes and power stations are accepted elements in the familiar experience of Spender. He can write of them not as one who consciously and determinedly sets out to prove that they may be made fit subjects for poetry, but as one who takes them for granted as part of existence and as proper material for poetic expression.

"Thinking, if these were tricklings through a dam,
I must have love enough to run a factory on,
Or give a city power, or drive a train."

This is no *tour de force*, no insistence upon an innovation in the esthetics of poetry; it is simply evidence— and evidence that does not even cry out for attention— that for the poet of the middle twentieth century there exists a larger and richer source of poetic thought and imagery than was ever before available.

Spender's poetry is grounded, then, in the world about him, in reality as he knows it:

"From all these events, from the slump, from the war, from the boom."

War and its aftermath, the extended use of machinery, the change from a predominantly agricultural society to one increasingly industrial—all these have disrupted the economic life of the twentieth century. Victims of it are the vast numbers of unemployed:

> "the silent crowd
> Who stand behind dull cigarettes
> These men who idle in the roads."

Of those who have work, many find increasingly unbearable the pressure under which they toil—and earn only enough to maintain a bare existence:

> "Time merely drives these lives which do not live
> As tides push rotten stuff along the shore."

Spender is close in sympathy to them. He knows the economic implications of his time and in his poetry gives clear and sure utterance to them.

He knows as well the political implications of his day. He is moved by the steadily growing number of those made to suffer because of a theory of politics and nationalism and of cruelly waged war, the swelling stream of refugees with

> "the pale unshaven stare of shuttered plants
> Exposed to a too violent sun."

Their plight, too, becomes the subject of his poems.

It is, then, a twentieth century Englishman who writes; and he writes out of the depth of his experience which is closely interwoven with that of other present-day men and women. It is not simply that Spender as a product of his century must of necessity—if unconsciously—be affected by it and so show, whether he will or not, its influences in his writing. His own attitude is a much more positive one than that; his writing is a conscious expression of that attitude. It is one of the strong convictions in his philosophy of life and art that the artist cannot cut himself off from society, from which, indeed, he gathers impetus and strength. "I suggest," he says,* "that at some time in his life an artist has got to come to grips with the objective, factual life around him. He cannot spin indefinitely from himself unless he learns how to establish contact with his audience by the use of symbols which represent reality to his contemporaries."

Just as some poets see in an ideal of beauty the reality on which to base their poetry and make its seeking their pursuit, so Spender sees in a society that is secure and free the foundation for his art and makes its achievement his purpose. Such a society does not in the present exist; but it must be created out of what does exist in the present. For the sake of the future, that present must be understood. If the poet has any hope of survival, of being able to continue to write, he must, Spender insists, "try somehow to understand that

* Spender: *The Destructive Element,* Houghton Mifflin Co.

objective life moving down on us like a glacier, but which, after all, is essentially not a glacier, is an historic process, the life of people like ourselves, and therefore our 'proper study.' "

His own steady determination to understand this "objective life" and to use it as the background for his art does not imply the absence from his poetry of all subjective material, the expression of intimate emotion, the revelation of his own inner being. Quite the contrary is true. A man of wide embracing sympathy and of deep concern for his fellows, Spender is still an intense individualist, to whom the subject of his own personality and its full development is of tremendous importance. He is aware of the inner struggle of man, the struggle to achieve the ideal of self, an achievement difficult—impossible—to attain because of the negative forces, particularly the will to death, which act against it:

"The 'great I' is an importunate intruder
  Quarreling with 'I tiring' and 'I sleeping'
  And all those other 'I's' who long for 'We dying.' "

It is a struggle to which he returns in a later poem, "Darkness and Light":

"To break out of the chaos of my darkness
  Into a lucid day is all my will.

.    .    .    .    .    .    .

Yet, equally, to avoid that lucid day
And to preserve my darkness, is all my will."

The resolution of this conflict,

>"the acceptance of that sun
>Which hews the day from night,"

is part of the process of growth. Growing up, maturing, developing—call it what you will—has two aspects. There is the realization that comes with added years that life, instead of being something swiftly and romantically experienced, is something slowly and painstakingly lived. That is a far from joyous discovery. With emphatic directness—and with restrained regret —Spender reveals it in one of his most forceful poems:

>"What I expected was
>Thunder, fighting,
>Long struggles with men
>And climbing.
>After continual straining
>I should grow strong;
>Then the rocks would shake
>And I should rest long.
>
>What I had not foreseen
>Was the gradual day
>Weakening the will
>Leaking the brightness away,
>The lack of good to touch
>The fading of body and soul
>Like smoke before wind
>Corrupt, unsubstantial.

The wearing of Time,
And the watching of cripples pass
With limbs shaped like questions
In their odd twist,
The pulverous grief
Melting the bones with pity,
The sick falling from earth—
These, I could not foresee.

For I had expected always
Some brightness to hold in trust,
Some final innocence
To save from dust;
That, hanging solid,
Would dangle through all
Like the created poem
Or the dazzling crystal."

Whatever sense of loss follows the disillusionment is to some extent offset by the other aspect of growth, the enriching realization of the self, not as a completely isolated and self-contained entity, but as the product of innumerable forces:

"My history is my ancestry
Written in veins upon my body";

and as the small part of a vast and multitudinous whole:

"Where I reflect the many, in my one."

Personality, Spender feels, reaches its height in love:

"I claim fulfillment in the fact of loving."

In tender lyrics, he sings his joy in the love "surrounding my life with violet skies." In poems like "Three Days," "Separation," "Two Kisses," he pours forth his feelings. But though love,

> "Shuttered by dark at the still centre
> Of the world's circular terror,"

brings quiet and peace, it does not silence forever Spender's questioning; it is not for him the permanent reality, the final answer, the goal to his search:

"The promise hangs, this swarm of stars and flowers,
And then there comes the shutting of a door."

Just as love is unable to solve his life's problem, so, too, does formal religion fail him. The religion of the churches, of dogma and creed, proves less than helpful:

"Religion stands, the church blocking the sun."

Nature, which for many has been the eagerly accepted substitute for organized religion, can neither suggest an answer nor even provide solace:

"I feel this huge sphere turn, the great wheel sing
While beasts move to their ease:
Sheep's love, gulls' peace—I feel my chattering
Uncared by these."

Where, then, can he turn? Where can he hope to find those realities which will enrich life and motivate his art? Religion and Nature failing him, he turns to his fellow man, to human society. But the society must be one that can be accepted with intellectual honesty and emotional whole-heartedness. Some poets, formulating the same solution to their wonderings and perplexities, have looked backward to an ideal state where all was well, to a Golden Age in the past when men were god-like. Spender looks to the future, to a society in which present wrongs will be righted or, at all events, lessened; in which men and women will be—not gods or heroes—but human beings free to develop to their utmost as human beings.

The contemporary state of society, of which Spender feels himself so integral a part, he analyzes with "the mind of a person whose sympathies are idealist and liberal in the present moment of history." He defines liberals as "those who care for freedom more than for the privileges which have given freedom of intellect to individuals in one particular class; those who are prepared to work toward a classless, communist society, if they are convinced that freedom will be enlarged in this way." He is unalterably opposed to Fascism with its attendant curtailment of political and social freedom. Bitterly he denounces it in any form, but particularly in the form of Naziism in "Von der Lubbe," in *Vienna*, in *Trial of a Judge*.

But even where Fascism does not operate, Spender

finds in society much that has to be changed. Political freedom must be supplemented by economic freedom and—eventually—by world freedom and peace. Only with economic freedom does Spender see the possibility of destroying forever those restraints which, molding the great mass of humanity according to the desires of the powerful, have prevented them from enjoying the best in life and from becoming the best of which they were potentially capable. "Palaces, an era's crown," must fall:

> "It is too late for rare accumulation
> For family pride, for beauty's filtered dusts."

The ills of the present, inherited from the past, are too grievous to be borne. The ruthless pressure of industry, the compulsion of profit, have mechanized the worker and destroyed in him even the power to feel:

> "They raise no hands, which rest upon their knees,
> But lean their solid eyes against the night,
> Dimly they feel
> Only the furniture they use in cells."

The farmer, who should be proudly free, is crushed by the same wheels of economic dependence; he is driven to cultivate "the marginal field,"

> "Where loss is exactly equalled by gain
> And the roots and the sinews wrestle with stone
> On the margin of just what can be done
> To eat back from the lands the man the land eats."

Children, underfed, underprivileged, become "stunted spirits in a fog." Poverty is stark, hideous:

"—There is no consolation, no, none
In the curving beauty of that line
Traced on our graph through history, where the oppressor
Starves and deprives the poor."

A new order must arise, in which such conditions are impossible. It is, however, not sufficient hopefully and patiently to await its development through the tedious process of minute changes. One must actively do one's share to hasten its creation. In the effort, the individual may have to be sacrificed for the larger purpose. For the good of the many, the sacrifice must be made; the goal pursued, even though

"Tomorrow Time's progress will forget us even here."

What promise does this new society make? Its program of "death to the killers, bringing light to life" is this:
"No man
Shall hunger: Man shall spend equally,
Our goal which we compel: Man shall be man."

The poem in which Spender makes this statement of social attitude—identified more easily by its opening line, "Not palaces, an era's crown," than by the prosaic numerical title "42," given it by the poet—and poems like "The Prisoners" and "The Funeral," in which he reveals his deep sympathy for the economically oppressed, have been called the first clear expression in English poetry of the Communist point of view. To accept this judgment, a very broad and general definition of Communism is indeed necessary. For, however strongly Spender avows his faith in an idealistic Communist society, as he does in his book, *Forward from Liberalism,* it is in a form of Communism quite different from the concept of political Communism as manifested in totalitarian Russia. The form it takes in his poetry, furthermore, is hardly startlingly new. It is an understanding sympathy for his fellow man and a passion for individual freedom, such as motivated the poets of the early nineteenth century; it is, primarily, a spirit expressing "the palpable and obvious love of man for man."

The mankind that stirs his love and sympathy is not a vague, indefinite abstraction. It is made up of real men and women, living in the world of today, "a world that revolves, dissolves, and explodes"—of men and women beset by the problems of that world, which the poet would help solve, and caught in the oppressions, which he detests and would destroy. Nor is it mankind in the mass about which his feelings center. He who bears "on rounded shoulders the weight of my humanity" is concerned above all with the individual. He admits the occasional necessity of the sacrifice of the individual, so that others may survive and develop. But any glorification of the mass above the individual is abhorrent to him, any aspect of totalitarianism, anything that reduces a human being to a cog in a machine, a figure in a statistical chart. The imagery of statistics, as a matter of fact, appears so frequently in Spender's poetry that it takes on the color of an obsessing symbolism, a representation of all that is detestable in a mechanized society:

> "This is festivity, it is the time of statistics
> When they record what one unit contributed."

Man is significant not as unit, but as personality. The important thing is

> "Never to allow gradually the traffic to smother
> With noise and fog the flowering of the spirit."

Spender looks to a liberalized society to promote this flowering. His ideal state—he has called it Communism—is one in which "the individual shall have the right to work, leisure and every form of self-expression which does not interfere with his neighbour's happiness." The economic implications of Communist philosophy are not for Spender its basic aims. They are the means of achieving his ideal, a society permitting genuine self-education and full individual development, one

> "Clean and equal like the shine from snow."

The poet has expressed faith that such a society can be achieved. He has confidence in the future. He looks with certainty to

"The beautiful generation that shall spring from our
  sides."

Obviously, this theme of a new world order of freedom and peace is not a theme new to English poetry.
Why, then, in Spender's poems, does it sound with fresh
fervor and effectiveness? Because Spender phrases it in
terms of modern politics and economics, because he derives his imagery from modern science and industry.

It is effective, too, because of the intensity of
Spender's feelings, an intensity that compensates for—
and possibly explains—the absence of any suggestion
of a sense of humor. The depth of emotion revealed
in such personal lyrics as "Exile," "Not to you I sighed,
No, not a word," and "Even whilst I watch him I am
remembering" is carried over and, if anything, intensified in his poems of social import. His emotions are
compelling and direct.

Equally forthright is Spender's poetic technique.
Simple and uncomplicated as it is, it still must not be
assumed to be haphazard. His method is deliberate, its
execution the result of plan and conscious purpose. One
can note differences in the poems between their first
appearance in some magazine or early collection and
their final appearance in the poet's published work.
Sometimes the difference is one only of title, as when
the poem "Mask" appears in *The Still Centre* as "View
from a Train" and gives up its original name to another
poem in the volume. Sometimes there are slight word
changes, like that in "Ultima Ratio Regum," wherein

the figure "intangible as rumor" is modified and becomes more vivid in its final form:

"Whilst his life, intangible as a Stock Exchange rumor,
    drifted outside."

Occasionally, as in "An Elementary School Class Room in a Slum," whole passages are changed, and a point of view becomes clearer.

This conscious craftsmanship is illustrated by the use of the same material in various forms or in different settings. An interesting instance of the reworking of a figure is shown by a quotation from the short story "Two Deaths." Spender is describing the Austrian government officials: "Behind him sat Minister Fey, a man with a face white and creased like a dirty handkerchief, shot through with bloodless lips and eyes like bullets." This explains the figure, much more compact and, possibly, a little obscure, as it appears in the poem, "Vienna":

"Seated below, Major Fey's strong white face
A wet handkerchief shot through with two lead
    bullets."

While Spender's poetic methods are deliberate, they are not prompted by a desire for innovation. He feels no compulsion to experiment; at the same time he enjoys the greatest freedom to do so. He is unrestricted in his choice of verse forms. He may use free verse, as in "The Prisoners"; quatrains, as in "Statistics";

stanzas of varying lengths, with an extremely short line as in "Old Wives in March":

> "Round fires sit
> Old wives, and knit";

an effective three-line stanza, made up of lines of different length, as in "Winter Landscape":

"Come home with white gulls waving across gray
  Fields. Evening. A daffodil West.
  Somewhere in clefts of rock the birds hide, breast to
    breast."

He uses, too, the measured sonnet; but in his use this form succumbs to his insistence upon poetic freedom. In the sonnet, "The world wears your image on the surface," there are several four-stress lines instead of the accepted pentameter. In "The Port," the usual octet is replaced by a nine-line stanza; and in "Exile," the customary order of the parts is reversed, the octet following instead of preceding the sestet.

These variations appear to be not studied efforts to create new effects, but the inevitable adaptation of methods to needs. The same impression is created by Spender's handling of rhyme. There are, of course, numerous poems written without rhyme. There are, on the other hand, poems written with conventional rhymed line endings; and even with the more subtle form of internal rhyme:

> "I love a friend
> Who is external: to him the sky is brass
> Solid the grass where his behaving runs.
> At night he sleeps well with limpid hands silent,
> His character rings like the single stroke of a bell."

Conventionally correct rhyme is, however, not the only tonal device employed by Spender. Assonance is present in his verse; so, too, is something that can best be described as a pleasurable association of sound, like *stop* and *gap* in the following lines:

> "My pen stops, and my laughter, dancing, stop
>   Or ride to a gap."

The use of formal rhyme and the less formal assonance within a single poem is well illustrated in this stanza:

> "This dwarfs our emerald country by its trek
>   So tall with prophecy:
>   Dreaming of cities
>   Where often clouds shall lean their swan-white neck."

However definitely a poet may be characterized by his use of such devices as meter and rhyme, he is still more highly individualized by the kind and variety of imagery that he employs. The former are tools fashioned for him in the past, tools which he may use in one manner or another; the latter, unless it is the meek acceptance of another's second-hand and time-worn material, is the outgrowth of his own experience and point of view. A clue to Spender's attitude toward the material of poetry and the source of imagery may be found in the fact that the poem of which the last quoted stanza is a part is entitled "The Pylons." To Spender no incongruity exists in using in a poem about poles for electric wires the picture of clouds with "swan-white necks." For him, there is, in fact, no distinction between imagery the source of which is hallowed by early and frequent use and that which grows out of present and newly created conditions. Whatever stirs the emotions is the fit source of poetry; whatever vivifies and gives point to a thought or feeling is the essence of the poetic. From material time-honored and admittedly "poetic," Spender may draw such figures as these:

> "The saddest of days drifts past like golden straw
> And the happiest swims like a star";

or

> "Life seems black against the snow";

or

> "—Those ladies like flies perfect in amber
> Those financiers like fossils of bones in coal."

With startling and convincing effect he uses such imagery in poems on contemporary, realistic, conventionally "unpoetic" subjects. "The Landscape near an Aerodrome" opens with these lines:

"More beautiful and soft than any moth
  With burring furred antennae feeling its huge path
  Through dusk, the air-liner with shut-off engines
  Glides over suburbs."

The Midland Express is described as

  "A juggler of the wheeling towns and stars."

A whole industrialized region is evoked in "View from a Train":

    "The face of the landscape is a mask
      Of bones and iron lines where time
      Has ploughed its character."

Nature, the source of so much imagery for poets from the earliest time to the present, is occasionally drawn upon. Spender can write of

  "Twittering Snow Bunting, Greenland Wheatear,
    Red-throated Divers; imagine butterflies
    Sulphurous cloudy yellow; glory of bees
    That suck from saxifrage."

Yet of his poetry can be said what he himself says of an express train:

  "Wrapt in her music as bird song, no, nor bough
    Breaking with honey buds, shall ever equal."

For much the greater part and by far the best of its imagery is derived from the contemporary scene. Sewing machines and bargain sales, for example!

"And my body seems a cloth which the machine-gun
    stitches
Like a sewing machine, neatly, with cotton from a
    reel";

and

    "Or they fall with Autumn leaves
    When fashions are blown out on white sales
    Before the models of another day."

Newspapers; printing presses, "stamping, cutting, sick-
ing out sheets from paper rolls"; moving pictures, "like
a quick spool of film"—all these are material from
which he creates pictures. Electricity provides a figure
for force:

    "Drink from here energy and only energy,
    As from the electric charges of a battery."

Propaganda, the insidious weapon of the moderns,

    "The furious words and minerals which kill life,"

motorcycles, radio, pumps, express trains—any of these,
all these, Spender feels may rightfully provide him with
the background of his poetry.

His diction and his figures of speech, then, are not
derived from literary tradition but are created out of
his direct experience of life in the twentieth century,
of life in the city, of life lived with men at work. Out
of his experience he has distilled the essence and provided a new set of symbols for his contemporaries. This

is, of course, consistent with his vivid interest in life
and, even more pointedly, with his expressed literary
philosophy. "But the poet," he writes in *The Destructive Element*, "must be conscious of the profound significance and meaning of imagery; his imagery must be
true. Images are not still-lifes to be hung on walls.
They are visions of the history of the race and of life
and death."

Out of the varied imagery of his poetry, two figures
appear with such frequency that they seem to bear special significance for the poet. They are those involving
the sun and time. The sun becomes the symbol of all
that is good and desired. It is the creative force. When
Spender writes of Beethoven's masterpieces, he says:

> "Then splitting skull and dream, there comes
> Blotting out lights, the trumpeter, the sun."

When he thinks "of those who were truly great," he
says of them: "Born of the sun they travelled a short
while toward the sun."

If the sun signifies the ideal of achievement, what
comes to symbolize the means of attaining it? Time
apparently plays that function. Time becomes "the general arbiter." But this does not imply a *laissez-faire* approach to life:

> "Time is a thing
>  That does not pass through boredom and the wishing,
>  But must be fought with, rushed at, over-awed
>  And threatened with a sword."

This is a philosophy of action, a philosophy of admiration for

"The will of those who dared to move
From the furrow, their life's groove,"

of admiration for "those who in their lives fought for life." More than this, it is a philosophy of optimism; for Spender believes firmly in the possibility of progress and improvement. Man has within himself vast resources of power:

"Different living is not living in different places
But creating in the mind a map
Creating in the mind a desert
An isolated mountain or a kinder health-resort."

Man working with Time will create the good:

"Time's ambition, huge as space, will hang its flags
In distant worlds, and in years on this world as distant."

The perfection to which Spender looks is a perfection of society in which the individual is free to develop to his finest. This is the ideal to which his poetry is an approach. It is, without question, a political and economic ideal. One finds, then, a merging of politics and art and a resulting problem which Spender must solve: that of the relationship between propaganda and poetry. But the problem is not so difficult as it may at first seem. The artist, like any other individual, must be free. He must not be forced to substitute for his independent judgment the fixed code of any political creed. His art must be free, its material unhampered by any interpretation imposed by the state. It is thus that Spender expresses * his own clearly defined attitude:

"It is destructive for an artist to say that he knows something which he only believes or hopes to be true. For example, to say that I am on the side of the proletariat, that I shall fight for their cause, may be just. To say that the proletariat is better than any other class, that the proletarian revolution is the historic future of the world, is to blind myself as an artist. It is the business of artists to insist on human values. If there is need for a revolution, it is these human values that will make the revolution."

Spender approaches the problem realistically. He recognizes the undeniable gulf at present existing between himself and the worker. But he feels that the test for both of them is the extent to which each is prepared to live for a world in the future that will unite the world of the poet with the worker's world. He looks to the time when both can meet in a classless society, one promising safety and security to all.

Such a society, firmly established and made up of individuals free and secure, is essential to Spender, not as politician, not as economist, but as poet. "The first aim of civilized men," he says in *Forward from Liberal-*

* Spender: *The Destructive Element*, Houghton Mifflin Co.

*ism,* "must be an unpolitical age, when conditions of peace and security are conducive to a classical art, rooted not in a small oligarchy but in the lives of the whole people."

The poet, however, is not to be merely a recipient of the good inherent in the ideal state. He has his responsibility as artist, the moral obligation to fulfill his function. His purpose is something more than simply to indulge in self-expression for his own gratification; he writes for an audience, to whom he must transmit a tradition evolved from the past and to whom he must present "an affirmation of the permanent in life, of real values."

> "Some old man's memory jumps to a child—
> Sparks from the days of energy."

Just so the poet communicates experience. Because of his peculiar intuition, the poet may be sensitive to new forms of life before they have been commonly accepted or even recognized. His is the duty to seek out the truth in these new forms and through his poetry to convey it to his fellows. This, as Spender * sees it, is the purpose of poetry as distinguished from prose:

"The result is that my prose is absorbed with problems of the will, and my poetry with that of crystallizing and contemplating a given situation, a situation which is permanent and yet contains within itself in-

* Spender: *Forward from Liberalism,* Random House, New York.

escapable truth, which is a seed of energy, planted in the mind of the reader."

Poetry thus becomes for Spender something quite different from an ego-centric outlet for personality. It has for him a moral purpose, a religious one, bound closely with his vision of a better form of society. It is not sufficient that it states the truths he finds; it must motivate men to action so that those truths may become effective and permanent. Linked in this fashion to a program of life, it forms a nucleus for his being:

"Not saving me from death, but saving me for speech."

Through the years when there has been need of comfort and consolation, poetry has given him release:

"This writing is my only wings away."

Always it has symbolized for him his hopes and desires; the ideal he has sought, the reality to which he would cling he has wished to be enduring, solid, "like the created poem."

POETICAL WORKS

| | |
|---|---|
| POEMS | *Random House, Inc.* |
| VIENNA | *Random House, Inc.* |
| TRIAL OF A JUDGE (Play) | *Random House, Inc.* |
| THE STILL CENTRE | *Faber and Faber* |

*ELINOR WYLIE*

## ELINOR WYLIE

AS one of those incongruities which frequently add piquancy to a life, it was in a crude little wooden cottage in the rurally remote settlement of Somerville, New Jersey, that Elinor Morton Hoyt was born on September 7, 1885. The incongruity lies in the contrast between the utter simplicity and unworldliness of her birthplace and the later sophistication of her life and writings. The Elinor Wylie who was the woman of the world was, however, in no sense a denial of her past; for the Somerville cottage was typical neither of the poet nor of her tradition and background. It was, as a matter of fact, almost in the nature of a whim of her parents who, after continuing in New York City the socially and culturally rich life to which they had been accustomed, had had financial reverses and, feeling the need of economizing, had given up their New York home for one in New Jersey in the same town to which a sudden vagary had taken them two years before on their honeymoon.

The marriage in January 1883 of Henry Martyn Hoyt and of Anne MacMichael united two old American families of English origin. Henry Hoyt, the poet's father, whose own father had been governor of Pennsylvania, came from an upstate Pennsylvania family;

313

her mother, the daughter of a banker, was a member of one of Philadelphia's oldest families, one that had given a mayor to that city. The Philadelphia wedding was to have been followed by a New England honeymoon; but in a mood of adventure, the pair had suddenly changed their plans and gone to the home of a relative in the New Jersey town. So, when prudence made it advisable for them to leave New York, it was to Somerville that they returned and it was there that their first child was born.

The little family was supremely happy, their lives filled with the domestic and social events of a small rural community. In 1887, the Hoyt finances permitted a return to more urban surroundings. They moved to Rosemont, a suburb of Philadelphia; and there, a son, Henry Martyn, and a daughter, Constance, were born.

The outward life of the Hoyt family was the usual one of most well-to-do people. But there existed also an inner life sensitive to impressions, a life made up of things small yet significant to the spirit; and in this life Elinor most keenly shared. First signs of spring, early blossoms and early berries, were matters of importance. Summers spent at Bar Harbor, Maine, a New England island resort, filled her life with experiences of beauty that became deep-rooted and remained always present. Long talks of family friends that she was permitted to listen to, talks that touched upon an infinite variety of subjects, opened her mind, even as a very young child, to the world outside her home. Literature enlarged that world still further. Her parents and grandparents were accustomed to read aloud to her; and while this habit delayed somewhat her own ability to read, it early made her familiar with books and devoted to them.

Books, for their content and probably, too, for their physical form, became her prized treasures. As a child of some nine or ten years, she chose as a birthday present from her grandfather a copy of *Hamlet*, bound in vellum and signed by Dr. Furness, the Shakespeare scholar. A significant choice, indeed! Her grandfather gave her, too, a claret-colored Keats when she was still a very young girl, "from which I have never been parted since." How deep and how lasting were the impressions made by books is shown by her own remembrance of her early reading. Particularly illuminating is it for the light it gives on her first acquaintance with Shelley, who ever after was for her a hero, an ideal, almost an intimate.*

"I first read 'The Cloud' and 'The Skylark' in my Third Reader, and I think I was seven years old. This was the same winter when my innocent young mother read 'Christabel' aloud to me. My admiration for it was so nearly pure horror that 'The Skylark' was a great consolation after dark. 'If we were things born not to shed a tear'; even a child can understand those words. Then when I was eleven we were no longer in that Victorian high-ceiled house in Philadelphia, where

* William Rose Benét: *Prose and Poetry of Elinor Wylie*, Wheaton College Press, Norton, Mass.

'The Skylark' first sang to me. It was September in Washington and the air was warm and sweet as if all the grapes and peaches of Maryland and Virginia had flavored it to my taste. I stood before the smallest book-case in the library, and from its shelves I drew Trelawny's 'Recollections.' The window was open; there was plenty of light and soft autumnal wind in the room. I did not move except to turn the pages. Even the black leather chair was too far away from the scene within the covers of the book. I stood quite still and turned the pages, and the curtains blew in at the window and a few golden leaves blew in between them.

"So I read for the first time of Shelley's death and burial. I can remember what I felt in that moment of past time, but never what I thought. It is therefore impossible to tell of it except to draw the picture of the room full of light and softer air and of the child standing in the center of the room and turning the pages of the book, afraid to move, afraid to cry for fear the scene within the pages of the book might be hidden from her eyes, wondering and wondering why the bright creature who had lived within that scene should have died and fallen into dust no stronger than the golden leaves blowing in at the window."

This familiarity with the poets early developed in the little girl a passionate love for words; an appreciation of their values, their shades of meaning, color, and tone; a feeling for them that was like that of a connoisseur of jewels.

316

"Poets make pets of pretty, docile words;
  I love smooth words, like gold-enamelled fish
  Which circle slowly with a silken swish,
  And tender ones, like downy-feathered birds;
  Words shy and dappled, deep-eyed deer in herds,
  Come to my hand, and playful if I wish,
  Or purring softly at a silver dish,
  Blue Persian kittens, fed on cream and curds.

I love bright words, words up and singing early;
  Words that are luminous in the dark, and sing;
  Warm lazy words, white cattle under trees;
  I love words opalescent, cool, and pearly,
  Like midsummer moths, and honied words like bees,
  Gilded and sticky, with a little sting."

Indeed, so early in her life had she made words her tools to express, as a poet would, her feelings and thoughts that she is said as a child of six in kindergarten to have described her mother's eyes as "clear brown lakes, fringed with rushes." *

Beyond the fact that such precocity was remembered and so must have been recognized as somewhat unusual, there seems no evidence that it was considered prophetic of the child's future. Rather than any future, it was the events of the immediate present that were important, the bustling, lively activities of the gay family. A sudden desire on the part of the parents to show

* Nancy Hoyt: *Elinor Wylie, The Portrait of an Unknown Lady,* The Bobbs-Merrill Co.

the nation's capital to the children led to a spring visit to Washington. As the result of a chance encounter there with a friend, Mr. Hoyt was introduced to President McKinley and shortly thereafter appointed by him as an Assistant Attorney-General.

This appointment led to the family's moving in 1897 from Rosemont to Washington. There Elinor attended Mrs. Flint's School, a typical day-school for girls. She became intensely interested in her school work and gave it such long and untiring devotion that she seemed in every danger of becoming a sober, over-intellectualized bluestocking.

Offsetting this intellectuality, however, and adding another element to a complex individual, was an interest of which teachers and family were both unaware. Without any harm to her studies, the young girl was spending much time writing verses and fostering that worship of Shelley which had begun some years before. But her emotional and esthetic needs had not yet crystallized; she had not yet decided upon the medium of expression which she would make her own. In addition to her writing, she was developing a talent for drawing, attending life classes at the Corcoran Gallery.

What for a time seemed like the danger of pedantry or even of single-minded scholarship was somehow averted. Elinor did not continue her academic work by going to college. Nor did she choose either literature or art as a career. Family life and Washington social life were offsetting influences. Two more children had been born in the Hoyt family, a boy and a girl to whom

Elinor was intensely devoted. The family circle was broken for a few months in the spring of 1903, when Elinor and a sister were taken abroad by their maternal grandfather and by that seasoned traveler were introduced to the cosmopolitan glories and delights of Paris and of London. On their return to the United States, the reunited family spent the rest of the summer at their Maine vacation place. Again, as for so many years before, the Maine seashore and countryside presented their simple but undying charms to the young girl.

She had been graduated from school, a slightly stern personage, somewhat austere, very dignified, and always with the suggestion of aloofness about her. Upon her formal presentation to Washington society, a seemingly completely different personality developed. Gaily and whole-heartedly she entered into the social life of the capital. Always beautiful, she now paid more and more attention to that beauty. In a manner that belied the years spent assiduously over books, she delighted in the frilly, flounced gowns of a fashionable young lady. She enjoyed with feminine enthusiasm the parties, and balls, the beaux, and admirers of a débutante. She became engaged without her parents' knowledge to Philip Hichborn, a young man but a few years older than herself, the son of an admiral. Shortly they were married.

But she was scarcely grown up or ready to accept the responsibilities that married life brings. A son was born to the couple. In spite of husband, child, and household, Elinor seemed to depend upon her own family—

the home she had left—for a sense of security. Differences in tastes and desires between her and her husband arose and increased. Her married life proved unhappy. Added to this as a source of grief was the death of her father. The world which she knew and which had protected her seemed to be crumbling.

In the midst of her unhappiness, the young Mrs. Hichborn took a step indicative of the conflict within her and indicative, too, of the courage to set and follow a course of action that she believed might soothe the conflict. She who had been brought up in the conventional, formal social world of Washington suddenly startled that world. In 1910 she left her husband and child and eloped with Mr. Horace Wylie, a man much older than herself and already married. Such total disregard for convention, such flouting of it, evoked sharp —and natural—criticism. But this is to be said of her action; it was not the result of a hasty, unconsidered impulse. She felt a deep abiding love, a sense of the essential rightness of her conduct, and, above all, the certainty in it of a personal integrity which she, in spite of vagaries, whimsicalities, and eccentricities, always maintained. Though she may have understood the world's disapproval, she was nevertheless sensitive and hurt by its criticism. The two people withdrew into themselves, each absorbed in the other, and retired to an inner world of their own creation.

Under the name of Waring, they left this country for Europe, spending the years in England, with occasional short trips to the continent. Their first home was in the little village of Burley about fifty miles from London, in a very old, white plastered cottage with thick walls and a mossy tiled roof, the whole set in a glowing flower garden. Their happy existence there was cut short by the chance visit of some Americans to the village, who promptly spread rumors about the American couple, rumors which the neighbors found difficult to believe. Sensitive, hurt, the "Warings" left Burley to find elsewhere a home that would be a refuge from malicious gossip. It was a procedure several times repeated, until finally, in June 1914, they bought a home of their own.

Life in each one of the little villages in which they stayed was supremely happy. The two people were engrossed in each other. They devoted a great part of their time to reading. For the rest, Elinor lived the life of an English country woman, sending to London for books and for gowns from Liberty's, the London store; attending the village church and helping to decorate it for services; visiting the village sick; giving and going to afternoon tea parties.

She draws a picture of her English country life in a short article "Shelley's Grandson and Some Others": *

"Once upon a time I lived in a very small English village. It was the most fairy-book place in the world and I hardly dare go back to England for fear it has changed. . . . The cottage had walls of cob and roofs of thatch, and there was a grey church and a green

* Elinor Wylie: "Shelley's Grandson and Some Others," *The Bookman*, August 1923.

churchyard, and a red and white inn called The Queen's Head. There were sherry glass elms with rooks in them, and a beechwood which was pink and purple in April, and bright holly bushes which were covered with scarlet berries in November.

"In this village I ate clotted cream, and smelled wall-flowers, and drank mead, all for the first time, and the cream and the wallflowers were heavenly, but I am sorry to say the mead was horrible."

One can imagine her ecstasy at discovering in this village a person who recalled to her the consuming interest and hero worship of her youth, a grandson of the poet Shelley! A little old gentleman, "he looked more like Shelley's grandfather," she declares in that adjustment of generations which the passing of time demands; and then goes on to explain her feelings. "Think of it—Shelley's grandson, and I have had tea with him frequently! He was an authentic eagle's feather; a somewhat small and whitish feather, but still Shelley's grandson. He was also Harriet's grandson, and I remember his looking very impish and saying gravely, 'You know, in this family, we don't think much of Mary.' I never dared ask him just how much he thought of Shelley, nor admit the extent of my own worship, for as a grandfather dear Shelley never had much chance."

The English years proved then not to be complete exile from those she loved. There was this contact with Shelley who was as real to her as though he were alive. There were, too, frequent visits to her by members of her family, who stayed with her for varying lengths of time. Over their last visit to her spread the dark shadow of the World War of 1914-1918. Her sister, Constance, who had married a German in the diplomatic service, was in the German embassy at Brussels. Naturally, she became the center of much concern. Her mother and her younger brother and sister, who had been spending the summer with Elinor, were after many difficulties able to find passage for America. Elinor and Horace Wylie threw all their sympathies on the side of the Allies. Elinor busied herself in war work in a camp for soldiers near her home in Witley. But the situation of the couple became increasingly difficult. They were occupying an anomalous position, which could not easily be explained to the English about them. Able-bodied, Horace Wylie, known as Mr. Waring, did not enlist in the English army; without a passport, their status and nationality were constantly under suspicion. Finally in the summer of 1916, they sold their house and returned to Boston. It was a return to the land which she held most dear. England she loved; but America had first claim on her heart:

> "Part of England lies beneath
>   Both the granite and the loam;
>   Let the divided heart come home
>   To half-content, and understand
>   His passion for a wilder land
>   Still untamed and still unfed
>   By flesh and bone that England bred."

During the years of the English sojourn, Elinor Wylie had done a little writing, but only a little. She had begun a novel, which, sent to her sister in Brussels, had somehow been lost and which was to prove her only attempt at fiction for eight years. She had written, too, a few poems, enough for a privately printed volume which she called *Incidental Numbers*. The book, printed in London in 1912 by the same company that had printed a very beautiful, much-admired edition of Blake's *Songs of Innocence,* was a small square volume of forty-three pages, bound in gray-blue. For each poem was noted the date of composition. The volume, slight though it was, gave definite indication of the strains that the poet was later to develop more thoroughly. There is the suggestion of the steady pursuit, in spite of the criticism of others, of what is believed to be right. One becomes aware, too, of the weapon that is to be used against opposition, the weapon which Eleanor was to wield in her struggles both against her own nature at odds with itself and against forces outside her, the weapon of intellect, and laughter:

"Inheritors of the relentness sword,
  The bright, indomitable sword of mirth,
  Dedicate from the instant of their birth
  To struggle with the dark powers."

From the small volume of work done in England, however, it would have been quite impossible to predict the literary activity of the following years. For very shortly after her arrival in this country, she began to write poem after poem which, almost perfectly formed in her mind, she was able to put down on paper with amazingly few changes. Why she was so suddenly able to find expression for thoughts and feelings it is difficult to say. Undoubtedly her marriage to Mr. Wylie (made possible finally by the death of Mr. Hichborn and the changed attitude of the first Mrs. Wylie) brought her a deep release from strain. Possibly, too, an impetus to poetry was provided by the renewal of her happiest memories, those of the Maine summers of her childhood. For she and her husband spent their first American summer in Maine, at first in her mother's home, and then in Somesville, a small settlement of little white houses built on classic Greek lines, that Elinor had known and loved from childhood. When winter set in, they closed their cottage and rented an apartment over the village grocery. There—and this forms another of those incongruous pictures in Elinor Wylie's life—in a room over the cracker barrels and tinned goods of a country store, she wrote such poems as "Sea Lullaby," which holds all the haunting terror of the sea, the eerie "Fire and Sleet and Candlelight," and that very lovely "Velvet Shoes" with its perfect picture of a muted snow-covered world:

> "We shall walk in velvet shoes;
>       Wherever we go
>   Silence will fall like dews

On white silence below,
We shall walk in the snow."

The New England sojourn was followed by a trip to the South and then by residence in Washington, her girlhood home. The Washington to which she returned was, however, a quite different place, a post-war Washington which had drawn to it vast numbers of people and which was the scene of much bustling activity. Elinor Wylie became the center of a group of people interested in literature. She entertained them in her home, where in her living-room she had gathered together furnishings which she held dear—"things" for their esthetic qualities were always precious to her—a blue velveteen sofa, an eighteenth century Sheffield mirror with candlesticks, Wedgwood lamps, fruit and flower pictures. Against this background of beauty, into which she herself fitted amazingly well, she received such people as Sinclair Lewis, who was writing *Main Street;* and William Rose Benét, then editing a journal for the Department of Commerce, but with literary contacts in New York. The talks were of literature; the interests were literary.

Under this influence, she began to write more prolifically. She received encouragement and recognition, as did so many other beginning poets, from Harriet Monroe, whose magazine *Poetry* was among the first to accept and print her poems. Soon there was enough material for a volume of verse and plans were made for its publication. The poet traveled frequently be-

tween Washington and New York to supervise her first
public appearance in book form.

In November 1921, *Nets to Catch the Wind* appeared. Over thirty, the poet was somewhat older than
are most when their first poems appear. But the volume,
which instantly won critical acclaim, showed the value
of the long apprenticeship she had served in her craft.
It contained poems practically perfect, poems like
"Wild Peaches," like the earlier "Sea Lullaby" and
"Velvet Shoes," like "August" which Louis Untermeyer
called "the complete fulfillment of design." Running
through the poems was a strain of mysticism, reminiscent of the poet Blake. Yet the mysticism was not one
of naïveté, for parallel to it was an equally strong
strain of sophistication. And throughout was the echo
of a woman struggling within herself and struggling
against an inflexible world. Was her soul daunted by
the struggle? This must be the answer:

> "But you have a proud face
> Which the world cannot harm,
> You have turned the pain to a grace
> And the scorn to a charm."

The Washington atmosphere, in spite of new found
friends and a few loyal old ones, was never completely
cordial. So, as the demand for her writings increased,
it seemed natural to leave that city for New York,
where she would be nearer the literary center of the
nation and, as it happened, freed from the restraints

of her past. With her arrival in New York in 1921 began the growth of the legendary Elinor Wylie, glamorous, mysterious, elusive, sometimes childish and petulant, but always charming.

The New York of the early nineteen-twenties was ready to receive and foster such a legend. The emotions that had been aroused by the war years were being expended in numberless directions. Men and women were enjoying a new freedom which they were expressing not only in manners and morals, but in the arts by experimentation in matter and in form. Novelists, poets, dramatists, artists flocked to New York where, particularly in Greenwich Village and the neighborhood of Washington Square, they made somewhat haphazard homes; formed congenial, intimate groups; devoted themselves to liberality in art and in life; and basked in a fervid glow of publicity turned on them by the general public.

This was the New York in which Elinor Wylie arrived. She established herself in a room off Washington Square, which her sister describes: * "I can't imagine where she slept in it, but I can remember that all her dressing-table equipment was neatly encased in a cupboard in the bathroom, and a tin outfit for cooking was also stowed away there with almost mathematical precision. In the dusk of early spring the lamps and candles glowed under the high ceiling of a drawing-room which

* Nancy Hoyt: *Elinor Wylie: The Portrait of an Unknown Lady.* Copyright 1935. Used by special permission of the publishers, The Bobbs-Merrill Company.

would have been suitable as one of a lady's twenty rooms but seemed slightly ridiculous and almost unbelievable as the only dwelling-place of a human being. Yet at 1 University Place were spent her gayest and most frivolous months." About her were the treasured possessions brought from her Washington home.

She loved elegance, not only in her surroundings, but in her life and in herself. She was beautiful, possessed of a "strange, unforgettable beauty." She had really remarkable bronze hair and large, glowing hazel eyes; her throat was lovely. She carried herself with dignity and grace. Of her appearance she was very vain, spending on it much time and energy. Hours were devoted to the proper choice of clothing; her dresses were gowns rather than mere dresses. Her visits to hairdressers partook almost of the nature of a rite. But this picture of worldliness is only a half-picture; for paralleling this sophistication in taste, there was—strange contradiction—a "johnny-cake side," a heritage from her Puritan ancestry.

"Down to the Puritan marrow of my bones
There's something in this richness that I hate."

Nor was this the only contradiction in her personality. While she possessed the cool detachment of a woman of the world, a superiority to the opinions of the vast majority of people, she could, at the same time, act with childlike impetuosity and she was always childishly sensitive, avid for praise and vulnerable to criticism. This criticism, one must hasten to add, could derive from herself just as well as from another. For she did not exempt herself from the standard of perfection that she set in all things. To the perfection of her work she applied herself even more assiduously than to the perfection of her appearance. She engaged in arduous research so that each minute detail of her writing might be exquisitely correct. She exercised a ceaseless and rigid discipline so that her work might be as nearly perfect in form as was humanly possible.

> "How many faults you might accuse me of
> Are truth, and by my truthfulness admitted!"

Thus she began an enumeration of her faults: but, she added, there is one "invulnerable point in this poor armor":

> "This strict ascetic habit of control
> That industry has woven for my soul."

She was a person of quickly changing, unpredictable moods.

> "Times she'll be docile as the gentlest thing
> That ever blinked in fur or folded wing,
> And then, like lightning in the dead of night,
> Fill with wild crackling, intermitting light
> My mind and soul and senses,—and next be
> Aloof, askance as a dryad in a tree."

So William Rose Benét described her. The conflicting elements in her, her role as a beauty and the demands it made, her intellect and its demands, her sensitivity as an artist and her courage, these in constant flux expressed themselves in the vagaries of her conduct. But never did her moods affect the essential core of her intelligence or her own stern code of honesty; and never, however they might resolve themselves into irony, did they result in complacency or in a lack of pity for her fellows.

How very well she understood herself she showed in "Portrait in Black Paint, With a Very Sparing Use of Whitewash," that autobiographical "Profile" which she wrote for *The New Yorker*.

" 'She gives herself'; there's a poetic thought;
  She gives you comfort sturdy as a reed;
  She gives you fifty things you might have bought,
  And half a hundred that you'll never need;
  She gives you friendship, but it's such a bother
  You'd fancy influenza from another.

  She does not give advice; that I admit;
  Here's her sole virtue, and I'll count it double,
  Forgiving her some crime because of it,
  But she gives tiresome and endless trouble.
  If you need rest, she'll straight contrive a racket;
  If gaiety, she'll fetch a padded jacket.

  And she gives love of the least useful kind
  At which advanced civilization mocks;
  Half, a Platonic passion of the mind,
  And half, a mad desire to mend the socks;

She's always wishing to turn back the page
And live with children in a golden age.

. . . . . . .

Doubtless, she gives her enemies the creeps
And all her friends a vast amount of worry;
She's given oblivion only when she sleeps;
She says she loves the grave; but she'd be sorry
To die, while it is vanity to live;
'She gives herself'; what has she left to give?"

It was, then, this creature of moods, of vivacity, of charm, who took her place in the life of one of New York's most conspicuous literary groups. It was a group composed of many significant people, among them Sinclair Lewis, William Rose Benét, Edna St. Vincent Millay, Edmund Wilson, John Dos Passos. Whatever their inner lives might have been, however secret and guarded to themselves, the details of their outer existence became public information; their tastes and activities became well known and the legendary Elinor Wylie grew beyond the bounds of her own chosen group of friends.

Her friends were not without influence on her own literary life. Through Edmund Wilson, she served for a time as poetry editor of the magazine *Vanity Fair*. Through Sinclair Lewis her interest was directed, after the long lapse of eight years, toward the writing of prose; and as a result of his persuasion she wrote *Jennifer Lorn*, her first finished novel, written with the same beauty, finesse, and delicacy as were her poems. Thereafter, her literary work was evenly divided between prose and poetry, a division rather more technical than actual, since in conception and in mood her novels closely approximated poetry.

With literature becoming the center of her existence, with new friends and new interests, she found the ties between her and her husband weakening. In the fall of 1923, after a vacation at the MacDowell Colony in Peterborough, New Hampshire, she divorced Horace Wylie and married William Rose Benét. Interestingly enough, she retained the name Wylie for her writing; and it was under that name, in the same year, that her second book of poems appeared, *Black Armour.*

Now, widely known, she saw her book most enthusiastically received. It showed the high, stern regard for craftsmanship which she exacted of herself. It showed, too, a careful and revealing self-examination. The conflict between brain and soul, between flesh and spirit, became more and more the subject of her thoughts:

> "There I walked, and there I raged;
>  The spiritual savage caged
>  Within my skeleton, raged afresh
>  To feel, behind a carnal mesh,
>  The clean bones crying in the flesh."

"Peregrine" presented in faint disguise another self-portrait made up of a tangled mass of contradictory details. In strong contrast to the moods of these two poems, but equally revealing of the person writing, was the moving poem, "The Hand." Her hand, the poet declared, was the tool of her will; perhaps, she added wistfully, though its perfect outline might have been marred, its worth would have been greater

> "If I had seen a thorn
>     Broken to grape-vine bud;
> If I had ever borne
>     Child of our mingled blood;
>
> Elixirs might escape;
>     But now, compact as stone,
> My hand preserved a shape
>     Too utterly its own."

One must not imagine, however, in spite of the suggestion in this last poem, that the poet was completely removed from the cares and exigencies of ordinary life. After her marriage to Benét, in addition to the demands of creative writing, she was subject to those of family existence. She devoted herself to the care of her three step-children, until, after a few years, they went to California to live with their maternal aunt. She was engrossed in the purchase, transformation, and financing of a home in New Canaan, Connecticut. She was worried by money cares and by poor health.

The New Canaan project was abandoned. The children were gone. She and her husband, returning to New York, resumed their former mode of life. There were occasional visits to Europe, where English ties were strengthened. And always there was steady application to her writing. In 1926 a third prose volume (*The Venetian Glass Nephew* having previously appeared) was published. This book, *Orphan Angel*, was Elinor Wylie's devoted offering at the shrine of her hero, Shelley. It was the highly imaginative tale of the English poet, whom she assumed to have been rescued from drowning and brought by an American boat to this country, where he preferred to stay incognito instead of returning to his wife and home. The book, chosen as a Book of the Month, brought its author the immediate sum of eight thousand dollars. What did she do with this money, so much more than royalties in the past had been? Her "johnny-cake side" must have suggested many practical, sensible uses to which it could be put. But, with a degree of appropriateness, if with a still greater degree of extravagance, she used a large part of it to buy some pages of the original manuscript of "Prometheus Unbound" and a check from Shelley to his father-in-law Godwin.

In 1928, appeared her third volume of verse, *Trivial Breath*. By now the poet seemed to realize that much of the witchery and glamor with which her earlier poems had been colored were the results of her own efforts to protect herself from the world by glorifying a life and world of her own. In *Trivial Breath*, she sounded a somewhat sterner note, a call to face life as it is:

"Go hence, for it is useless to pretend."

Whether she felt that the core of existence might more easily be reached and appreciated away from the surface activity of New York, one cannot be sure. At all events, her mind and heart turned to England as the place in which to establish a home. In May 1928, she sailed for Europe and, after much searching, found in Chilmark, a small village nine miles from Salisbury, the little cottage which she decided to buy. Her husband was to join her in midsummer. Meanwhile she was at work on plans for her house and for a fourth volume of poems. Her friends, of whom she had many in England, included her in their busy social life.

It was in early summer, during a visit to one of them, that she fell down a flight of stairs. The fall was evidence of the illness from which she had been suffering. Weakened by that illness and by the shock of her accident, she returned to London. After some while, she let her family in America know what had happened. Her husband joined her in England, and found her much recovered and most enthusiastic about the poems which, with increasing ease, she was creating.

When it was necessary for him to return to New York, she stayed behind so that the flow of poetry should not be interrupted. Alone now in England, she worked feverishly.

The strain told on her. She awoke one morning in October to find that in the night she had been stricken by a partial paralysis, which affected the muscles of her face. She was informed, to spare her the shock of hearing the word "stroke"—which she doubtless suspected in spite of such precautions—that she was suffering from a facial neuralgia and must rest. The beauty on which she set such store was marred. Her vanity was terribly wounded.

But she had promised to spend the Christmas holidays with her family. She dreaded the meetings with her old associates. Nevertheless, she gathered up her things, including the manuscript of *Angels and Earthly Creatures,* and on December 1 sailed for New York. Those who met her found the disfigurement less than they had been led to expect; one half of her mouth was set in a permanent involuntary smile, a little wry and ironic.

Though she was tired, and exhausted, she continued work on her poems, getting them ready for publication. *Angels and Earthly Creatures* proved to be the culmination of her art, the final perfection of her genius. Meaning and style were completely and irrevocably fused. The book contained a sonnet sequence, "One Person," which was the supreme expression of her love. Carl Van Doren * sketches the background of these poems. Elinor Wylie, as she had herself told him, had at last found a man whom she loved absolutely; but unable—or unwilling—again to break and re-create her life, she kept this love a thing apart. She poured into these poems her deepest feelings, the tenderest emotion of loving rather than being loved, her sense of profound humility in the experience. The book contained, too, that stately but tender poem, "Hymn to Earth." With what premoni-

* Carl Van Doren: "Elinor Wylie: A Portrait from Memory," *Harper's Magazine,* September 1936.

tion, one wonders, did the poet write this, her own leave-
taking?

"Hail, element of earth, receive thy own,
  And cherish, at thy charitable breast,
  This man, this mongrel beast:
  He ploughs the sand, and, at his hardest need,
  He sows himself for seed;
  He ploughs the furrow, and in this lies down
  Before the corn is grown;
  Between the apple bloom
  And the ripe apple is sufficient room
  In time, and matter, to consume his love
  And make him parcel of a cypress grove.

Receive him as thy lover for an hour
  Who will not weary, by a longer stay,
  The kind embrace of clay;
  Even within thine arms he is dispersed
  To nothing, as at first;
  The air flings downward from its four-quartered tower
  Him whom the flames devour;
  At the full tide, at the flood,
  The sea is mingled with his salty blood:
  The traveller dust, although the dust be vile,
  Sleeps as thy lover for a little while."

On the morning of Sunday, December 16, 1928, the
poet telephoned her sister that her book was at last
ready for the printers. That evening she asked for some

water. As her husband gave it to her, she said, "Is that all it is?" and died. Her work had been perfected. In view of that, one could not have asked for longer life for her who, with her beauty marred, however slightly, and with her strength impaired, would have felt mere duration of years intolerable.

Thus much of biography can scarcely explain or even completely depict the poet. It may well be that she must ever elude complete delineation; that there was no single, unified Elinor Wylie; that the woman she seemed to one observer was quite as real as the totally different woman she seemed to another, the woman of one time and mood quite as real as that of another time and mood; that, indeed, it was this very conflict, this interplay of personalities within a single individual that was the essence of her being. Yet however much such biographical information falls short of completeness, it will help somewhat to illumine the poetry that was the rich legacy she left.

It is readily apparent, then, that the conflict between spirit and intellect that underlies the thought of so many of her poems had a very real source within herself. On the one hand were the body, sensations, emotions warm and vibrant, what she sometimes called the "soul"; on the other were cold, objective thought and intelligence. The forces they exerted could be equally strong. She who cried out

"My body is weary to death of my mischievous brain"

saw the struggle as never ending.

This double sensitivity, a sensitivity through the feelings and through the mind, endowed her with peculiar power of insight. She was able to look into a situation and see it clearly, stripped of irrelevancies and falsities. But in re-creating it for her readers, frequently—particularly in her earlier poems—she presented it in a mood and manner that were not hers when she first apprehended it. Sometimes, her mind over-intellectualized it. Sometimes, her very sensitivity made her shrink from the stark truth she found. To save herself hurt, in self-protection, she built a hard, glittering wall, a defense against blows. Like the animal in "The Tortoise in Eternity," whose shell is its "armour to his need," she had her own "darling roof."

The rôle, which at times she filled, that of sophisticated woman of the world, made its own demands. Such a one must dominate a situation; she must not too openly reveal her feelings lest they provide a target for the aim of others. Such emotional control resulted in delicate restraint, such as that of the wistful "On a Singing Girl":

> "Musa of the sea-blue eyes,
> Silver nightingale, alone
> In a little coffin lies:
> A stone beneath a stone.
>
> She, whose song we loved the best,
> Is voiceless in a sudden night;
> On your light limbs, O loveliest,
> May the dust be light!"

But, in another mood, it resulted in a light pretense of indifference, the pretense of "Speed the Parting," which conceals its true feelings until its last lines:

> "You will die, I suppose, before long.
> *Oh, worser, sooner than later!*"

A woman of the world should be tolerant:

> "As one by one our faiths are shaken
>     Our hatreds fall; so mine for you.
> Of course I think you were mistaken;
>     But still, I see your point of view."

Wit and a lightness of touch must season her understanding and appreciation.

> "When the skies are low an' the earth is frozen,
> Ye'll be gay an' glad for the leddie ye've chosen,
> When ower the snow I go prinkin' an' prancin'
> In my wee red slippers were made for dancin'."

The part could be perfectly played; the feelings held in such complete subjection that the real person might escape, prove utterly elusive:

> "I need not die to go
>     So far you cannot know
>     My escape, my retreat."

But that is only one of the facets of the diamond-like poet. It must not be thought that she was timorous or hesitant always in self-revelation. When she willed, she dispassionately studied herself and the hurts that she herself suffered; then candidly she made patent her feelings; as she did in such tender, subjective poems as "Desolation is a Delicate Thing":

"This sorrow, which I believed a gravestone over my
        heart,
  Is gone like a cloud; it eluded me as I woke;
  Its crystal dust is suddenly broken and blown apart;
  It was not my heart; it was this poor sorrow alone
        which broke."

and "Now That Your Eyes Are Shut":

  "My casual ghost may slip,
    Issuing tiptoe, from the pure inhuman;
  The tissues of my lip
    Will bruise your eyelids, while I am a woman."

It was, indeed, in her love songs, particularly in the "One Person" sequence, that most whole-heartedly, without fear or artificiality, she poured forth her feelings, revealing her own vulnerability and exulting in it. The love she glorified was an outgoing emotion, a feminine love, humble and submissive:

  "And am I not your child who has come home?
  And am I not your hound for faithfulness?"

She sounded in them a note of deep humility:

  "I have entreated you to grant me time
    To memorize the pure appointed task;

Today it is Eternity I ask
In which to learn the lesson of this rhyme:
Its liberal periods are not too wide
To educate me fitly for your bride."

Does that seem like quite a different person? If one must reconcile these contradictory personalities, seeking some basic underlying unity, one may perhaps find a clue in "Love Song":

"Had I concealed my love
And you so loved me longer,
Since all the wise reprove
Confession of that hunger
In any human creature,
It had not been my nature."

In this strict adherence to the dictates of her nature lies the key both to her varying aspects and to her philosophy. Under the protean Elinor Wylie that the world knew was a basic self of which she—and perhaps she alone—was aware; one that did not deny any phase, but included them all; one to which she tried to be true. That so tempestuous, so unpredictable a nature must be productive of difficulties was inevitable; but these consequences, though she could not always foresee them, though she could not always welcome them, she did bravely accept:

"Five-petalled flame, be cold:
Be firm, dissolving star:

343

Accept the stricter mould
That makes you singular."

There was no compromise in her soul. From her first book, in "The Eagle and the Mole," through to her last book, in "Nonsense Rhyme," runs the same admonition, variously expressed:

"Beware the moderated soul
That climbs no fractional inch to fall."

Life is to be lived and lived with courage; it is to be measured by activity rather than by number of years:

" 'And he who shortens his life in time
May lengthen it in living.' "

For time passes quickly, and life is brief. In that very brevity all life is one:

"One thing comes and another thing goes:
Frosts in November drive away the rose;
Like a blowing ember the windflower blows
And drives away the snows."

How did the poet face this inexorable passing of time? She offered no belief in personal immortality as a solace in confronting death. But in the absence of such belief she did not feel the need of fearing death. For her it seemed the opportunity of a complete merging, more or less mystical, with all the universe. The noble "Hymn to Earth" and the more lightly mannered "Letter to V——" suggest it. "Farewell, Sweet Dust" more explicitly states it:

"Farewell, sweet dust; I was never a miser:
  Once, for a minute, I made you mine:
  Now you are gone, I am none the wiser
  But the leaves of the willow are bright as wine."

In the light of such belief, death could never be "other than a friend."

The strain of mysticism in Elinor Wylie that gave glimpses of the ultimate unity of the universe must not be interpreted in terms of a maudlin sentimentality. True, as in "Cold-blooded Creatures," she felt that animals bear sorrows of life, just as do men; but she did not identify herself with them. Nor did she identify herself with all people; her discrimination, her esthetic judgment dictated choices for her, as she somewhat ironically made clear in "Preferences." But her mystical apperception did prevent her from withdrawing from people; it enabled her to feel a tie with them and filled her with a great pity and forbearance for them. "A Crowded Trolley Car" suggests the divinity she saw in man, a divinity which all men shared. She could not agree with all men; she raged against some; but she could hate none:

"If any have a stone to throw
It is not I, ever or now."

345

Her feelings stirred her; but her intellect controlled her feelings, gave her perspective, and helped her to be tolerant:

> "But none has merited my fear,
>   And none has quite escaped my smile."

Little in her philosophical outlook is intrinsically modern. What, then, makes her a modern poet? Her life could have been lived as it was lived only in the twentieth century and her life indubitably colored her thoughts and feelings; that is part of her modernity. But what is more important—and here again the paradoxical and incongruous appear—she is modern because, with characteristic modern courage and independence, she defied the conventions of what a modern poet should be and should write. She was true to herself, not to what her contemporaries laid down as standards. They might concern themselves with machinery, and industry, with labor, with war and peace, and with the social wrongs of civilization, making them all fit subject for poetic treatment. Not Elinor Wylie. Her spirit was not the spirit of modern industrialized society; it was more at home in the past then it was in the present. And that is the spirit that her poetry reflects.

There is throughout her poems a hovering sense of another time and place, of a romantic era of beauty and weird doings. Ghosts, witchcraft, enchantment, falconry, knight errantry, alchemy, astrology, these furnished her with modes of thought.

"I have been accused
Of gold and silvery trickery, infused
With blood of meteors, and moonstones which
Are cold as eyeballs in a flooded ditch."

This accusation of witchcraft could be supported by such poems as "The Madwoman's Miracle" and "Incantation." "The Devil in Seven Shires" might have come direct from the Middle Ages. The essence of the romantic and fabulous past is distilled in "King's Ransom." Her ideas were expressed not so frequently in the language of her own times as in that of the systems of thought of other centuries. Phrases culled haphazardly from her poems have about them the aura of the past: "my bands of silk and miniver," "planetary war," "the only engine which can fabricate." These most certainly are not the language of everyday speech. Nor are such phrases as "translucent dream," "veiled, prismatic plain," "lacquered, nacred curve," "ordered bruit," "sarcastic sigil"; or such forms of words as blessèd, unslakèd, confusion pronounced in four syllables, or imagination in six.

This was a complete reversal of the principle governing the writing of much modern poetry, that of employing the language and rhythm of ordinary speech to create new beauty. But, on the other hand, it was not evidence of a practice against which that principle protested; it was not the slavish following of a mold already set, the easy acceptance of trite, worn "poetic diction." There was no element of the ready-made about

347

it. The words may have had connotations of another age; but their use was Elinor Wylie's own. Her manner was not borrowed; it was peculiarly hers. "I have found a certain way to write," she said while she was at work on her novel, *Jennifer Lorn*, "and I don't know where it comes from. Do you think it can be a throw-back to some ancestor?"

However deep in her unconscious was the source of this individuality of manner, its perfection—and the perfection of all her work—was not spontaneous. Her craftsmanship was the result of constant exercise and discipline. Writing was work and could be, at times, very hard work. For her, poetry was not the fruit of idleness. "People are always worrying about the hardships of artificial flower makers and rollers of scented cigarettes," she explained, "and a really hard-worked sonneteer may be a shocking sight when he is sweating over the sestet."

Training, added to her genius—for training, alone, could not have accomplished it—gave her exquisite control of poetic technique. Her rhymes, for example, are original, clever, and witty, but not tortured. She frequently used the feminine rhyme form, the rhyming of two or more syllables; but the effect was robust, not fragile. Surprise and strength, both are present in such rhymes as: *never is, precipice; Chelsea, palsey; lozenges, in these; ovens, province; slowly as, magnolias.* How delicately her ear was attuned to sound can be suggested by thus lifting rhymes from their context;

348

but it is more vividly shown by quoting entire lines, such lines, say, as

> "I've chaines o' coral like rowan berries,
>   An' a cramoisie mantle that cam' froe Paris."

or these, with their nice balance of rhyme and alliteration:

> "Yea, through your body pale as glass
>   I saw the petals of the grass
>   Wave in the wind and softly stir
>   As seaweed under seawater."

Frequently, as in the poem "To a Book," words are used almost as embroidery, an intricately patterned, painstakingly stitched decoration. The decoration then becomes an intellectual one. "Lucent circle," "archangelic levity," "sidereal blossom," "terrestrial malfeasance," "lunar quietude"—these are but a few of the ornamental phrases in that poem. Quite as frequently, words are used for their sensory value. There is the sense of smell in "apple-scented rain." In the sense of sight, color was, possibly, the strongest element. The poet's particular fondness for silver is shown in her title "Silver Filigree." Silver runs like a gleaming thread throughout her poems; there are silver skies, silver rings, carved silver, silver leaves, "silver-pointed willow boughs." A startling study in color, this instance in black and white, is the poem "Incantation":

"A white well
In a black cave;
A bright shell
In a dark wave.

.　　.　　.

A bright spark
Where black ashes are;
In the smothering dark
One white star."

And, to be quite paradoxical, rarely has sound ever been better suggested than by that picture in terms of its opposite, that perfect picture of silence, "Velvet Shoes."

This unerring instinct for the proper detail manifests itself in an exactness of phrase that is unforgettable. Eyes are "starred with salt"; the sea is "wind-spun"; trees are "reverential"; a hand is "sudden as an asp." The phrase grows into a metaphor, as in the red carpet that the poet would lay down in homage to Shelley:

"I would unroll the rounded moon and sun
And knit them up for you to walk upon."

Or, the building up of details presents such perfect pictures, as in "Miranda's Supper":

"Between the proud and painted stalks,
Plucked from Corinth, Miranda walks;
Pale, elegant, at point to vanish;
Her shoes are French, her shawl is Spanish;
Her silk in pure Manchurian rustles;

350

Three novices went blind at Brussels
To weave the enigma of her scarf;
Her lawns amazed the India Wharf
With webbed enchantment like a witch's
Before they flew in feather-stitches
To flounce her meanest petticoat."

In that other element of poetic technique, meter, she showed an equal sureness. Frequently, she seemed to write poems to tunes that were singing in her head. Poems in old ballad form, like "Robin Hood's Heart" and "The Puritan's Ballad," suggest the songs her old Scotch nurse sang to her when she was a child. Another of her favorite verse forms was a compact form, short-lined, with staccato rhythm. "The Eagle and the Mole" with its quatrains of iambic trimeter couplets illustrates this use of short, close-rhymed lines; so, too, does "Peregrine" with its two-stress lines:

"Liar and bragger
He had no friend
Except a dagger
And a candle-end."

Quite in contrast to these quick, racing meters is that other of her favorite forms, the sonnet. From "Atavism," her earliest sonnet, through those like "Unwilling Admission," "False Prophet," "A Red Carpet for Shelley," to the culminating "One Person" sequence of nineteen poems, she showed consummate skill.

Fixed verse forms, however, never constrained her. She felt herself free to experiment. A thoroughly delightful result is "Little Sonnet," wherein tetrameter lines are substituted for the pentameter. Equally satisfying is a poem like "Shepherd's Holiday," experimental and flexible, in which two five-lined stanzas are followed by this stanza made up of seven lines of varying lengths:

"Too silent for the neighbors, too simple for the towns-
    people,
  What shall we do who love each other so?
  I'll teach your gray sheep
  To guard you from the steep,
  You'll catch me back from drowning where my dark
    lake lies deep,
  I'll pluck a feather pillow that shall sing you to sleep
  Up among the rocks where the blueberries grow."

It is strange, in view of the poet's skill, to find occasional flaws in the perfect structure of her poems. Carl Van Doren in an introduction to her sonnets * points out that a line is missing in the octave of "One Person," an omission which he did not notice when he heard it read by the poet. There is a similar omission in the third sonnet of "Wild Peaches," a deficiency on which no comment seems ever to have been made. That the poet, meticulous as she always was, did not discover and correct these errors suggests the force of feeling

* Carl Van Doren, editor: *The Borzoi Reader,* Alfred A. Knopf.

that carried her beyond the dictates of rules of poetics. The same force of feeling sweeps over the reader who, too, is usually unaware of such errors until some syllable-counting critic makes them known.

Such rare discrepancies as crept into Elinor Wylie's poetry are unimportant; they serve primarily to point up the perfected art and beauty of her poems. Technical rules for rhyme and meter—rules kept or broken—cannot explain the beauty of a poem like the very brief, very tender "Little Elegy":

> "Withouten you
> No rose can grow;
> No leaf be green
> If never seen
> Your sweetest face;
> No bird have grace
> Or power to sing;
> Or anything
> Be kind, or fair,
> And you nowhere."

In that, as in so many of her poems, there is a unified completeness. Within herself, spirit and intellect may have struggled. In her poetry they became reconciled; subject and form complemented each other and became one.

## POETICAL WORKS

| | |
|---|---|
| NETS TO CATCH THE WIND | *Harcourt, Brace and Co.* |
| BLACK ARMOUR | *George H. Doran Co.* |
| TRIVIAL BREATH | *Alfred A. Knopf, Inc.* |
| ANGELS AND EARTHLY CREATURES | |
| | *Alfred A. Knopf, Inc.* |
| COLLECTED POEMS | *Alfred A. Knopf, Inc.* |

*WILLIAM BUTLER YEATS*

## WILLIAM BUTLER YEATS

A T a dinner in Dublin in 1935, a toast was proposed
to a man who had "served Ireland honestly
and fearlessly in serving his art." The man was
William Butler Yeats; the occasion, the dinner tendered
him by the Irish Academy of Letters in celebration of
his seventieth birthday. The dinner was perhaps unusual as a contradiction of the saying that a prophet is
not without honor save in his own country. The toast
definitely was unusual in its accuracy of statement.
With a nice regard for values, it described Yeats's work,
giving importance to what was important. For, dear
as were Ireland and its cause to the poet's heart, he
saw his service to his country always in terms of his
art and in that service, in spite of pressure to do otherwise, he made no compromise with his art.

To understand Yeats and his work, it is necessary, if
not to accept, at all events to acknowledge the possibility of certain points of view. However insistent one may
be that for himself the five senses alone are the ultimate
test for validity of experience, one must realize that
there are others who have faith in intuition, in mystical
experience, in supernatural knowledge. Such a person
was Yeats. He believed that the coming of seabirds was
an omen of death in his family; he heard disembodied

357

voices reproving him for some thought or act; he knew —or almost knew—of thefts of mortals by fairies. "I did not believe with my intellect," he acknowledged, "that you could be carried away body and soul, but I believed with my emotions—the belief of the country people made that easy." Out of this emotional belief, the world of faery and of Irish mythology took on reality for him; esoteric cults and mystic systems of thought produced a philosophy of life. For Yeats, the world of emotions and beliefs was fully as important as the world of external events. To appreciate this fact is fundamental to an understanding of the poet and his poetry.

William Butler Yeats, named for his paternal grandfather, the rector at Tyllylish Downs, Ireland, was born June 13, 1865, at Sandymount, near Dublin. His father was John Butler Yeats, a painter, a man of strong feelings and definite convictions. His mother was one of the Pollexfen family of Sligo, a family of seamen and merchants, one with a background of substantiality and of aristocracy; her mother, in turn, had been a Middleton, a family interested in the ways of the Irish folk, believing strongly in their superstitions and in supernatural happenings.

Yeats was the oldest of a family of three boys and two girls, of whom one boy died as a child. The young family spent most of their early years with their Pollexfen grandparents at Sligo. It is a picture of a sensitive, timid child that Yeats draws of himself in his autobiography. In spite of sisters and brothers, horse, pony, dogs, and garden, he felt the pangs of loneliness. In spite of kindness, he came to fear his grandfather, William Pollexfen, whom "it was the custom to fear and admire"; in fact, he confesses, "I think I confused my grandfather with God." His boyish thoughts were colored by a fear of death. In his adult memory, his childhood loomed as a long unhappiness, an unhappiness, however, created not so much by others as by his own mind.

It is quite obvious that these youthful years could not have been years of continuous misery. There were joyous episodes, play in the garden, adventures on the water, visits to Middleton relatives. There was the warm friendship with the Pollexfen stableboy, who opened for him the world of poetry through a book of Orange rhymes. There was, too, his congenial uncle, George Pollexfen, with whom there developed a close and warm relationship and who was later to be his fellow adventurer in mystic experiments.

Important for his later development as poet was his boyhood contact with the Irish countryside; his awed hearing of old Irish tales of kings and heroes, of the wonders of fairies—euphemistically called "the others" —of the inexplicable behavior of certain country folk— inexplicable, indeed, save to those who knew what fairies could accomplish—of the superstitious relating of events in this world to those in another.

Important, too, as a possible explanation for the conflict of forces within Yeats's own temperament was the conflict which he felt existed between his father and his mother's family. His father was an artist, with an artist's outlook on life; he did not force himself to fit into any conventional world of thought; and he was very far from being the financially solid business man or man of affairs which the Pollexfen family held in approval. Alert possibly to the disapproval of his in-laws and perhaps even acknowledging some justification for it, he had told his son, "You must do everything well that the Pollexfens respect, though you must do other things also." The Pollexfens, people of property, were evidently sure of themselves and of their position in life. Certainly that was manifested in their good-by to the little boy who, with his family, was leaving Ireland for London: "Here you are somebody. There you will be nobody at all."

It was a ten-year-old nobody who found himself in London, in a London, however, not wholly unfamiliar to him. A few years before, he had spent some time there, living alone with his father, meeting his father's friends, sharing his father's experiences. That existence was quite different from the new one which he entered. Now both parents, his sisters, and his brother were with him.

With the settling of his family in London, Yeats went to the Godolphin School at Hammersmith, there continuing the education which had been begun at a dame's school in Sligo. He did not adjust himself readily or well to his new school. He was overwhelmed by a feeling of strangeness and of inferiority. His Irish birth and background marked him as different from the other boys. That was sufficient cause to provoke innumerable fights; and these fights continued until one day by chance he showed his skill at swimming and diving and thus was able to command some respect for his abilities. Scholastically, too, these early school years were difficult. Late in learning to read, he proved to be only a fair student. What scholastic interests he then had were chiefly scientific, aroused first by reading an old eighteenth century encyclopaedia and manifested by the collecting of moths and butterflies.

Much more important than school to his growth and development was the influence of his father and his father's friends. Those early contacts with the artistic life which he had known a few years before were renewed; and the artistic life of London at that time was an awakened and lively one. A new spirit animated art, a desire to bring it nearer to the individual, to have it mold the forms of ordinary, domestic life. The period was one of discussions of esthetic theories and of formulation of new doctrines. The young Yeats met his father's friends, among whom were the poets William Morris and Edward Dowden and the artist and novelist William De Morgan. He listened to their animated conversations and so acquired an education that no formal school could have given him.

But even if there had been no such group of able and interesting people, association with his father, alone, would have educated the boy. The elder Yeats read him poetry, emphasizing always drama and action, poems like "The Lay of the Last Minstrel" and "Lays of Ancient Rome"—"the first poetry that had moved me after the stable-boy's *Orange Rhymes.*" He read him *Ivanhoe.* He took him to the theater where, among other performances, he saw that of Sir Henry Irving as Hamlet. (Incidentally, the boy immediately chose Hamlet as an ideal, indeed dramatizing himself as that hero.) So much did Yeats learn with his father's help, learn thus through his ears and eyes that in later years he said of himself, "I have remembered nothing I read, but only those things that I heard or saw."

However stimulating and glamorous London may at times have seemed, it did not bring the boy happiness. His school years were colored by a basic dislike for England and by a nostalgic turning toward Ireland. Love for Ireland was kept alive and fostered by his mother, who made this one exception to her customary disapproval of any display of emotion. His was a love so terrific and enveloping that walking along a London street, a child no older than ten, he longed for a piece of earth from the road at Sligo that he might kiss it.

Ireland was still home to Yeats, particularly that part of Ireland about Sligo. He visited there each year at his grandparents' home. Finally, when he was fifteen, his family left London to return to his beloved country, moving to Howth, a town a short distance from Dublin.

A good-looking youngster, tall and lanky, with shaggy black hair, he went in to Dublin each day to the Erasmus Smith School, established in a building that had once been Dean Swift's mansion. He seemed to fit in easily with his Irish schoolmates, who proved much more cordial to the newcomer than the boys in England had been.

Strangely enough, in view of his later interests, he was a bad student in history and in literature, and a good one in geometry. He was interested in mechanics and perfected—of all things!—a burglar alarm. He continued his youthful interest in science, spending long afternoons with his schoolmates on the cliffs of Howth in search of specimens for scientific collections. That interest was colored by the controversy then raging over Darwin's theory of evolution. Frankly a materialist at this time, Yeats accepted the theory and argued on its behalf.

In Dublin, as in London, Yeats's formal schooling was supplemented by what he learned from his father. The trip from Howth each morning was made early enough for him to breakfast with his father in his Dublin studio. His father continued his habit of reading aloud to him from the English poets, discussing points of style, stressing over and over the elements of drama and passion.

The association between father and son was very close. At his father's urging, Yeats, after finishing school, studied art. But technical methods taught at the art school were different from those practiced by his father. Indeed, the whole atmosphere was different from the artistic atmosphere to which he was accustomed. He found at the school no critical judgment of pictures and but little learning at all as a background for art. He, alone, of all the students, for example, had any knowledge of English life and of current English literature.

Gradually, out of his studies at school, his association with his father, and his own independent thinking, he developed a theory of art and, in so doing, took his first step away from the scientific materialism which, somehow, he had begun to hate. Differing from his father who insisted that one must paint what one saw, he felt that only beautiful things should be painted. Rejecting an art based on realism, he longed for one which in symbolism and associative value might be allied to poetry.

Soon, indeed, his interest in poetry superseded his interest in pictorial art. He began to write poems, poems that were for the most part marked strongly by the influence of Shelley and of Spenser. His father, with paternal and so, perhaps, forgivable pride, suggested that these early writings had almost—if not completely —all the perfection of the poet's later work. "He had a great faculty! He could do anything that he liked in verse." Yeats, himself, realized that success was not so easily achieved, that those first attempts at writing left much to be desired, much that could be accomplished only through struggle and discipline. "My lines," he said, "but seldom scanned, for I could not understand the prosody in the books, although there were many lines that taken by themselves had music."

What phases of his developing personality thus sought expression in verse? A fond relationship with his uncle, George Pollexfen, who was absorbed in studies of the occult, turned Yeats's interests in the same direction. Yeats took part in psychical research; he became a member of the Theosophical Society, a cult then growing into prominence as a reaction against the rationalistic, scientific materialism of the mid-century. He had experienced, too, an adolescent love affair with a girl who was engaged to someone else. Tenuous at best, and probably at no time very real, it came to an end and in its ending created in him a spirit of aloofness and withdrawal. This was intensified by his enthusiasm for Thoreau's *Walden,* which he had come to know through his father and which produced a desire to retreat from the life about him and live alone on an island called Innisfree.

These feelings and yearnings, first formulated in his youthful years, were to appear not only in his early poetry but many years later in his more mature work. How long he was able to store up poetic material before transmuting it into poetry is indicated by an episode of his teens. He asked a cousin to take out a boat with him at midnight that he might learn the early dawn habits of certain water birds. "I had wanted the birds' cries," he later wrote, "for the poem that became fifteen years afterwards 'The Shadowy Waters.'"

At nineteen, then a student at Dublin University, he had the satisfaction of seeing his first printed poem, "The Island of Statues," published in *The Dublin University Review.* The poem was an Arcadian play, a weak imitation of Spenser.

The poet had not yet found himself or his material.

He was still seeking subjects other than those near and familiar to him. From the unreal, pastoral life of Spenser, he turned to a period remote in time and in place, that of the Spanish Inquisition, and used it as the subject of a dramatic poem, *Mosada,* published when he was twenty-one.

But just about this time another influence entered his life, one that was to re-direct it and give it a center of thought and activity. Through Ellen O'Leary he became acquainted with her brother John, an ardent Irish patriot, whose enthusiastic follower he became. At the O'Leary home he met men and women, eager workers in the cause of Ireland, who became his lifelong friends. Imbued with their zeal, he joined the Young Ireland Society, a workman's club to which he gave talks on Irish history and Irish literature. Through debates and discussions with O'Leary, through reading Irish books, his very early fascination with Ireland and things Irish was kindled anew; he was stirred by a great purpose, that of formulating a distinctive and worth-while Irish literature.

In the late 1880's, definitely abandoning the art of his father for literature, he left Dublin and took up residence once more in London. As a young journalist, he received one of his first commissions through the poet, W. E. Henley, to write some Irish articles for *Chambers' Encyclopaedia*. He was now part of the active intellectual life of the city. Through William Morris, of whom he said, "I would choose to live his life, poetry and all, rather than my own or any other man's," he attended meetings of the Socialist League, where he met, among others, George Bernard Shaw. Bedford Park, the community in which he lived, had a small theater adapted for amateur performances. He became interested in drama; he became friends with others similarly interested, particularly with Florence Farr and Maude Gonne, both of whom took part in the performances. Under the kindly criticism of his first sponsor, Henley, he continued to write poetry.

He was already formulating a philosophy of poetry dependent on a sense of the past. Poetry seemed to him the heritage of the emotional experience of men of gone-by ages; it should, he felt, find forms and rhythms old enough and familiar enough to become part of the innate rhythm of man. An expression of this belief was his narrative poem, published in 1889, *The Wanderings of Oisin* (sometimes spelled Usheen). It told the story of the pagan Irish mythological hero, Oisin, of his three-hundred-years absence from this world in the world of make-believe and of his final return to a Christianized Ireland. Yeats was turning for subject matter to his own spirit's home—to Ireland. The story of Oisin was familiar to his countrymen. In its ready-made subject he found the means of expressing emotions common to all men and, very particularly, his own desire for escape from the world about him. It was this desire, stirred by the sight of a fountain in a Fleet Street shop window, that found expression about the same time in "The Lake Isle of Innisfree," "my first lyric with anything in its rhythm of my own music."

Developing thus material and method, he began to write freely. His work brought him in contact with other writers in London, with Ernest Dowson, Richard Le Gallienne, Arthur Symons, Ernest Rhys. To save themselves from bitter rivalry and envy of each other, and to develop their work through mutual criticism, these men with others formed "The Rhymers Club," meeting in the Cheshire Cheese, hallowed by memories of Samuel Johnson. Of the club Yeats wrote in 1892 to *The Boston Pilot*, to which he contributed literary letters: "They all believe that the deluge of triolets and rondeaus has passed away, and that we must look once more upon the world with serious eyes and set to music—each according to his lights—the deep soul of humanity." *

Yeats could share whole-heartedly in this purpose of looking "upon the world with serious eyes." But he could not see the soul of humanity in terms of social movements, of political or economic theories. So he quarreled with the manner of such poets as Swinburne, Browning, and Tennyson, who made evident in their poetry their concern with politics, science, history, and religion. Yeats would have none of this; he desired to create a poetry pure, distilled, refined from all purpose and thesis.

With all his intellectualizing, there still remained in Yeats something of the child, acting a part. If he no longer dramatized himself as his old hero, Hamlet, he

* Yeats: *Letters to the New Island,* edited by Horace Reynolds, Harvard University Press.

dramatized himself as his idea of a poet. He let his black hair grow so long that it swept over his forehead to his deep, penetrating eyes. He wore brown velveteen coats, loose flowing ties, and—a particular favorite— a voluminous cape which had been discarded by his father some twenty years before.

The poet, however affected and stylized he might have appeared, led an active, well-filled life in London. Yet his heart was not there. "Any breath of Ireland," he wrote to a friend, "in this hateful London, where you cannot go five paces without seeing some wretched object broken either by wealth or poverty, is good." He was able to escape from detested London to Ireland during the summer. From his contacts there and even more from his desires, he created a Utopian, dream Ireland which became for him the real one.

Yeats's life from the time of this journalistic period is a little difficult to present. Even in his autobiography, the chronological detailing of incidents is not clear. Yet, though one cannot see the ordering of events, the nice fitting with jig-saw puzzle precision of cause and effect, one can see beginning at this time those main threads of thought and of action which, however seemingly opposed, wove themselves into a basic, recognizable pattern. Of these, two were outstanding: one, his work for Ireland; the other, his interest in the occult and in esoteric forms of thought. Together they formed the foundations of his life and his art; for with Yeats, life and art were one.

The predilection for the mystic and metaphysical was

innate with Yeats, his individualized manifestation, perhaps, of the tradition for religion which characterized his father's family. In spite of that tradition, it is true, his father adhered to no fixed formal religion. The younger Yeats, troubled from earliest years by problems of death and sin, could find no answer either in any of the historic faiths. Contemporary science, furthermore, which for a time won his loyalty, was upsetting to conventional religion. But Yeats, after his first adherence to Darwinism, found the materialism of Victorian science too devastating for his spirit. The Celtic strain in him, with its natural leaning toward the mystic, could not tolerate a mechanical explanation of the universe. Without a religion to cling to, unable to accept a scientific theory in its stead, Yeats still felt the need of a system of thought to explain, guide, and comfort. He turned toward Oriental religions, mystic cults, systems of magic, all of them offering to those who will believe some explanation of an otherwise inexplicable universe.

One after another of these semi-religions claimed his attention. While a student in Dublin, as a member of a group called the Hermetic Students, he came under the influence of a Persian, a professor of Oriental languages at Trinity College, who talked persuasively of the magicians of the East. Next a Brahmin philosopher from London engaged his interest. In London, he was attracted by the growing faith of Theosophy. He attended spiritual séances held by Mme. Blavatsky, the leader of the movement, at which séances messages were supposed to be received from spirits of the dead. He became a believer in a system of visual symbols which, handed down from antiquity and shrouded in mystery, still had the power to wake specific thoughts and mental images. He accepted the idea of automatic writing, writing prompted by some power outside the writer, himself. Long before the popularizing of Freudian psychology, he became a student of the unconscious.

Toward all these systems he tried to be objective and critical, maintaining what is called a "margin of scientific doubt," and criticizing others who believed implicitly. But in them were elements congenial to his spirit. These he absorbed and modified, constructing of them at last an involved philosophy for himself. This philosophy he finally expressed in *A Vision*, a confused and complicated exposition of an all-inclusive belief in a cycle of mankind corresponding somehow to the twenty-eight phases of the moon.

Of more significance, however, to his poetry was his belief in a Divine Mind, which he had formulated in his earlier years, and explained thus in his article on "Magic" in *Ideas of Good and Evil:*

"(1) That the borders of our minds are ever shifting, and that many minds can flow into one another as it were, and create or reveal a single mind, a single energy.

"(2) That the borders of our memories are as shifting, and that our memories are a part of one great memory, the memory of Nature, herself.

"(3) That this great mind and great memory can be evoked by symbols."

371

To Yeats's way of thinking—further explanation may not be amiss—each personal imagination is a part of this Mind. Scholars and visionaries contribute their thoughts to it and in turn draw from it inspiration for the expression of beauty and truth. It is a vast fund, built up and handed down through the ages. In the light of this theory, folk-lore and myths assume a new importance, since they represent the accumulated wisdom of the past; and symbols play a unique part because they are an accepted form for expressing thoughts quickly and vividly and for evoking deep emotions.

Poetry, as part of the Great Mind, partook of its nature and used its methods. Poetic truths seemed to him the nearest approach to authoritative religion. Poetry became a form of religious magic, a means of conjuring up the beauty and truth of the past, of distilling it, and of presenting it to the present in a new form to pass again into the general mind. The poet, for him, became a combination of magician, seer, and priest.

This concern with the abstract and theoretical ran parallel in time and in interest with Yeats's active work for Ireland, that poor relation of England, that land of poverty and distress, of turmoil, economic unrest, and political agitation. The fire of Irish spirit, kindled in him earlier by John O'Leary, had not died. In London, Yeats had been a member of the Irish Literary Society of London, made up of London residents of Irish birth. In Dublin, he became one of the founders of the National Literary Society, which, affiliated with local Young Ireland Societies in small towns, had for its purpose the distribution of books on Irish subjects. From the very beginning of his work for Ireland, Yeats concentrated his efforts on the literary aspect. Land reform and political propaganda he regarded only as sources of bitterness and disruption; in the shared heritage of Irish literature, alone, he saw a chance to re-create the soul of Ireland.

With this resurgence of the Irish soul, the Celtic Renaissance, Yeats was most closely identified:

> "Know that I would accounted be
> True brother of a company
> That sang, to sweeten Ireland's wrong
> Ballad and story, rann and song."

In his life-long devotion to Irish literature, he made clear that his concept of it was something quite different from the conventional notions held by most non-Irish. It differed just as much from the idea of the patronizing presentation of an awkward oaf as it did from the sentimental one of a "convivial Ireland with the traditional tear and smile." It differed, furthermore, from the chauvinistic ideas of some of the Irish themselves, with their insistence upon the revival and use in Irish literature of the Gaelic language and upon the necessity of making Irish literature primarily an instrument of political propaganda. For him Irish literature was founded in the Irish spirit as molded by and manifested in centuries of Irish folk-thinking; for him it was part of the great body of English literature and so should be written in English.

This effort to present Ireland to the world and to unite Ireland itself through this literary presentation engrossed Yeats and gave direction not only to his socialized, organizational work but to his own literary activity. His first contribution in that direction was the editing of *A Book of Irish Verse,* a collection which he hoped would "lead a world sick with theories to those sweet well waters of primeval poetry, upon whose edge still linger the brotherhoods of wisdom, the immortal moods."

His interest in Irish folk-lore cannot be mentioned without mentioning Lady Gregory, of Dublin, who directed and fostered that interest. Lady Gregory was a kindly and generous influence in his life. Over a period of twenty years, he spent many months at her home in Coole, which became the center of his memories and desires. She lent him money that enabled him to write without feeling financial pressure. "Because of those summers, because of that money, I was able through the greater part of my working life to write without thought of anything but the beauty or the utility of what I wrote." * She helped him in his work in the theater, which formed the next phase of his Irish literary activity.

The Irish, themselves, received the books distributed among them without enthusiasm. So the leaders of the

* Yeats: *The Autobiography of William Butler Yeats,* The Macmillan Company.

National Literary Society realized that some other means was necessary to renew interest in their literary heritage. The Society decided that if the Irish would not read literature, they would, at any rate, listen to it; so plans were made for an Irish theater. In the late eighteen-nineties, the Irish Literary Theatre (which shortly was renamed the Irish National Theatre and, a few years later, became the Abbey Theatre group) was formed for the purpose of producing Irish plays by Irish playwrights. Here, too, the insistence was placed upon works of pure literature. Notice was sent to those submitting plays: "We do not desire propagandist plays, nor plays written mainly to serve some obvious moral purpose; for art seldom concerns itself with those interests or opinions that can be defended by argument, but with realities of emotion and character that become self-evident when made vivid to the imagination."

Consistent with this purpose, on May 8, 1899, the Theatre produced in the Antient Concert Rooms in Dublin as its opening bill two plays: *The Heather Field* by Edward Martyn; and *Countess Cathleen,* by Yeats, which he had written in 1892. The latter told the story of a pious countess who sold her own soul to the devil so that with the money food might be bought for the starving peasants on her lands. Because of this central incident, the play was attacked by the religious as a libel on Catholic womanhood. The storm of controversy that it aroused was but one of many that centered in the theater.

In spite of discussions and quarrels, Yeats continued with his connection with the Theatre and with his mission of spreading knowledge of Ireland through its literature. Inextricably bound to his name in this work are those of Lady Gregory, who was the Theatre's chief sponsor, and of John Synge, whom Yeats persuaded to write for the Theatre. Yeats, himself, wrote a number of plays, some in prose and some in verse. To further the main purpose of all this dramatic work, he made a number of trips, including several to the United States, lecturing about the Celtic movement and arousing tremendous interest in it.

The work did not proceed smoothly. Dissension arose. There was disillusionment about people. There were bitter quarrels over methods. There were disappointments at failures.

All these are reflected in his poetry, in the marked change of manner that distinguishes his later from his earlier writing. For it was in his writing that the two strands interwove: the zeal for the Celtic cause and the mystic element in his temperament. His service to the cause he saw in terms of his literary work; and his work, particularly his poetry, he expressed in accordance with his belief in the Great Mind.

Where did he find the fund of beauty and truth? the symbols that could evoke them? He discovered them anew in his Irish inheritance, in Irish folk-lore, mythology, manner of living, in the very atmosphere of Ireland.

So, after his first tentative poems cast in imitation

of others, he put his belief into practice and developed a manner of his own. Association, in his visits to Paris, with writers of the French Symbolist school of literature had served to strengthen his belief in the efficacy of symbols; and gave further emphasis to his insistence that a symbolic phrase or figure had power beyond itself, power to suggest more than was inherent in it. He wrote and wrote incessantly. Neither his work in London on *The Savoy,* a magazine with Arthur Symons as editor, nor his work in Dublin with the Irish Theatre interrupted the creation of plays and poems.

Always, as he had so early and clearly manifested, his interest lay in his art; always his work was for art's sake. As a result, he found himself at variance with other writers of the late nineties and nearly nineteen-hundreds, who were using their literature for the promulgation of pet social and political theories.

The World War of 1914-1918 broke. There was a shattering of all that Yeats held dear. Fantasy, beauty, peace were destroyed by the stark reality of warfare. Political unrest in Ireland deepened and broke out in open rebellion. External events seemed almost more than the poet could stand. The war gave him the inspiration for no poem. A natural disposition to withdraw from life now became more marked. However, in 1917, he married a Miss Georgia Lees; to them were born a son and a daughter. But the small family, instead of living in London or in Dublin, made their home in an old, sequestered farmhouse and tower, Thoor Ballylee, on the coast of Ireland.

"I, the poet William Yeats,
With old mill boards and sea-green slates,
And smithy work from the Gort forge,
Restored this tower for my wife George;
And may these characters remain
When all is ruin once again."

Yet it must not be thought that he lived in complete self-imposed isolation. He continued to give himself to his countrymen. With the founding of the Irish Free State, he was appointed to its Senate, the Dail Eireann, in which he served from 1922 to 1928, until his poor health necessitated his resigning. He was active in that body, urging the passage of liberal bills. He was active, too, in answer to the demands made on public men, inspecting schools, attending meetings, judging exhibitions.

His literary life, steadfastly pursued during these years, won him acclaim. In 1923, he was awarded the Nobel Prize for Literature "for his consistently emotional poetry, which in the strictest artistic form expresses a people's spirit." He received honorary degrees from Oxford, Cambridge, and the University of Dublin. In 1935, as has been noted, the Irish Academy of Letters, which he together with Bernard Shaw had been instrumental in founding, honored him on his seventieth birthday. In 1937, he was given the Gregory Medal by the Academy; and that same year a medal by the International Mark Twain Society—a fact made known to the public only after his death.

That occurred on January 28, 1939. The illness that had forced him to resign from the Irish Senate had compelled him to spend his winters in warm climates. So it was away from his beloved Ireland, in France, in Roquebrune, a little town on the Riviera, that death found him.

What kind of person was this man whom his own nation honored? Physically, he fulfilled the conventional concept of a poet. Tall, stooped, long-haired, flowing tie, an air of abstraction—it was almost as if a caricaturist had drawn him. More than any other feature, his eyes immediately stamped him. "His dark eyes," a writer in the *New Republic* * described him, "oblique and set far into his head, gave him a cryptic and remote suggestion. His pursed lips closed as on a secret. He opened them for utterance almost as in a dream."

With a flavor of theatricality, he put himself in settings that emphasized the mystic element of his poetry and then proceeded to live up to the settings. His rooms, dimly lit by candles, were barely furnished, a long, deal table, cluttered by manuscripts and books, holding the center of the place. Kneeling before this table, the poet would read to chance visitors, intoning his words, absorbed completely in his art, totally unaware of whether his listeners were active or asleep, staying or departing.

Such indifference or unawareness of others was a de-

* F. H.: "Books and Things," *New Republic,* November 24, 1923.

vice he had created for his own protection. He withdrew into himself, a completely introspective, subjective person. St. John Ervine, the Irish writer, called him "extraordinarily aloof from life"; and after an acquaintanceship of ten years felt that he knew him little better than when they had first met.

Some clues to this attitude are given in his writings. He tells us that he was a most self-conscious individual. He had joined a group studying French and somehow had felt himself expand. When his sister asked to join the group, too, he delayed giving her an answer, "for I knew that the new and admirable self I was making would turn, under family eyes, into plain rag-doll." If his family made him acutely aware of himself, his Irish compatriots made him equally so. For, years later, imagining himself to be unpopular in Ireland, he asked his publishers not to send any of his books to Ireland for review, "a decision kept for many years." "Gradually," so he wrote in *Letters to the New Island,* "I overcame my shyness a little, though I am still struggling with it and cannot free myself from the belief that it comes from lack of courage, that the problem is not artistic but moral."

Undoubtedly, a contributory cause for this shyness was that early uprooting from the Irish environment of which he felt himself so much a part. To compensate for the feeling of not belonging, of insecurity or inferiority, his imagination was called into play, supplying him with what he missed in actuality. The real and the unreal lost their distinguishing characteristics.

While his imagination, on the one hand, encouraged him in his divorce from reality, another quality steeled him to face it. He possessed the ability to discipline himself; and once aware of a weakness, exerted himself in an effort to overcome it. He realized that he felt ill at ease among people he did not know well; so he "would often go to a strange house where I would spend a wretched hour for schooling sake." The same motive prompted him in his Dublin days to join a discussion club.

During these years of inner unrest and efforts to overcome it, the search for peace and security manifested itself in two forms. On the one hand was the eager desire for a feeling of permanence, of the continuation of identity, the persistence of self; on the other, was a striving for something outside himself, the pursuit of an ideal of beauty.

For the former, a sense of attachment, whether to family or to place, was necessary. Yeats recalled that even as a little boy he realized that "all the well-known families had their grotesque or tragic or romantic legends, and I often said to myself how terrible it would be to go away and die where nobody would know my story."

For the latter, the quest itself was important, the tireless seeking for a perfection that could never be achieved, for the

"Far-off, most secret, and inviolate Rose."

For Yeats was enough of a Celt to share in the description of the Celtic race given by the French literary critic, Renan: "The essential element of the Celt's poetic life is the *adventure*—that is to say, the pursuit of the unknown, an endless quest after an object ever flying from desire."

This search for the ideal of beauty, for Yeats the beauty of poetry, was marked always by a sense of integrity, a steadfast refusal to compromise. Art for him had to be free from what he called "impurities," from speculation about social problems, from propaganda, from any purpose other than the creation of beauty. He decried the "moral uplift" which he felt marred much of American writing. "A great artist," he said, "has only one consideration—that is reality. If he is a poet, it will be the reality of inner life." It was his inner life that he put into his verse; and with such uncompromising loyalty to his ideals that of him may be said what he wrote of his comrades:

> "But never made a poorer song
> That you might have a heavier purse
> Nor gave loud service to a cause
> That you might have a troop of friends."

Yeats's choice of poetry as his medium of expression must have been the result of some inner, not to be denied compulsion. His early training had been in pictorial art; yet that he rejected. He rejected it so definitely, in fact, that his verse reflects very little of it; it is a verse of moods rather than of pictures. Furthermore, he had deficiencies which had to be overcome before he could write successful poetry. He confessed to having no ear for music; yet, at its best, his verse is most musical. This could be achieved only as the result of unwavering discipline. He deliberately trained himself in poetic craftsmanship. The progress that he made is suggested by two quotations from his prose, both concerned with his method of writing. The first is from his autobiography, about the time of his early work in Irish literature:

"Metrical composition is always very difficult to me, nothing is done upon the first day, not one rhyme is in its place; and when at last the rhymes begin to come, the first rough draft of a six-line stanza takes the whole day. At that time I had not formed a style, and sometimes a six-line stanza would take several days, and not seem finished even then; and I had not learnt, as I have now, to put it all out of my head before night, and so the last night was generally sleepless, and the last day a day of nervous strain."

The second is from "The Bounty of Sweden," written after he had received the Nobel Prize:

"Every now and then, when something has stirred my imagination, I begin talking to myself. . . . When I begin to write I have no object but to find for them some natural speech, rhythm and syntax, and to set it out in some pattern, so seeming old that it may seem all men's speech, and though the labour is very great,

I seem to have used no faculty peculiar to myself, no special gift."

That the labor was great is shown by the various forms that some of his poems took. As a result of his deliberate craftsmanship, material was reworked. Changes were made from one edition to another. Just as Yeats's father was never able to consider a picture finished, so Yeats, himself, found it difficult to finish a poem.

> "The friends that have it I do wrong
> Whenever I remake a song,
> Should know what issue is at stake;
> It is myself that I remake."

Motivating him, always, was his search for perfection.

The changes in the poems took several forms. Sometimes it might be a change of title only, as when "Breasal the Fisherman" appeared in the *Collected Poems* as "The Fish." Sometimes the change consisted of the substitution of one word for another, the reworking of a line or two. For example, "The kings of the old time are fled," a line in the original "The Song of the Happy Shepherd," was changed in the 1933 edition of the poems to "The kings of the old time are dead." How much was achieved by this painstaking jeweler-like artistry may be seen by comparing two versions of "The Sorrow of Love." The earlier version is as follows:

"The brawling of a sparrow in the eaves,
  The full round moon and the star-laden sky
  And the loud song of the ever-singing leaves
  Had hid away earth's old and weary cry.

  And then you came with those red mournful lips
  And with you came the whole of the world's tears
  And all the trouble of her labouring ships
  And all the trouble of her myriad years.

  And now the sparrows warring in the eaves,
  The curd-pale moon, the white stars in the sky,
  And the loud chaunting of the unquiet leaves,
  Are shaken with earth's old and weary cry."

This is its final form:

"The brawling of a sparrow in the eaves,
  The brilliant moon and all the milky sky,
  And all that famous harmony of leaves,
  Had blotted out man's image and his cry.

  A girl arose that had red mournful lips
  And seemed the greatness of the world in tears,
  Doomed like Odysseus and the labouring ships
  And proud as Priam murdered with his peers;

  Arose, and on the instant clamorous eaves,
  A climbing moon upon an empty sky,
  And all that lamentation of the leaves,
  Could but compose man's image and his cry."

If Yeats has been compared to a jeweler because of the delicacy and precision of his work, in still another respect the comparison has force. Just as a jeweler may place a precious stone now in one setting and now in another, so Yeats frequently treasured a motif, using it more than once in the course of years, developing it in various ways. "Hanrahan Laments Because of His Wanderings" is one of Yeats's earlier poems:

> "O where is our Mother of Peace
> Nodding her purple hood?
> For the winds that awakened the stars
> Are blowing through my blood.
> I would that the death-pale deer
> Had come through the mountain side,
> And trampled the mountain away,
> And drunk up the murmuring tide;
> For the winds that awakened the stars
> Are blowing through my blood,
> And our Mother of Peace has forgot me
> Under her purple hood."

Notice how much of it is easily recognized in the later poem, "Maid Quiet":

> "Where has Maid Quiet gone to,
> Nodding her russet hood?
> The winds that awakened the stars
> Are blowing through my blood.
> O how could I be so calm
> When she rose up to depart?

Now words that called up the lightning
Are hurtling through my heart."

Sometimes, it must be admitted, the changes were not improvements. The last stanza of "A Cradle Song" in its final version:

"I sigh that kiss you,
   For I must own
   That I shall miss you
   When you have grown."

lacks the directness and poignancy of the earlier form:

"I kiss you and kiss you,
   My pigeon, my own;
   Ah, how I shall miss you
   When you have grown."

The variations in editions consist not simply of word changes. There are modifications of manner. "The Lamentations of the Old Pensioner," for example, has two completely different forms: the earlier, simple and direct; the latter, more studied and obviously wrought. There are indications, too, of changed feelings and attitudes on the part of the poet. No poem, perhaps, shows that more clearly than "The Dedication of a Book of Stories Selected from the Irish Novelists." Originally, it was a poem delicate, gracious, full of love for Ireland. In its final version, written after discouragement over his work for Ireland, it contains these lines heavy with bitterness:

"I tore it from the barren boughs of Eire,
   That country where a man can be so crossed;

   Can be so battered, badgered and destroyed
   That he's a loveless man."

Yeats's writing—not only his poetry, but his prose
and plays, too—underwent constant revision. "The
Shadowy Waters" was altered innumerable times
through the years. The play, *The Hour-Glass,* was
written both in prose and in verse, and with different
endings. A single situation was used more than once.
In two different plays, *The Full Moon* and *The King
of the Great Clock Tower,* a poor unknown arrives at a
royal court and announces his determination to look
upon the Queen and dance with her. The idea

   "That only God has loved us for ourselves"

is the motif of two completely differently treated poems,
"The Hero, the Girl and the Fool," and "For Anne
Gregory."

This method of writing, of changing forms and of
using material in various ways, should prepare one for
the fact that the volumes of Yeats's published works
are of the most bewildering variety. English editions
are different from American editions. Titles change. A
single work may appear in several collections. Collections may partially duplicate one another. Over a
period of some forty years, Yeats constantly presented
his work in new forms or in new combinations.

The question might arise whether such re-working of material implies a paucity of ideas. In the case of Yeats, it was rather the method of folk-lore, the endless modification of some known fact or accepted thought. It was the application of Yeats's own belief in the Great Mind as the source of all imagination and, particularly, of poetry. "People do not invent, they remember," he said. Writing for him implied not so much creating something new as perfecting what already existed, crystallizing it in as perfect a form as possible so that it might more easily become part of the memory and imagination of men in the future.

In view of such a concept of his art, it cannot be surprising that over the period of his writing career Yeats should manifest definite changes in manner and in attitude. His very earliest poems were well received. A review in 1899 by Arthur Symons said, "Mr. Yeats is the only one among the younger English poets who has the whole poetical temperament, and nothing but the poetical temperament." By that time there had been published *The Wanderings of Oisin, Poems,* and *The Wind Among the Reeds.* The poems were, for the most part, poems of escape; the articulate desire of one who, ill at ease in this world, desires to flee to another world, shadowy, unreal—but better. They were unreal in manner, artificial, affected. They were either filled with faery, shadowy and mysterious with the colors of Irish landscape dimmed by twilight, or else they were lush and extravagant. On the one hand they abounded with subdued notes like *dove-grey* and *moth-hour;* or, on the other hand, they told of lips like a sunset,

"A stormy sunset on doomed ships,"

or of the angel Michael, who

"would go weave out of the stars
A chaplet for your head."

The poems were studded with instances of the then current poetic diction, "honey-pale moon," "lilies of death-pale hope, roses of passionate dream," "thought-woven sails."

*In the Seven Woods,* which appeared in 1904, was written in much the same manner; yet, even in that volume, in such a poem as "The Old Men Admiring Themselves in the Water," sharp, clear-cut, unornamented, were hints of a change about to take place. The change occurred sometime around the year 1912, a deliberate conscious modification of method:

"Years afterwards when I had finished The Wanderings of Oisin, dissatisfied with its yellow and dull green, with all that overcharged color inherited from the romantic movement, I deliberately reshaped my style, deliberately sought out an impression as of cold light and tumbling clouds. I cast off traditional metaphors and loosened my rhythm, and recognizing that all the criticism of life known to me was alien and English, became as emotional as possible but with an emotion which I described to myself as cold."

This fundamental change was announced poetically in "A Coat." The poet, deploring that "fools" have caught and worn the richly embroidered coat of his poetry, declares:

> "Song, let them take it,
>   For there's more enterprise
>   In walking naked."

The new method showed itself in poems in *The Green Helmet and Other Poems* and in *Responsibilities*. The extraneous ornamentation was shed, its place taken by clarity, directness, and simplicity, a new austerity, as in "A Drinking Song":

> "Wine comes in at the mouth
>   And love comes in at the eye;
>   That's all we shall know for truth
>   Before we grow old and die.
>   I lift the glass to my mouth,
>   I look at you, and I sigh."

Increased simplicity showed itself, too, in the details chosen for the poems. The early poetry was filled with mythical beings quite remote from any known on earth; in the later poems, these beings possessed at least some human qualities. No early poem would have included such homely details as these:

> "The gods were sitting at the board
>   In their great house at Slievenamon.

> They sang a drowsy song, or snored,
> For all were full of wine and meat."

This approach toward reality suggests one other manifestation of the change in Yeats's attitude. He found a new source of inspiration for his poems. In addition to his own yearnings and reveries, he began to use as subjects for his poetry his feelings toward people—real people—and toward public events. So, for example, it was a living, flesh-and-blood woman, a friend, of whom he sang in "No Second Troy"; and it was an actual Dublin incident that he decried in "To a Wealthy Man Who Promised a Second Subscription to the Dublin Municipal Gallery If It Were Proved the People Wanted Pictures." No hazy introspection could have prompted such a poem as "To a Friend Whose Work Has Come to Nothing," a poem meant for Lady Gregory to console her for her defeat in her work for the Irish Theatre.

That poem showed a new note that had crept into Yeats's poetry, a note of bitterness and cynicism. The disappointment that almost invariably comes to one engaged in public work did not escape Yeats in his activity for Ireland. Disillusionment arising from his disappointment colored his poetry:

> "Romantic Ireland's dead and gone,
> It's with O'Leary in the grave."

But the regret was not always thus mildly expressed. Deepened and sharpened, it became satire—satire increased, at times, by humor, as it was in "To a Poet, Who Would Have Me Praise Certain Bad Poets, Imitators of His and Mine," wherein the suggestion that he praise was parried by the question

"But was there ever dog that praised his fleas?"

With age and its increasing disillusionment with life, the real world continued to be a sad place for him. But mere imaginative escape from it no longer sufficed. Through his own experience he grew somewhat—if only a little—closer to humanity in general. The realization that his problems were not unique checked still further the wildness and exuberance of his emotions and mannerisms. Still greater restraint entered his poetry, a new quietness of manner, almost conversational in tone.

*The Wild Swans at Coole* contains poems in this mood, such poems as "An Irish Airman Foresees His Death" and the series called "Upon a Dying Lady." Two later volumes, *The Tower* and *The Winding Stair and Other Poems,* exemplify it further. That Yeats, aware always of his art, recognized this change is shown in a statement he made in his book, *A Vision:* "And I put The Tower and The Winding Stair into evidence to show that my poetry has gained in self-possession and power."

There is no diminution of either even in his last book, the posthumously published *Last Poems and Plays.* "The Three Bushes," "What Then?", "Are You Content?" are evidence of this perfected simplicity; so, too, is "Under Ben Bulben," with its closing epitaph:

*"Cast a cold eye*
*On life, on death*
*Horseman, pass by!"*

In the evolution of his manner, Yeats was not restricted by the use of any one single form of writing. Long narrative poems, shorter ballads, lyrics—these all lent themselves to his pen. So, too, did poetic drama. But Yeats was essentially a lyric, not a dramatic poet; so his poetic plays, lacking in dramatic quality, may be considered primarily as poetry and grouped with his poems in a study of his art.

From the time, then, of the writing of "The Lake Isle of Innisfree," the first poem in which the poet actually found himself, Yeats employed a great variety of poetic forms and displayed a number of varying poetic mannerisms. Did he, as a result, fail to stamp his poetry as unmistakably his? Quite the contrary is true. Through variation and development, there remained some fundamental characteristics, uniquely Yeats's. Outstanding is the rhythmic subtlety of his verse, a wavering, deliberately uncertain pulsation, based on natural speech:

> "The trees are in their autumn beauty,
>   The woodland paths are dry,
>   Under the October twilight the water
>   Mirrors a still sky;
>   Upon the brimming water among the stones
>   Are nine-and-fifty swans."

Yeats's meters sound inevitably right to modern ears; lines have not been tortured to fit into rigidly marked compartments. But, in evolving them, Yeats did not feel that he was creating something new. Rather he was seeking to revive the old, compelling effect of ancient chants; he sought—and found—"metrical forms that seemed old enough to have been sung by men half-asleep or riding upon a journey" and, therefore, fundamental enough to be incorporated into the rhythm of today.

Masterly, too, was his use of words not only for their meaning, but for the sheer beauty of their sound:

"I hear lake water lapping with low sounds by the shore."

Alliteration as it is employed in that line or in a line like

"She passed the salley gardens with little snow-white feet"

is a by no means unusual poetic device. But consider its intricate manipulation in the subtle interplay of initial and mid-word *l*'s and *w*'s in:

"Autumn is over the long leaves that love us,
And over the mice in the barley sheaves;
Yellow the leaves of the rowan above us,
And yellow the wet wild-strawberry leaves."

395

The great effectiveness of sound as sound reaches an amazing height in the opening stanza of "The Lover Tells of the Rose in His Heart," with its monosyllables. its harsh *c's*, and—in the third line—its *p's:*

"All things uncomely and broken, all things worn out
    and old,
  The cry of a child by the roadway, the creak of a lum-
    bering cart,
  The heavy steps of the ploughman, splashing the
    wintry mould,
  Are wronging your image that blossoms a rose in the
    deeps of my heart."

The tonal rightness of words makes terminal rhyme less necessary. There is actual rhyme, of course; but assonance and exact repetition are also used. The use of all three in a single poem is illustrated in "Lines Written in Dejection," wherein the rhyme scheme is as follows: *on, bodies, moon, ladies, tears, gone, vanished, sun, vanished, years, sun,* with repetition of *vanished* and *sun* instead of rhyme.

Extended, this device of repetition leads to refrain, varying from that of a single line, through the variations of two lines as:

"And never was piping so sad,
    And never was piping so gay"

to the four-line chorus of "The Stolen Child":

"Come away, O human child!
 To the waters and the wild
 With a faery, hand in hand,
 For the world's more full of weeping than you can
   understand."

Other technical devices of the poets, figures of speech
—similes and metaphors—Yeats also used. One finds
throughout the poems such comparisons as "angers that
are like noisy clouds" and the unforgettable last lines
of *The Countess Cathleen:*

"The years like great black oxen tread the world
 And God the herdsman goads them on behind
 And I am broken by their passing feet."

More individual than these—than rhythm, sound,
figures of speech—was still another characteristic, an
outgrowth of his theory of poetry, his use of symbols.
It cannot be too emphatically stated that these symbols
were affected first by Yeats's Irish inheritance. Though
he wrote in English, though he was first influenced by
English writers, Yeats was essentially an Irish poet; his
poetry, Irish poetry.

Irish landscape gives color to the background of his
poems:

"The grey cairn on the hill, when day sinks drowned in
   dew."

Details of Irish life vivify them:

> "He'll hear no more the lowing
> Of the calves on the warm hillside
> Or the kettle on the hob
> Sing peace into his breast,
> Or see the brown mice bob
> Round and round the oatmeal-chest."

Specific Irish places and landmarks are mentioned. Irish characters, eccentrics and simple persons, are the center of many poems, of such poems as "The Ballad of Father O'Hart," "The Fiddler of Dooney," and the moving "The Ballad of Father Gilligan."

But the Irish quality of Yeats's poetry consisted of something more than Irish natural beauty, geography, and people. It was something less tangible, but more important—the spirit of Ireland, its culture, its way of thinking and feeling.

In expressing this spirit, Yeats was playing the rôle of poet as he had conceived it in his philosophy. He was a new mouthpiece for old thoughts and fancies. In Irish folk-lore and myth he found the accumulated treasure of past imagination, the source of present poetry. So he wrote poems based on ancient legends: his early "The Wanderings of Oisin," "Fergus and the Druid," "The Old Age of Queen Maeve," and those numerous ones with Cuchulain as their hero.

This share of the common Irish inheritance is, according to his theory, part of the *anima mundi*, the Great Mind, "which has a memory independent of indi-

398

vidual memories, though they constantly enrich it with their images and thoughts." Because of their familiarity, these stories, by association of ideas, suggest more than simply what their words say. Memories crowd in. Emotions are evoked. Imagination is stirred anew. The stories themselves have become symbols for something other than themselves.

It is this symbolism that is the hallmark of Yeats's poetry. It is possible, of course, to use a symbolic method of writing without using specific symbols; any method of suggestion does this. Thus in poems like "The Everlasting Voices," "Into the Twilight," "Two Trees," "The Hasting of the Sidhe," "The Song of the Happy Shepherd," there is suggested, implicit not expressed, a dream of a more perfect beauty than exists in this world.

But Yeats's symbolic method was something more than this. Symbols were the means of evoking the Great Mind and the Great Memory. "I cannot now," he wrote,* "think symbols less than the greatest of all powers whether they are used consciously by the masters of magic, or half unconsciously by their successors, the poet, the musician, and the artist."

Some of the symbols that Yeats employed are quite obvious. That the rose personified for him eternal beauty and truth is readily apparent. With not too much difficulty one can recognize in the frequently used figure of the hound and deer the representation of—

* Yeats: *Ideas of Good and Evil*, The Macmillan Co.

whatever the quest—pursuer and pursued. Sometimes a brief suggestion, made by the author himself or gained from a knowledge of his life, is sufficient to clarify an otherwise bewildering symbol. Thus towers and winding stairs take on added significance when the nature of Yeats's home is recalled; and a poem like "Blood and the Moon," otherwise difficult, becomes clearer as a result of Yeats's note that his home Thoor Ballylee had an empty room at its top and that butterflies often entered the tower only to die against its window-panes.

Frequently, however, the symbolism is so obscure as to baffle the average reader, a fact that Yeats recognized. In the 1909 edition of *The Wind Among the Reeds,* he wrote: "Being troubled by what was thought a reckless obscurity, I tried to explain myself in reckless notes, into which I put all the little learning I had and more wilful fancy than I now think admirable, though what is most mystical seems to me the most true." The "recklessness" of some of the notes is suggested by his explanation that in his "Secret Rose" poems, he uses Michael Robartes to represent fire reflected in water; Hanrahan, fire blown by wind; Aedh, fire burning by itself. Surely such meaning could not be guessed by the uninitiated and even when it is explained, it is scarcely intelligible! The symbol of the "hound with one red ear," so obviously weighty with significance for Yeats, means nothing to the reader. A phrase of almost cabalistic incomprehensibility in "The Mother of God,"

"a fallen flare
Through the hollow of an ear"

takes on meaning only when someone versed in early
Christian pictorial symbolism suggests that this refers
to the method whereby early painters depicted the An-
nunciation to the Virgin. Symbolism, however, should
not be synonymous with obscurity. When it must be
bolstered up by explanations, it defeats its own purpose of compressing great meaning into small compass.

If, as too often occurred, obscurity clouded Yeats's
poems, it was the result of the excesses of a devotee
and practitioner of a cult, indifferent to those not initi-
ated. It was the flow of uncontrolled enthusiasm in
carrying out the theory of the nature and function of
art. It derived from the belief in the mystical Mind and
Memory and from the efforts mystically to draw upon
those images "in the Great Memory stored." That, according to Yeats, was the poet's function:

"Where got I that truth?
Out of a medium's mouth,
Out of nothing it came,
Out of the forest loam,
Out of dark night where lay
The crowns of Nineveh."

Yeats's conception of the proud place of the poet in
the scheme of things is shown nowhere more clearly
than in *The King's Threshold,* wherein Leanchon, the
poet, sacrifices himself so that rulers and people would

recognize the rights of poets to sit in the councils of kings. The words of the poet bear the stamp of truth; they present values that are permanent:

> "The notes they waken shall live on
> When all this heavy history's done."

Yet, as has been earlier said, however much Yeats believed in the value of poetry to bring light to the world, he did not readily lend his talents to any cause. The request for a poem during the World War of 1914-1918 resulted in his refusal, "On Being Asked for a War Poem." Since he had "no gift to set a statesman right," he felt that

> "He has had enough of meddling who can please
> A young girl in the indolence of her youth,
> Or an old man upon a winter's night."

True, matters of contemporary public interest did provide material for his poems. *Last Poems and Plays* contains, for example, poems about Roger Casement and about the Irish Easter Rebellion. But his attitude toward the proper subject of poetry was in general that of "Politics":

> "How can I, that girl standing there,
> My attention fix
> On Roman or on Russian
> Or on Spanish Politics?
> Yet here's a travelled man that knows
> What he talks about,
> And there's a politician

That has read and thought,
And maybe what they say is true
Of war and war's alarms,
But O that I were young again
And held her in my arms!"

His poetry, then, was derived less from topical incidents than from a wide, general inheritance linking the past and the present. It came to have a traditional quality based on Irish folk-lore and on the vast body of Irish supernatural beliefs and superstitions. In plays, as in *The Land of Heart's Desire,* in poems, as in "The Old Age of Queen Maeve" and "The Shadowy Waters," old stories form the theme. The vague, unworldly beliefs of a mystic race are suggested in many poems. Remnants of superstitions fill them; curlews are rebuked because they are omens of ill fortune; fairy folk capture mortal beings. Tokens of folk-lore, assuming validity through centuries of use, are incorporated into his poetry: the mystic number three is used to denote the number of centuries Oisin was absent from this world; it is his contact with earth that made him mortal again.

These accepted ways of thinking, crystallized into readily understood symbols, provide a quick reference to widely experienced thoughts and feelings. These are the true coin of Yeats's realm:

"I have no speech but symbols, the pagan speech I made
Amid the dreams of youth."

Truly symbolic of Ireland and of her poet-son was the Irish concept of fairyland. For Ireland, fairyland was the land of fancy that the geographical land could never be. For Yeats, it was the symbol for imagination itself, the escape from the real world in which he never felt truly at home. Again and again it appears in his poems: in "A Fairy Song," "The Man Who Dreamed of Fairyland," "The Hasting of the Sidhe." The human world is a world of sorrow:

"For the world's more full of weeping than you can understand."

Mortals are called, or of their own volition flee, from this world to the fairy world. The two worlds are constantly opposed.

This opposition was typical of Yeats's own desire for escape. It was the cry that rang in his early poems, in "The Lake Isle of Innisfree" and in "To an Isle in the Water." Always he yearned for a place

"Where Time would surely forget us, and Sorrow come near us no more."

What was the reason for this desire to withdraw? The knowledge of the imperfections of this life. This world is not an ideal place; the ideal cannot be found therein. Yet it was the relentless pursuit of the ideal that marked Yeats's life. Like Wandering Aengus in his poem, he could not be deterred, even by age, from his search:

> "Though I am old with wandering
>   Through hollow lands and hilly lands,
>   I will find out where she is gone,
>   And kiss her lips and take her hands;
>   And walk among long dappled grass,
>   And pluck till time and times are done
>   The silver apples of the moon,
>   The golden apples of the sun."

Yet he knew that his quest was vain. "Why should not old men be mad?" he asks in the realization of the discrepancy between potentiality and actuality. Not only is the ideal not obtainable; even its approximation fails to endure. Beauty dies:

> "Everything that man esteems
>   Endures a moment or a day."

Once, indeed, Yeats did give promise of some sort of permanence for the things we value:

> "All lives that has lived;
>   So much is certain;
>   Old sages were not deceived;
>   Somewhere beyond the curtain
>   Of distorting days
>   Lives that lovely thing
>   That shone before these eyes
>   Targeted, trod like Spring."

Not in this world, but only in another world do beauty and truth persist. Death, perhaps, will grant him what this world has failed to give. In death, and only in death, can love be permanent. He knows

> "that his head
> May not lie on the breast nor his lips on the hair
> Of the woman he loves, until he dies."

Death thus became acceptable to him.

> "Through winter-time we call on spring,
>   And through the spring we summer call,
>   And when abounding hedges ring
>   Declare that winter's best of all;
>   And after that there's nothing good
>   Because the spring-time has not come—
>   Nor know that what disturbs our blood
>   Is but its longing for the tomb."

Death, indeed, was more than accepted. It was welcomed because of life's deficiencies. It was another refuge from life.

It was not only the negative aspect of life that Yeats deplored. It was not simply that it lacked what he desired. What was much worse, it presented a conflict with the ideals of his poetry:

> "The intellect of man is forced to choose
>   Perfection of the life, or of the work."

A choice between the two must be made; one cannot have both. Lovers of life do not sing; "those that love the world serve it in action." Succinctly Yeats puts the conflict:

> "I might have thrown poor words away
> And been content to live."

But words were his compelling force. Throw them away, he could not. So, according to his view, a life of action was impossible for him. As a substitute, however, he offers only dreams and vague ideals. In spite of an effort to build a sustaining philosophy, in so perplexing a poem, for example, as "The Phases of the Moon," in spite of weird systems and strange ideas, no guiding principle is offered.

> "The abstract joy,
> The half-read wisdom of daemonic images,
> Suffice the aging man as once the growing boy."

These are but poor sustenance to souls crying for food. His poetry, then, offers no vitalizing faith, no direction to life, or even consolation for it. But it does express, and expresses movingly, a mood common at some time to all mankind.

One misses, however, a sense of warm human sympathy. However great the insistence that the poet serves some extra-human function, some mystical seer-magician-priest rôle, there is no suggestion that that service is done through love of mankind, through any feeling of brotherhood.

The poet, indubitably, withdrew from life and from his fellow men. But it would be wrong to infer that there was a complete lack of contact with others, a total retirement into the misty world of his own thoughts and feelings. There are in his poetry reflections of his association with others. True, such early love poems as "Down by the Salley Gardens" and "When You Are Old" are wraith-like, poems to ghosts of lovers, or to what one might youthfully dream lovers to be. But the later lyrics, "A Woman Homer Sung," "His Phoenix," leave no doubt of the actuality of the women he loved or admired. His friends—and they were many—are recalled in poems like "In Memory of Major Robert Gregory" and "All Souls' Night." His family and his home life in Thoor Ballylee also provided him with material for poems. The titles of his books published in 1928 and in 1933, *The Tower* and *The Winding Stair and Other Poems,* are in themselves significant since they refer to his tower home. The section in *The Tower,* called "Meditations in Time of Civil War," throbs with thoughts of his domestic life; "My Descendants," in particular, dwells on his feelings toward the members of his family and their place in the continuity of existence. For his son and his daughter he wrote poems like the moving "A Prayer for My Son" and "A Prayer for My Daughter."

However many the poems in which Yeats celebrated his relationship with family and with friends, however deeply he felt the joys of those relationships—

"Think where man's glory most begins and ends,
And say my glory was I had such friends."—

he has come to be identified with something more inclusive than these—with Ireland, itself. That came not simply from service to his country—in his early days in the Irish theater, in his later life in the Irish Senate. It was an identification, furthermore, not with the people of Ireland so much as with the spirit of Ireland. Politically, intellectually, he may not have been one with its people; but poetically, emotionally, he was one with its soul.

"I am thinking of a child's vow sworn in vain
  Never to leave that valley his fathers called their
    home."

The child's vow may have been physically, but it was never spiritually, broken. Yeats was Ireland.

> "Out of Ireland have we come.
> Great hatred, little room,
> Maimed us at the start.
> I carry from my mother's womb
> A fanatic heart."

That heart he kept alive in the poetry he wrote. Among the poems, unforgettable ones, that pulsate with Ireland's as well as Yeats's spirit are "Red Hanrahan's Song About Ireland," the familiar "The Lake Isle of Innisfree," "A Cradle Song," "A Faery Song," "The Cloak, the Boat, and the Shoes," "Down by the Salley Gardens," "The Meditation of the Old Fisherman." Tender, wistful, longing for something other and better than the familiar, they reveal Yeats the poet and the Irishman. "Among School Children" epitomizes that man's life: the visit of

"A sixty-year-old smiling public man"

to a school, the memories aroused by his sight of the children, the philosophical musing upon the oneness of the universe called up by sight and recollection:

> "O chestnut tree, great rooted blossomer,
> Are you the leaf, the blossom or the bole?
> O body swayed to music, O brightening glance,
> How can we know the dancer from the dance?"

It was a long life over which he mused, a life that held more than fifty years of writing. In age, as in youth, he was zealous in his art. In 1935, when he was seventy, he wrote in his preface to *The King of the Great Clock Tower:* "A year ago I found that I had written no verse for two years; I had never been so long barren; I had nothing in my head, and there used to be more than I could write." With that sturdy determination that characterized his early years of apprenticeship in writing, he forced himself to write. The play was one result of that determination; other results were several poems, among them this:

> "God guard me from those thoughts men think
> In the mind alone,
> He that sings a lasting song
> Thinks in a marrow bone;
>
> From all that makes a wise old man
> That can be praised of all;

O what am I that I should not seem
For the song's sake a fool.

I pray—for fashion's word is out
And prayer comes round again—
That I may seem though I die old
A foolish, passionate man."

"For the song's sake," Yeats led his life. He was passionate in his fidelity to the belief that ran through his life like the scarlet thread of authenticity that

"Words alone are certain good."

It was to the service of words that Yeats dedicated himself. How great a span that service covered Yeats revealed in describing the medal presented to him when he received the Nobel Prize: *

"It shows a young man listening to a Muse, who stands young and beautiful with a great lyre in her hand, and I think as I examine it, 'I was good-looking once like that young man, but my unpracticed verse was full of infirmity, my Muse old as it were, and now I am old and rheumatic and nothing to look at, but my Muse is young.' "

### SELECTED LIST OF POETICAL WORKS

(The numerous editions in which Yeats's poetry appeared make a complete list of his poetical works unwieldy and unhelpful.)

| | |
|---|---|
| COLLECTED POEMS | *The Macmillan Co.* |
| LAST POEMS AND PLAYS | *The Macmillan Co.* |

* Quoted in Louise Bogan: "William Butler Yeats," *The Atlantic Monthly,* May 1938.